Normativity and Variety of Speech Actions

Poznań Studies in the Philosophy of the Sciences and the Humanities

VOLUME 112

The titles published in this series are listed at *brill.com/ps*

Normativity and Variety of Speech Actions

Edited by

Maciej Witek and Iwona Witczak-Plisiecka

BRILL

RODOPI

LEIDEN | BOSTON

Cover illustration: Created by geralt. Retrieved from: https://pixabay.com/pl/osobowych-portret-ludzi-kobieta-943888/. Illustration falls under the CC0 Creative Commons license.
Poznań Studies is sponsored by the University of Warsaw.

The Library of Congress Cataloging-in-Publication Data is available online at http://catalog.loc.gov
LC record available at http://lccn.loc.gov/2018041876

Typeface for the Latin, Greek, and Cyrillic scripts: "Brill". See and download: brill.com/brill-typeface.

ISSN 0303-8157
ISBN 978-90-04-36650-3 (hardback)
ISBN 978-90-04-36652-7 (e-book)

This book is printed on acid-free paper and produced in a sustainable manner.

Contents

Editorial to the Special Issue of *Poznań Studies in the Philosophy of the Sciences and the Humanities*: Normativity and Variety of Speech Actions

Iwona Witczak-Plisiecka and Maciej Witek

Although it has been nearly a century since John L. Austin promoted a speech act-theoretic functional perspective on language use, the fact that there are things that can be done 'linguistically,' i.e. by saying, can often be found surprising, contentious, or mysterious. On the one hand, a human being is primarily a *homo loquens* and a *homo significans*, who, as claimed by Anna Wierzbicka, "lives on expression and communication of meaning;" (Wierzbicka 1987, pp. 1–2) on the other hand, in communicating with others every person constantly performs not just descriptive speech acts, but socially significant actions. People may be able to walk and eat, to construct and to demolish without using much language, but it is thanks to language that they can promise and deny, that they can invite and order, name and nominate. In the Searlean expansive view, the entire social world is dependent on performative language use (e.g. Searle 1995, 2010) where speech acts form a basis for a construction of social reality in the broadest possible sense. It is the significance of the performative character of speech that motivated compilation of the present volume.

Even though speech acts have been present in the history of civilisation since it began, the philosophical and linguistic literature devoted to performative language use really started in the twentieth century, and in the Anglo-Saxon world was marked with Austin's lectures posthumously published in a book format under the meaningful title – *How to Do Things with Words* (Austin 1962/1975). Although there had been numerous references to performative language use over the centuries, both prior to Austin and during his lifetime (cf. e.g. the overview in Witczak-Plisiecka 2013b), no other account has ever had a bigger or an equal impact. It is since Austin's times that speech act theory has been growing to embrace various themes and to expand its methodology. It is now common to talk about speech actions next to speech acts (cf. e.g. Mey 2001; 2010; 2011), and virtually all rudiments of Austinian speech act theory have been analysed in depth and often further developed, but the various modifications and developments only function to emphasise the significance of the original reflection.

In compiling the present volume, as editors, we wanted to show this rich variety in contemporary speech act-theoretic research. It has not been our ambition to present a holistic view, as even a speech act theory-based bibliography would have to exceed the length of the book, but we have hoped that the volume will further enrich the field and may entice further research programmes. In our editorial work we have been guided by a general speech act-theoretic reflection – a reflection thoroughly Austinian in spirit – that speech is primarily a type of action. Having much appreciated the legacy of J.L. Austin (1962/ 1975; 1964; 1970), we also accepted as evident that his theory, partly construed posthumously on the basis of his lecture notes, provides an open-ended framework for analysis of much varied language-oriented phenomena. It is our belief that speech act theory is by no means a simple construct indicating through its tri-partite – locution-illocution-perlocution – perspective some transparent distinctions between the form, the function, and the results of an utterance, an image that one may often draw from introductory linguistics accounts. Instead, we believe that the emphasis on performative language use opens a path to varied research, research that can elucidate important aspects of social interaction. We have been exploring speech act-theoretic issues (e.g. Witek 2005; 2009; 2011; 2013a; 2013b; 2015a; 2015b; 2015c; 2016; Witczak-Plisiecka 2007; 2009a; 2009b; 2010; 2011; 2012; 2013a; 2013b; 2013c; 2014; Witczak-Plisiecka and Witek 2009; Budzyńska and Witek 2014; Jaszczolt and Witek 2018) and having seen its richness eventually decided to put together a collection of papers that could do justice to the variety found in the field.

The discussions presented in the present volume address directly problems related to types of norms operative in speech act-theoretic contexts, speaker's intentions and commitments, speaker-addressee coordination, speech actions in discursive practice, in literal and non-literal language, with regard to irony, presupposition, and meaningful significant silence; the problems are analysed with reference to the data culled from natural conversation, mediated political discourse, law, and literary language. Among the approached problems there is a question of the origin of the performative force, whether it (at least mainly) resides with the speaker's intention, or rather the speaker's original intention is not a primary factor in determining the actual force and the meaning of the speech act which can be dynamically determined (cf. Matczak, this volume) or interactionally negotiated (cf. Corredor, this volume) in the course of subsequent linguistic practice. Let us emphasise once again that it has been the editors' intention that the volume should present a wide spectrum of speech act-theoretic problems, which could shed light on the nature of speech act theory in general and the status of its particular rudiments as applied in different research programmes. Hopefully, next to being a presentation of genuine research in the field of speech acts, the volume may provide an indication with regard to what speech act theory really is or can be in the twenty first century.

The volume has been divided into two main sections, of which the first focuses on the normative character of speech actions (*Part One: Normative Aspects of Speech Actions*) and the other one includes papers which concentrate on more situated aspects either in the sense of manner or the field of application (*Part Two: Varieties of Speech Actions*).

In chapter one, '*Varieties of Speech Act Norms*,' Marina Sbisà discusses three types of norms that govern the practice of making illocutionary acts: constitutive rules, maxims, and objective requirements. Following John R. Searle (1969, p. 33), she claims that the function of illocutionary constitutive rules is to create the possibility of new forms of linguistic behaviour by defining the conditions under which the utterance of a certain sentence constitutes the performance of a certain illocutionary act; the violation of a constitutive rule, then, results in making the purported act void and null. What she calls 'maxims,' in turn, are regulative rather than constitutive rules. Their function is to advise interlocutors how to perform successful speech acts in a way that is optimal from their subjective perspectives in discourse. The flouting of a certain maxim – e.g., the flouting of the Gricean Maxim of Quality (Grice 1989), Searle's sincerity condition (Searle 1969), or Williamson's Knowledge Rule (Williamson 2000) – results in loss of the speaker's credibility or damage to her reputation. Objective requirements, by contrast, define the conditions under which speech acts of a certain type qualify as correct or righteous independently of the current perspective of the interlocutors; the violation of a certain objective or *perspective-transcendent* requirement results in the negative assessment of the speaker's utterance as not being the right thing to say in the speech situation she finds herself in. In short, the three types of norms under discussion differ in function, and the different roles that constitutive rules, maxims, and objective requirements play in the dynamics of illocutionary practice correspond to different kinds of penalty that results from their violation.

Discussing the nature and function of constitutive rules, Sbisà notes that Austin's conditions for the felicitous performance of illocutionary acts – i.e., his famous A and B rules, originally designed to capture the conditions "necessary for the smooth or 'happy' functioning of [performatives]" (Austin 1975, p. 14) – can be regarded as templates for open-ended systems of constitutive rules. She also draws a distinction between constitutive rules in the strong sense and constitutive rules in the weak sense. According to Sbisà, to say that a given rule is constitutive in the strong sense – or, for short, that it is *strongly* constitutive – is to assume that its violation results in making the speaker's purported act void and null; in other words, a successful performance of an illocutionary act depends on our compliance with the constitutive rules that jointly define its type. By contrast, the speaker's violation of a rule that is constitutive in the weak sense – or, for short, that is *weakly* constitutive – does not result in the nullification of her act, but subjects her to certain forms of criticisms, e.g., it exposes her to accusations of being insincere or inconsistent. In general, a given rule is *weakly* constitutive for a certain act only if it contributes to the definition of the type to which the act belongs, but the non-compliance with it does not result in making the act null and void. Sbisà argues that many rules that are constitutive in the weak sense – e.g., Austin's rule templates Γ1 and Γ2, Searle's sincerity rule, and Williamson's Knowledge Rule – are in fact maxims that encode "regulative advice for optimal speech act performance in the perspective of the participants in the current verbal interaction" (Sbisà this volume, p. 33).

According to Sbisà, constitutive rules and maxims should be carefully distinguished from what she calls *objective requirements*. Objective requirements introduce a third dimension of evaluation of illocutionary acts. In certain respects they behave like maxims, i.e., their violation subjects the speaker to certain forms of criticisms. Unlike the standards for optimal speech act performance set by maxims, however, the standards of correctness established by objective requirements are independent of the particular perspective of the interacting agents. In general, they are perspective-transcendent and allow for the assessment of a speech act in respect of their 'correspondence with facts' or, in other words, for the evaluation of the act as 'the right thing' to say with regard to the actual state of the world rather than the interlocutors' mental states. Sbisà argues that this kind of assessment applies not only to assertions, but "to speech acts of any kind of illocutionary force." (Sbisà this volume, p. 33) Every illocutionary act that fails to meet the objective requirements appropriate to its type – e.g., a *false* statement, *bad* advice, *unmerited* congratulation, or *incorrect* promise – subjects the speaker to an accusation of making an incorrect conversational move.

Sbisà claims that constitutive rules in the strong sense are conventional in that they exist and function by virtue of a collective agreement on the part of the participants in a linguistic interaction (for a discussion of this issue, see Sbisà 2007; 2009); maxims and objective requirements, by contrast, are not conventional: rather than being established by a tacit agreement, they seem to be derived from general principles of optimal and successful cooperative transactions.

Having discussed the relationship between constitutive rules, maxims, and objective requirements, Sbisà turns to considering the phenomenon of accommodation as it occurs in linguistic communication in general, and in illocutionary interaction in particular. Contrary to Lewis (1979; cf. Witek 2016; 2015c; 2013a), she argues that accommodation – construed of as a context-adjusting mechanism guided by the need to maintain the default assumption that the speaker's utterance qualifies as 'correct play' – involves no rules apart from the constitutive rules governing the illocutionary act type in question. (Sbisà this volume). In other words, even though accommodating processes function against the background of certain norms and rules, they are not governed by specific rules of their own. (Sbisà this volume, p. 42). According to Sbisà, they are better viewed as involving the operation of general cognitive mechanisms responsible for pattern recognition and default attribution of mental states and deontic roles to others.

In *'Commitment and Obligation in Speech Act Theory,' Brian Ball* examines the explanatory role that normative concepts play in our theorising about speech acts. In his analyses, he focuses on assertions and the notions of commitment and obligation. Following Searle (1969, p. 29), Ball assumes that to make an assertion is to undertake a commitment to the truth of the proposition asserted. He argues, however, that the notion of commitment involved in the above-mentioned description of assertions is to be analysed along the lines of Timothy Williamson's (2000) epistemic foundationalism rather than in terms of Robert B. Brandom's (1983) discursive coherentism. According to Brandom, a felicitous assertion changes the normative situation of the participants in a speech situation by, first, obligating the speaker to provide independent evidence for the asserted proposition if her original speech act is challenged and, second, entitling the hearer to assert this proposition as well as its immediate consequences. According to Williamson, by contrast, to undertake a commitment to a proposition in asserting it is to incur an obligation to *epistemically* ensure its truth or, more specifically, to incur an obligation to *know* that it is true; in other words, viewed from the standpoint of epistemic foundationalism, every felicitous assertion results in the speaker's becoming obliged to know the truth of the proposition asserted. Even though he limits his discussion to assertions, Ball claims that the notion of undertaking a commitment as 'incurring an obligation to ensure' plays a key role in explaining other illocutionary act types; for example, in making a promise the speaker incurs an obligation to ensure thorough action – this time practical rather than epistemic – that the promised state of affair occurs.

Ball starts his paper by motivating the general idea that assertion involves undertaking a commitment. He argues that we need this idea to make sense of a view – which he finds uncontroversial – that assertions can be retracted. To retract an assertion that *p*, i.e., to make it null and void, is not to make it the case that the assertion was never made; rather, it is to bring it about that the speaker is no longer committed to the truth of the proposition that *p*. Therefore, to maintain the idea that assertions can be retracted we have to distinguish between the act of making an assertion and its normative effect that consists in the speaker's being committed to the truth of what she asserts: it is the latter, not the former, that is nullified in the act of retraction. Next, Ball examines critically the position of discursive coherentism and claims that it is not general enough, i.e., it accounts only for some cases of assertions; in other words, it is not the case that all felicitous assertions authorise further assertions and commit speakers to justify and vindicate their original claims. According to Ball, rather than defending the view in question by adding new epicycles, it is better to reject it in favour of Williamson's epistemic foundationalism. In the central part of his paper, Ball distinguishes between descriptive and normative accounts of assertions – thereby simplifying MacFarlane's four-fold taxonomy of views – and argues that it is the latter, not the former, that provides an adequate and uniform explanation of assertoric talk. After a critical discussion of Stalnaker's descriptive account, he claims, contrary to what MacFalene seems to suggest, that the Knowledge Rule (KR) – i.e., 'one must assert that p only if one knows that p' – does individuate assertion as a normative kind. According to Ball, what all assertions have in common is their specific dynamics that is built into the deontic modal verb that occurs in (KR), i.e., the fact that every felicitous assertion results in the speaker's incurring an obligation to epistemically ensure the truth of what she asserts or, in other words, in her being obliged to know that the proposition she asserts is true.

In '*Coordination and Norms in Illocutionary Interaction,*' *Maciej Witek* uses the framework of the interactional approach to speech acts (Witek 2015a; 2013b) to account for the coordinative function of language conventions and the normative aspect of illocutionary practice. The interactional approach results from integrating elements of the Austinian theory of speech acts (Austin 1975; Sbisà 1992; 2002; 2009; 2013) within the framework of Ruth G. Millikan's biological model of language (Millikan 1984; 2005). Its central idea is that the force of an act depends on the response the act invites *by convention* (Austin 1975: 117), where the Austinian phrase 'by convention' means 'in accordance with the conventional pattern that the speaker and the hearer jointly reproduce.' The idea of speaker-hearer conventional patterns comes from Millikan (1984; 2005). She claims, that language conventions proliferate through a mechanism of counterpart reproduction, which involves the speaker's utterance of a certain linguistic form in a context and the hearer's cooperative response to it; the response is a *conventional outcome* of the act – or, as Witek puts it, its *international effect* – and occurs either at the level of belief-formation (if the speaker's act is an assertion) or at the level of behaviour-production (if the speaker's act is a directive). According to Millikan, speech acts and language conventions can be described and classified by their proper functions or purposes. Roughly, the proper purpose of a speech act is to evoke its interactive effect understood as the hearer's *cooperative*, conventionally determined response; the proper function of a speaker-hearer conventional pattern, in turn, is to help achieve *coordination* between the interacting agents. It remains to be examined, however, what type of cooperative response speech acts are designed to invite or elicit, and what type of coordination problems language conventions are designed to solve.

In Sections 2 and 3 of his paper, Witek elaborates on the ideas of the cooperative function of speech acts and of the coordinative function of language conventions. He distinguishes between primary and secondary interactional effects of speech acts and, consistently, between primary and secondary speaker-hearer patterns. The force of an act depends on what counts as its primary interactional effect, *e.g.*, *believing* or *complying with* what the speaker is told (depending on whether the act is an assertion or directive, respectively); we refer to its secondary effects – that can be described in terms of rhetorical relations in the sense of Asher and Lascarides (2001; 2003) – to explain those forms of cooperation that cannot be described as cases of straightforward trust and compliance. Next, Witek puts forth a hypothesis according to which the proper function of language conventions is to help achieve mental coordination between the speaker and the hearer. More specifically, conventional patterns proliferate because they help produce and maintain a preferred correspondence between what the interacting agents take to be their publicly recognizable beliefs, desires, intentions, expectations, and so on. Producing and maintaining mental coordination between the interacting agents consists, then, in keeping their own representations of their publicly recognizable mental states sufficiently aligned. One way to achieve this end is to interact in accordance with speaker-hearer conventional patters, whose general structure involves the speaker's forming a certain mental state, her utterance of an appropriate linguistic form in a certain context, and the hearer's forming a mental state that stands in a preferred correspondence relation to the one revealed by the speaker.

In Section 4 of his paper, Witek uses the interactional model of mental coordination to account for the normative aspect of illocutionary practice. Roughly, speech acts construed as moves made in an illocutionary game are subject to *norms* (Williamson 2000; Sbisà this volume; Ball 2014a; 2014b; this volume) and produce *normative effects* (Sbisà 2009; 2013; this volume; Witek 2015c). In particular, illocutionary acts are subject to sincerity rules such as the belief rule 'One must: assert that p only if one believes that p' and the desire rule 'One must: order the hearer to do A only if one desires the hearer to do A;' they also produce normative effects by modifying the domain of the commitments, obligations, rights and entitlements of the conversing agents. Witek argues that the normative character of sincerity rules can be accounted for in terms of the Normal conditions – 'Normal' in Millikan's (1984) technical sense – for proper functioning of speech acts: the Normal condition under which the reproduction of a certain pattern results in achieving mental coordination between the speaker and the hearer is that the speaker's act is sincere; he also suggests that the normative effects of speech acts construed of as illocutionary contributions to a language game can be spelled out in terms of constraints their performance put on the scope of allowable subsequent moves.

Part Two of the volume gathers papers which jointly exhibit the tremendous variety found in speech act-theoretic research; the variety that pertains both to the subject matter and theoretical and methodological commitments.

Chapter four, entitled *'Speech acts in discourse'* and authored by *Anita Fetzer*, takes up a long-standing and difficult problem of marrying speech act theory and discourse studies. The paper starts with two main distinctions, *viz.* the speech act and discourse dichotomy, and the discourse and context dichotomy, and the claim that utterances function as linking threads between what we recognise as speech acts and as discourse. In other words, both speech act theory and discourse studies deal with utterances, but there are differences in 'how' such utterances are treated within the two fields. Being an expert on context (cf. e.g. Fetzer 2004; 2007), the author emphasises that all speech acts are necessarily situated in social context, which is also crucial for discourse. Fetzer builds her discussion around three main research questions; she asks:

1)   Is discourse primarily descriptive and, for this reason, not relevant to speech act theory?
2)   Is the concept of discourse incompatible with speech act theory?
3)   Does discourse constitute some kind of macro speech act composed of concatenated micro speech acts; and is discourse only one macro speech act, or is it a combination of both micro and macro speech acts?

The final conclusion is that discourse is in fact inherently pragmatic in the sense that it constitutes matters with which people 'can do things.' In this light, discourse is compatible with speech act-theoretic perspective; it is indeed rather speech act-theoretic in nature and characterised by features such as rationality, intentionality, and cooperation. By definition discourse is 'large' and consequently can be successfully conceived of as a macro speech act (or should we say 'action'?) that can be approached using the tripartite division into locution, illocution and perlocution, a macro speech act that is composed of internal acts with the provision that an act in such a context should not be directly identified with one utterance, i.e. a speech act may sometimes be realised by one utterance, but on many occasions one speech act may be matched with a number of utterances. The author concludes that it is more convenient to adopt the Gricean notion of 'discursive contribution' which would always have: (1) illocutionary force, (2) propositional content, and (3) textual meaning. This notion is supposed to secure researchers against the inherent but much varied fuzziness of the contributions; it should also facilitate analysis of various sub-discourses within which a macro speech act, and one form, may be applied to perform different functions.

Among interesting points included in the discussion there is Fetzer's interest in a less frequently discussed class of expositives as originally discussed by Austin, as well as her ethnomethodology-inspired analysis of speech acts as 'doubly contextual,' being always parts of 'larger plans.' In this text Austin's speech act theory is also, *inter alia*, confronted with de Beaugrande and Dressler's (1981), van Dijk's (1980a; 2008), and Schegloff's (1995) functional views and pioneering work. There are rather few firm claims in the text, but the discussion will certainly invite response from researchers working within discourse studies and in the interface of discourse and performativity.

Dennis Kurzon's text – '*Silence as Speech Action, Silence as non-Speech Action: A Study of Some Silences in Maeterlinck's Pelléas et Mélisande*' – uses speech act-theoretic tools to talk about silence that may be actional in nature. It focuses on literary language and fictional world, which was originally rejected as data in Austin's framework, but later found its way into speech act theory. In this text Kurzon draws on his own model of silence and its different types (cf. Kurzon 1998; 2007).

Kurzon puts emphasis on the fact that meaningful silence, and silence in general, will always be interpreted with reference to the context in which it appears. Unlike linguistic, i.e. actually 'uttered,' utterances, it can never receive interpretation that is (just) semantic, but meaningful silence, where it constitutes action, may be paraphrased semantically. According to Kurzon, silence may constitute a speech action or a non-speech action, and in the former case it is intentional – just like any other linguistic performance. This performative type of silence is marked by the fact that the speaker decides not to say something even when he or she is participating in the interaction and such silence may be modally 'glossed' as 'I will not/may not speak,' often under some external pressure (cf. Kurzon 1998). Unintentional silence, in turn, is shown as silence which may be psychologically motivated, e.g. by the emotional state of the person.

Using Maeterlinck's play as data for analysis of performative silence is novel research and a real challenge as silence stands as an important element in Maeterlinck's own art, as explicitly stated in his essay of 1896 (Maeterlinck 1902) where he suggests that silence can be more meaningful than ephemeral words, and that silence, being meaningful, can actually be dangerous. Thus, the analysis presented by Kurzon really brings together speech act theoretic reflection and a symbolist's (and a Nobel Prize winner's) reflection on language and its meaningfulness. It points to the depth of meaningful performance that may be found in silence embedded in actual human interaction and it (implicitly) confirms that performance is primarily social.

There are references to other playwrights and authors who deliberately used silence in their work, such as Chekov, Beckett, or Pinter, as well as to Adorno's post-war dictum: 'Nach Auschwitz ein Gedicht zu schreiben ist barbarisch,' but for the actual analysis of the play Kurzon concentrates on three types of silence selected from his own theory where there are four main types (Kurzon 2007), viz. conversational silence, textual silence, situational silence and thematic silence. The first and most frequent type, conversational silence, occurs in interaction where a person, for instance fails to answer a question, or respond to an offer. Textual silence happens when someone reads a book, e.g. in a classroom or in a library, or recites a prayer. Situational silence is similar to the previous type, but does not involve any activity such as reading or reciting; it is explained as mainly institutional and may happen at, e.g. remembrance ceremonies or even surprise parties. The fourth type of silence is thematic silence and it is technically different from the other three as it cannot be timed. Thematic silence is always silent 'about' something and as such it is hardly 'silence' at all. Instances of thematic silence can be easily found in political discourse and in other discourses where certain topics are being avoided. Eventually, Kurzon identifies a number of 'silences' in the play to classify them as actional (ones that may be replaced by words, i.e. conversational and thematic silences) or non-actional (situational silence in the play).

The text authored by *Cristina Corredor, 'The Dynamics of Conversation: Fixing the Force in Irony. A Case Study,'* is another example of a study which attempts to extend traditional speech act theory to systematically include conversational analysis with special attention paid to the performative character of suggested meaning, especially irony. The author uses the frameworks of the interactionalist view of communication and discourse analysis to account for an actual case of negotiating the force of a public statement. The analyzed case involves an ironic utterance initiating a sequence of interaction in which the speaker's original ironic intention, in spite of being correctly recognized, was not accepted as the primary factor in determining the force and meaning of his speech act. Corredor argues that the actual force of the act under discussion was determined through a dynamic process of meaning negotiation and fixation, which can be adequately accounted for along the lines of the interactionalist view of communication. According to the latter, what plays a decisive role in determining the force and meaning of at least some speech acts is not the speaker's original intention, but the hearer's uptake (Austin 1975; Sbisà 2009; 2013; Carassa and Colombetti 2009; Witek 2015a; 2013a; 2013b). Following Schegloff (2006), Corredor assumes that the interactional process of meaning negotiation involves a sequence of three turns that starts with the speaker's proposal, moves thorough the addressee's response of accepting or rejecting the speech act the speaker purports to make, and ends with the final turn of validation or repair from the speaker.

According to Corredor, irony as seen in the analyzed case can be spelled out as follows. At first, the speaker makes an utterance that is intended as a parodic irony; in this particular context he *pretends* to be a negationist and an anti-Semitic person and intends to get his audience to identify – in virtue of their recognition of this pretense – his intended ironical meaning which has "to do with pointing at the extraordinary power of the Internet to spread and make believe almost anything." (Corredor this volume, p. 150) In the second turn, the addressee recognizes the communicative plan behind the speaker's utterance, but refuses to accept it as the primary factor in determining the force and meaning of his words; rather, the addressee takes them at their face value and holds the speaker accountable for the consequences of their literal meaning (more specifically, what the addressee critically evaluates and re-jects as non-acceptable is the speaker's instrumental use of the negationist and anti-Semitic opinions). In the third turn, the speaker explicates the de-tails of his original communicative plan but acknowledges that the addressee literal reading of his words was available in the sequence. In short, the force of the speaker's initiating move is determined through the process of inter-actional negotiation that involves the interplay of two factors: the speaker's intention and the hearer's uptake; what is more, at least in some cases it is the latter, not the former, that plays a decisive role in determining actual forces and meanings.

Besides developing the interactionalist account of parodic irony – according to which ironical utterances should be described and accounted for in terms of indirect and negotiated illocutionary forces – Corredor discusses other the-oretical approaches to the phenomenon being investigated. She distinguishes between the one-stage approach, such as the echoic theory developed by the proponents of Relevance Theory (Wilson 2013; Wilson and Sperber 2012), and the two-stage approach, represented by the theories proposed by Giora (2003) and Attardo (2000). Corredor argues that it is the two-stage approach that of-fers a better theoretical framework for explaining parodic irony; namely, it al-lows for the fact that the two alternative senses of an ironic utterance – literal and non-literal – are available to the interpreter and, as the corollary of this, can be used in the process of meaning negotiation.

The next text aims to emphasise the performative potential found in the context of mediated interviews with Czech politicians. In '*Forms of Aggressive Speech Actions in Public Communication*,' the author, *Milada Hirshova*, points to the phenomenon of aggression found in speech actions performed in public communication events. In particular, she analyses extracts of both hostile aggressive verbal behaviour and instrumental verbal aggression, and selected interactions that combine both of them, culled from the recordings of the Czech public TV stations CT1, namely the weekly talk show *Máte slovo* (Eng. 'The floor is yours') and CT24 – daily news and commentaries (*Studio 24*).

Taking a general speech act-theoretic stance, Hirshova briefly introduces the notions of 'speech act' and 'speech action' to move towards politeness-related phenomena, i.e. politeness, impoliteness, rudeness, and, finally, verbal aggression. Rudeness and verbal aggression are described as instances of vulgar behaviour. The extracts chosen for analysis are discussed against the relevant political background of the Czech Republic. The author points to the macro designs of the analysed interactions; she identifies instances of clearly instrumental aggression and instances of aggression that seem rather incidental. In her discussion she includes elements such as participants' and the audience's emotions, values, and conventions. There is an interesting conclusion as Hirshova suggests that in the 2010s in Czech TV shows that deal with political topics, aggressive communicative patterns of behaviour have become almost standard. In fact such aggressive patterns seem to function as the most important verbal instrument for politicians to publicly forward their attitudes and position. The author claims that her analyses of the chosen dialogues, being extracts from TV shows and from a recording of an interview, jointly demonstrate that aggressive, and even openly offensive communication can be seen not just as a borderline case of impoliteness but, more accurately, as a parallel phenomenon, a communicative strategy which can use vulgarities, but can dispense with them as well. She believes it is quite evident that within this strategy, speech actions such as accusations, i.e. statements concerning the past or the current opponents' activities, defamations, and rhetorical questions that carry offensive presuppositions, are all among the most frequent types of actions used in mediated political discourse.

Milada Hirshova's text includes numerous references to works from outside speech act theory, linking the performative perspective with other functional research programmes, some of which lean towards discourse analysis rather than philosophy-based speech act theory (e.g. van Dijk 1980b), and some are explicitly based on politeness theory in the tradition of Brown and Levinson (1987) with its further developments towards impoliteness (e.g. Spencer-Oatey 2005; 2007; Culpeper 2011).

In a much different text entitled '*A Theory that Beats the Theory? Lineages, the Growth of Signs, and Dynamic Legal Interpretation,*' Marcin Matczak takes issue with the static approach to legal interpretation and argues in favour of an alternative, dynamic approach. The static approach is represented by a theory called 'originalism,' which comes in two versions: *originalism of original intentions* and *originalism of original conventions*. According to the former, what plays a key role in constituting the content of a legal text is the intention with which it was enacted by the lawmaker; according to the latter, in contrast, the meaning of the text is determined by the conventions prevailing at the moment of its enactment. What these two views have in common is the idea that the meaning of the words used in legal texts does not change over time; for example, the term 'cruel punishment' occurring in the eighth amendment to the US Constitution – i.e., "Excessive bail shall not be required, nor excessive fines imposed, nor cruel and unusual punishments inflicted" – is to be read in accordance with the semantic standards that were established *either* by the lawmaker's original meaning-constituting intention *or* by the linguistic conventions that were in force at the end of the eighteenth century. Matczak argues that the static approach, despite its *prima facie* credibility, fails to provide an adequate account of legal interpretation and, for that reason, it is to be replaced with the dynamic approach, which is represented by a theory called 'living constitutionalism.' According to this theory, the meaning of a legal term evolves over time or, more specifically, is continuously qualified and amended through an objective and social process that involves legal disputes and judicial practice; in short, "*law in action* influences the meaning of *law on the books*." (Matczak this volume, p. 203).

In his discussion, Matczak focuses on two objections that are traditionally raised against living constitutionalism and other dynamic theories of legal interpretation. First, the proponents of the static approach often claim that living constitutionalism lacks a sufficient support from the philosophy of language, whereas originalism is a well-grounded theory justified by the philosophical doctrine of semantic internalism; in other words, there seems to be no sufficiently robust philosophical theory of *meaning-constitution* or *meaning-fixation* that could ground dynamic theories of legal interpretation. Second, it is also argued that dynamic theories of legal interpretation can be used to undermine the stability of the law and increase the interpreters' discretionary powers. According to Matczak, these objections can be dealt with by developing a philosophical theory of legal interpretation that results from integrating Ruth G. Millikan's (1984; 2005; cf. Witek 2015a; this volume) model of linguistic conventions as lineages and Charles S. Peirce's (1878; 1931–36; 1998) conception of the growth of signs; the resulted framework – Matczak claims – is robust enough to provide a theory that can beat the theory. (Matczak this volume)

Millikan defines language conventions as *reproductively established families* (Millikan 1984) or *lineages* (Millikan 2005; cf. Witek 2015; this volume) of historical uses of sentences, words and other linguistic items that: (*a*) are equivalent with respect of their proper function; and (*b*) proliferate due to the weight of precedent. In short, every language convention is a lineage established by a precedent whose form is subsequently reproduced by cooperative speakers and hearers. According to Matczak, one example of the mechanism underlying the evolutionary development of conventional reproductively established families is the Kripkean causal chain of communication that preserves the reference of proper names; he argues, however, that the externalist framework provided by Millikan, unlike the ones offered by Kripke (1980) and Putnam (1975), can be used to account for the meaning-stabilizing mechanisms of legal terms such as 'cruel punishment;' in other words, it provides a sufficiently robust alternative to semantic internalism and the form of originalism it supports.

Perice's theory of the growth of signs, in turn, provides a philosophical justification of the idea of dynamic legal interpretation. According to Matczak, legal terms such as 'cruel punishment' change their content over time. More specifically, their meanings are subject to the process of semeiosis in Peirce's sense. Matczak argues that historical uses of the term 'cruel punishment' make up a conventional lineage whose elements are dynamic interpretants in Perice's sense; that is to say, they have been translated into each other in the course of legal practice and, as a result, form a sequence of increasingly richer meanings.

A central tenet of the Percean-Millikanian model of legal interpretation developed by Matczak, then, is that to determine the meaning of a term occurring in a legal text is to recognize the historically constituted lineage to which it belongs; in other words, the lawmaker's original intentions and the semantic standards prevailing at the moment of the text's enactment are no longer regarded as primary factors constituting the meaning of the term. Rather, the meanings of the words used in a legal text are dynamically determined and amended in the course of permanent semeiosis, which is "a traceable, relatively transparent and verifiable process: the individual interpreter's discretionary authority over meaning is thus strictly curtailed." (Matczak this volume, p. 181).

The final paper, '*Are Implicative Verbs Presupposition Triggers? Evidence from Polish,*' by *Mateusz Włodarczyk*, is an account of the results based on the experiment researching reinforceability of conversational implicatures and presuppositions. In the reported study within, subject analysis of variance (ANO-VA) was used for statistical analysis. The experiment involved four different presupposition triggers, *viz.* factive verbs, implicative verbs, change of state verbs, and temporal clauses. The final result of the mean score of 3.31 on the redundancy scale for sentences with reinforced indirect messages linked with implicative verbs have been shown to suggest that in contrast to presuppositions carried by other triggers, those indirect messages (or assumptions) can be reinforced without producing a sense of anomalous redundancy. The author argues that the results could be explained using the notion of accommodation and that assumptions linked to implicative verbs could be treated as default meanings rather than presuppositions.

This text integrates older approaches, a neo-Gricean approach, and in particular Kasia Jaszczolt's theory of default semantics (Jaszczolt 2005; 2010) with a broadly speech act-theoretic perspective where meaning is seen as dynamic, situated, i.e. context-dependent, and perspectival. The linking thread between traditional speech act theory and the reported analysis may also be found in the author's concentration on the class of implicative verbs, in which he follows Karttunen (1971) and Levinson (1983). Włodarczyk starts with the original account, and acknowledging the fact that implicative verbs have sometimes been classified as conventional implicatures (Abbott 2006, Potts 2007), he moves to test the class using Jaszczolt's original theory of default semantics. While this text can hardly be recognised as strictly speech act theory-oriented, it serves to show that the spirit of the speech act-theoretic attitude is present both in studies on presupposition and in novel semantics theories such as default semantics.

It is the editors' hope that the variety of topics and approaches found in the present volume will invite further discussions on speech act theory and the performative dimension of language use.

Finally, the editors would like to thank the authors for contributing to this thematic volume and allowing their speech act-theoretic research programmes to become part of it. We would also like to extend our thanks to the large group of reviewers of the volume, who performed tremendous work in selecting and profiling the articles. Last but not least we would like to express our gratitude to Professor Katarzyna Paprzycka-Hausman and the *Poznań Studies in the Philosophy of the Sciences and the Humanities* team for making this project possible by offering us space in the journal.

Bibliography

Abbott, B. (2006). Where have some of the presuppositions gone. B.J. Birner and G.L. Ward (eds.), *Drawing the boundaries of meaning: Neo-Gricean studies in pragmatics and semantics in honor of Laurence R. Horn*, 1–20. Amsterdam: John Benjamins

Asher, N. and A. Lascarides (2001). Indirect Speech Acts. *Synthese* 128, 183–228.

Asher, N. and A. Lascarides (2003). *Logics of Conversation*. Cambridge: Cambridge University Press.

Attardo, S. (2000). Irony as relevant inappropriateness. *Journal of Pragmatics* 32, 793–826.

Austin, J.L. (1962/1975). *How to Do Things with Words*. 2nd ed. [first published in 1962]. Oxford: Oxford University Press.

Austin, J.L. (1964). *Sense and Sensibilia (Reconstructed from the manuscript notes by G.J. Warnock)*. Oxford: Clarendon Press.

Austin, J.L. (1970). *Philosophical Papers*. 2nd ed. [first published in 1961; ed. by J.O. Urmson & G.J. Warnock]. Oxford: Oxford University Press.

Ball, B. (2014a). On the Normativity of Speech Acts. In P. Stalmaszczyk (ed.), *Semantics and Beyond. Philosophical and Linguistic Inquiries*, pp. 9–26. Berlin/Boston: De Gruyter.

Ball, B. (2014b). Speech Acts: Natural or Normative Kinds? The Case of Assertion. *Mind & Language* 29 (3), 336–350.

Ball. B. (this volume). Commitment and Obligation in Speech Act Theory. In. M. Witek and I. Witczak-Plisiecka (eds.), *Normativity and Variety of Speech Actions*, pp. 51–65. Leiden: Brill (*Poznań Studies in the Philosophy of the Sciences and the Humanities* 112).

Brandom, R. (1983). Asserting. *Nous* 17 (4), 637–650.

Brown, P. and S.C. Levinson. (1987). *Politeness*. Cambridge: Cambridge University Press.

Budzyńska, K. and M. Witek (2014). Non-Inferential Aspects of *Ad Hominem* and *Ad Baculum. Argumentation* 28, 301–315.

Carassa, A. and M. Colombetti. (2009). Joint meaning. *Journal of Pragmatics* 41, 1837–1854.

Corredor, C. (this volume). The dynamics of conversation: fixing the force in irony. A case study. In. M. Witek and I. Witczak-Plisiecka (eds.), *Normativity and Variety of Speech Actions*, pp. 140–158. Leiden: Brill (*Poznań Studies in the Philosophy of the Sciences and the Humanities* 112).

Culpeper, J. (2011). *Impoliteness*. Cambridge: Cambridge University Press.

De Beaugrande, R-A. and W.U. Dressler. (1981). *Einführung in die Textlinguistik*. Tübingen: Niemeyer.

Fetzer, A. (2004). *Recontextualizing Context: Grammaticality meets Appropriateness*. Amsterdam/Philadelphia: John Benjamins.

Fetzer, A. (ed.) (2007). *Context and Appropriateness: Micro meets macro*. Amsterdam/Philadelphia: John Benjamins.

Giora, R. (2003). *On our mind: salience, context and figurative language*. Oxford: Oxford University Press.

Grice, H.P. (1989). *Studies in the Way of Words*. Cambridge, Mass.: Harvard University Press.

Jaszczolt, K.M. (2005). *Default Semantics: Foundations of a Compositional Theory of Acts of Communication*. Oxford: Oxford University Press.

Jaszczolt, K.M. (2010). Default Semantics. In B. Heine and H. Narrog (eds.), *The Oxford Handbook of Linguistic Analysis*, pp. 193–221. Oxford: Oxford University Press.

Jaszczolt, K.M. and M. Witek (2018). Expressing the Self: From Types of *De Se* to Speech-Act-Types. In M. Huang and K. Jaszczolt (eds.), *Expressing the Self: Cultural Diversity and Cognitive Universals*. Oxford: Oxford University Press, pp. 187–221.

Karttunen, L. (1971). Implicative Verbs. *Language* 47, 340–358.

Kripke, S. (1980). *Naming and Necessity*. Cambridge, Mass.: Harvard University Press.

Kurzon, D. (1998). *Discourse of Silence*. Amsterdam: John Benjamins.

Kurzon, D. (2007). A typology of silence. *Journal of Pragmatics* 39, 1673–1688.

Levinson, S.C. (1983). *Pragmatics*. Cambridge: Cambridge University.

Lewis, D. (1979). Scorekeeping in a language game. *Journal of Philosophical Logic* 8, 339–359.

Maeterlinck, M. (1902). Le silence. In *Le Tresor des Humbles*, pp. 2–25. Paris: Mercure de France.

Matczak, M. (this volume). A theory that beats the theory? Lineages, the growth of signs, and dynamic legal interpretation. In. M. Witek and I. Witczak-Plisiecka (eds.), *Normativity and Variety of Speech Actions*, pp. 180–205. Leiden: Brill (*Poznań Studies in the Philosophy of the Sciences and the Humanities* 112).

Mey, J. (2001). *Pragmatics: An Introduction*. Oxford: Blackwell.

Mey, J. (2010). Reference and the pragmeme. *Journal of Pragmatics* 42, 2882–2888.

Mey, J. (2011). Speech acts in context. In A. Fetzer and E. Oishi (eds.), *Context and Contexts: Parts meet whole?*, pp. 171–180. Amsterdam/Philadelphia: John Benjamins.

Millikan, R.G. (1984). *Language, Thought and Other Biological Categories*. Cambridge, Mass.: MIT Press.

Millikan, R.G. (2005). *Language: A Biological Model*. Oxford: Oxford University Press.

Peirce, C.S. (1878). How to Make Our Ideas Clear. *Popular Science Monthly* 12, 286–302.

Peirce, C.S. (1931–36). *The Collected Papers*. Volumes 1–6. Eds. Charles Hartshorne and Paul Weiss. Cambridge Mass.: Harvard University Press.

Peirce, C.S. (1998). *The Essential Peirce*. Volume 2. Bloomington I.N.: Indiana University Press.

Potts, C. (2007). Into the Conventional-Implicature Dimension. *Philosophy Compass* 2 (4), 665–679.

Putnam, H. (1975). The Meaning of 'Meaning.' *Minnesota Studies in the Philosophy of Science* 7, 131–193.

Sbisà, M. (1992). Speech Acts, Effects and Responses. In. J. Searle et al., *(On) Searle on Conversation*, pp. 101–112. Amsterdam/Philadelphia: John Benjamins.

Sbisà, M. (2002). Speech acts in context. *Language & Communication* 22, 421–436.

Sbisà, M. (2007). How to read Austin. Pragmatics 17(3): 461–473.

Sbisà, M. (2009). Uptake and Conventionality in Illocution. *Lodz Papers in Pragmatics* 5 (1), 33–52.

Sbisà, M. (2013). Locution, illocution, perlocution. In. M. Sbisà, K. Turner (eds.), *Pragmatics of Speech Actions*, pp. 25–75. Berlin/Boston: De Gruyter Mouton.

Sbisà, M. (this volume). Varieties of speech act norms. In. M. Witek and I. Witczak-Plisiecka (eds.), *Normativity and Variety of Speech Actions*, pp. 23–50. Leiden: Brill (*Poznań Studies in the Philosophy of the Sciences and the Humanities* 112).

Schegloff, E.A. (1995). Discourse as an Interactional Achievement III: The Omnirelevance of Action. *Research on Language and Social Interaction* 28 (3), 185–211.

Schegloff, E.A. (2006). *Sequence Organization in Interaction*. Cambridge: Cambridge University Press.

Searle, J.R. (1969). *Speech Acts: An Essay in the Philosophy of Language*. Cambridge, Mass.: Cambridge University Press.

Searle, J.R. (1979). *Expression and Meaning*. Cambridge: Cambridge University Press.

Searle, J.R. (1995). *The Construction of Social Reality*. New York: Free Press.

Searle, J.R. (2010). *Making the Social World: The Structure of Human Civilization*. Oxford: Oxford University Press.

Spencer-Oatey, H. (2005). (Im)Politeness, Face and Perceptions of Rapport. Unpackaging Their Bases and Interrelationships. *Journal of Politeness Research: Language, Behaviour, Culture* 1, 95–119.

Spencer-Oatey, H. (2007). Theories of Identity and the Analysis of Face. *Journal of Pragmatics* 39, 639–665.

Van Dijk, T.A. (1980a). *Macrostructures*. Hillsdale, NJ: Earlbaum.

Van Dijk, T.A. (1980b). *Text and Context*. London: Longman.

Van Dijk, T.A. (2008). *Discourse and Context. A Sociocognitive Approach*. Cambridge: Cambridge University Press.

Wierzbicka, A. (1987) *English Speech Act Verbs: A semantic dictionary*. Marrickville: Academic Press Australia.

Williamson, T. (2000) *Knowledge and its limits*. Oxford: Oxford University Press.

Wilson, D. (2013). Irony comprehension: A developmental perspective. *Journal of Pragmatics* 59 (A), 40–56.

Wilson, D. and D. Sperber (2012). Explaining irony. In D. Wilson and D. Sperber (eds.), *Meaning and Relevance*, pp. 123–145. Cambridge: Cambridge University Press.

Witczak-Plisiecka, I. (2007). *Language, Law and Speech Acts: Pragmatic Meaning in English Legal Texts*. Łódź: WSSM.

Witczak-Plisiecka, I. (2009a). A linguistic-pragmatic note on indeterminacy in legal language. *Linguistica Copernicana* 1 (1), 231–243.

Witczak-Plisiecka, I. (2009b). Speech acts and the autonomy of linguistic pragmatics. *Lodz Papers in Pragmatics* 5 (1), 85–106. doi: 10.2478/v10016-009-0008-8.

Witczak-Plisiecka, I. (ed.) (2010). *Speech Actions in Theory and Applied Studies*. [*Pragmatic Perspectives on Language and Linguistics, Vol. I.*]. Newcastle: Cambridge Scholars Publishing.

Witczak-Plisiecka, I. (2011). Performatywność jako znaczenie wyłaniające się w kontekście w świetle pojęć emergencji i amalgamatów językoznawstwa kognitywnego. In A. Kwiatkowska (ed.), *Przestrzenie kognitywnych poszukiwań*, pp. 195–206. Łódź: Wydawnictwo Uniwersytetu Łódzkiego.

Witczak-Plisiecka, I. (ed.) (2012). *Research in Language* 10 (3): Special Issue *Cognitive and pragmatic perspectives on speech action* (available on-line at deGruyter Open: http://www.degruyter.com/view/j/rela).

Witczak-Plisiecka, I. (2013a). Speech action in legal contexts. In M. Sbisà & K. Turner (eds.), *Pragmatics of Speech Actions* [Handbook of Pragmatics; Part 2], pp. 613–658. Berlin/Boston: Mouton de Gruyter.

Witczak-Plisiecka, I. (2013b). *From Speech Acts to Speech Actions*. Łódź: Łódź University Press.

Witczak-Plisiecka, I. (ed.) (2013c). *Research in Language* 11 (2): Special Issue *Researching Meaning, Context and Cognition* (available on-line at deGruyter Open: http://www.degruyter.com/view/j/rela).

Witczak-Plisiecka, I. (ed.) (2014). *Pragmatic and Cognitive Aspects of Speech Actions*. Frankfurt am Main: Peter Lang.

Witczak-Plisiecka, I. and M. Witek (eds.) (2009). *Lodz Papers in Pragmatics* 5 (1): Special Issue on Speech Actions (available on-line at deGruyter Open: http://www.degruyter.com/view/j/lpp).

Witek, M. (ed.) (2005). *Philosophica* 75: Special Issue *Truth, Knowledge and the Pragmatics of Natural Language* (available on-line at: http://logica.ugent.be/philosophica/).

Witek, M. (2009). Scepticism About Reflexive Intentions Refuted. *Lodz Papers in Pragmatics* 5 (1), 69–83.

Witek, M. (2011). *Spór o podstawy teorii czynności mowy*. Szczecin: WN US.

Witek, M. (2013a). How to Establish Authority with Words: Imperative Utterances and Presupposition Accommodation. In A. Brożek, J. Jadacki & B. Žarnic (eds.), *Theory of Imperatives from Different Points of View* (2) [*Logic, Methodology and Philosophy of Science at Warsaw University*, Vol. 7], pp. 145–157. Warszawa: Semper.

Witek, M. (2013b). Three Approaches to the Study of Speech Acts. *Dialogue and Universalism* 23 (1), 129–142.

Witek, M. (2015a). An Interactional Account of Illocutionary Practice. *Language Sciences* 47, 43–55.

Witek, M. (2015b). Linguistic Underdeterminacy: A View from Speech Act Theory. *Journal of Pragmatics* 76, 15–29.

Witek, M. (2015c). Mechanisms of Illocutionary Games. *Language & Communication* 42, 11–22.

Witek, M. (2016). Accommodation and Convention. *Polish Journal of Philosophy* 10 (1), 99–115.

PART 1

Normative Aspects of Speech Actions

∵

CHAPTER 1

Varieties of Speech Act Norms

Marina Sbisà

Abstract

This paper explores the field of speech act norms, shedding some light upon their variety, in particular as regards the different roles they play in the dynamics of illocution. A threefold distinction is proposed: constitutive rules, upon which the performance of illocutionary acts depends; maxims, based on rational motivations, encoding regulative advice for optimal speech act performance in the perspective of the participants; and objective requirements for the overall correctness of the accomplished speech act with regard to the situation in the world to which it relates. These three kinds of norms engender three different sorts of penalty when not complied with. Some examples applying the proposed distinction to speech act types provide a very limited test of its potential as a descriptive framework. Of the three kinds of norms, only constitutive rules can be said to be conventional, since they establish procedures that are repeatable and recognizable from one occasion to another and whose function (bringing about changes in the deontic roles of the participants) is only exercised against a background of social agreement: therefore, one may conceive of all speech acts as conventional for certain aspects and non-conventional for others.

1 Introduction

The aim of this paper is to explore the field of speech act norms, shedding some light upon their variety, in particular as regards the different roles they play in the dynamics of illocution, that is, in the interactional mechanisms that make it possible for the utterance of one interlocutor to bring about an illocutionary effect, recognized by the other interlocutor.[1] I propose a

---

1 An early version of this paper was read at the 9th International Pragmatics Conference (held in Gotheborg, 8–13 July 2007) at a workshop on Speech Act Norms coordinated by Mitchell Green. I am grateful to the participants for discussion and comments. Once I resumed the project, I have greatly profited from comments and objections by Maciej Witek, whom I would also like to thank wholeheartedly. I thank also Rae Langton for discussion about Lewis on accommodation, and two anonymous referees for their critical comments and suggestions.

threefold distinction between constitutive rules, maxims, and objective requirements. In my perspective, constitutive rules are those speech act norms which, when complied with, enable us to perform the acts they define; they organize procedures or routines that are repeatable and recognizable from one occasion to another and whose function (the production of illocutionary effects) is only exercised against a background of intersubjective agreement. Maxims encode regulative advice for optimal speech act performance in the perspective of the participants in the current verbal interaction. Objective requirements set standards of assessment (specific to each illocutionary act type) that the speech act performed should meet, irrespective of the perspective of the participants, in order to qualify as correct (or proper, or good, or if suitable, true).

Since Wittgenstein (1953) and his language games, many have considered speech as a rule-governed activity. Even philosophers and linguists with no sympathy for Wittgenstein's perspective admit that speech acts obey to norms. While at first sight one might think that the rules or norms applying to speech all belong to one and the same kind, this paper argues that it is not so. Linguistic rules such as rules of syntax or lexical semantics and rules of polite verbal behaviour do not function in the same way as the rules for the performance of illocutionary acts. Moreover, even the latter (upon which this paper will focus attention) do not all work in the same way.

When paying attention to differences, one might even come to doubt whether all the rules that play a role in accounts of how speech acts work are indeed norms and, therefore, whether there is indeed a single, all-encompassing object of inquiry such as the field of speech act norms. In this paper, I will not discuss in a general way whether all rules are also norms, but I presuppose that 'speech act norms' are a field worth investigating and within it examine those speech act rules that play some kind of normative role with respect to one or other of the aspects or phases of speech act production and understanding (among which I take as salient the performance and recognition of the illocutionary act). I do not assume, however, that all norms have to be formulated as rules and that is why I prefer the label 'speech act norms' for my current object of inquiry. Distinctions between the functions that speech act norms may play can be grounded in remarks concerning illocutionary act dynamics and, most importantly, in the description of what happens when the norm is violated. Indeed, when a norm is violated some penalty follows, and the kind of penalty is generally correlated with the function served by the norm.

I intend to keep my discussion on norms and their functions separate from the issue of the origin and nature of norms (both in general and with respect to speech acts).[2] I think that the analysis of the norms applying to speech acts as they appear to our consciousness and practical experience is a significant task in itself, regardless of other, more directly explanatory attempts, which in any case presuppose the explananda and their properties.

2   Constitutive Rules

Taking inspiration (and borrowing the name) from the speech-act theoretical tradition, I call a first kind of speech act norms 'constitutive rules'. Constitutive rules are widely recognized as rules without which a certain act type would not exist and performances of acts of that type could not occur. Acts that are so constituted need not be speech acts, but all speech acts, *qua* illocutionary acts, must have constitutive rules.

The most classic reference for constitutive rules in speech act theory is John Searle's chapter on constitutive and regulative rules (Searle 1969, pp. 33–42). Searle claims that constitutive rules "'do not merely regulate, they create or define new forms of behaviour'", creating as it were their "'very possibility'." (Searle 1969, p. 33). Thus the activities to which these rules apply are logically dependent upon them. While regulative rules establish how something should be done, constitutive rules establish how one can do something and thus, in the case of speech acts, when a certain utterance amounts to the performance of a certain illocutionary act.

Searle takes constitutive rules to comprise all the conditions, individually necessary and jointly sufficient, for the felicitous and non-defective performances of an illocutionary act and, after specifying the conditions for promising, specifies also those of various other illocutionary act types (Searle 1969, pp. 54–71). It is instructive to compare what he says about constitutive rules with Austin's discussion of how saying can 'make it so' (Austin 1962, p. 7 and pp. 13–38), which also involves the specification of a set of rules, primarily meant to account for performativity in explicitly performative utterances, but actually extendable to the performance of illocutionary acts and therefore functionally similar to Searle's constitutive rules.[3] Austin's rules, however, are

---

2 A recent discussion of this issue, not unrelated to the speech-act theoretical perspective developed here, is due to Witek (2015b). In the same vein, Witek (this volume) argues for a naturalistic account of some normative aspects of illocutionary acts.

3 That Austin intended those rules to apply to illocutionary acts is clear from the fact that he takes the defects and failures in performing illocutionary acts to be infelicities (that is, defects due to the violation of one or other of the rules in question) (cf. Austin 1962, pp. 105–106

cast in a generic form, with variables to be filled in to yield the rules for specific illocutionary acts, for example:

> There must exist an accepted conventional procedure having a certain conventional effect, that procedure to include the uttering of certain words by certain persons in certain circumstances. (Austin 1962, p. 14)

Obviously, the actual constitutive rules of an illocutionary act should specify the procedure that is required to exist and its effect. Thus, Austin's rules are not themselves constitutive rules of any illocutionary act, but are templates for sets of such rules.

Austin distinguishes three main kinds of rules (or rule templates), which he calls A, B and Γ: A rules are concerned with the existence of a procedure and the appropriateness of participants and circumstances (they require the existence of a procedure and the appropriateness of persons and circumstances to that procedure), B rules with the execution of the procedure (they require its correctness and completeness), and Γ rules with the sincerity and consistency of the participants. However, Austin does not present these rules as (templates for) jointly sufficient conditions, but leaves the performance of illocutionary act tokens open to unforeseen forms of defeasibility. Thus, one of the main differences between his speech act theory and Searle's resides in the alleged completeness of the Searlean set of rules as opposed to the advertised incompleteness of that of Austin. It is indeed in the effort to be exhaustive that Searle posits rules requiring, for example, normal conditions of communication to obtain, introduces the 'essential' condition, and a further condition we may call 'meaning-intention' condition requiring the speaker to entertain a Gricean meaning intention in her utterance of the linguistic means designed for the performance of the act she intends to perform (Searle 1969, pp. 60–61; cf. Grice 1989, p. 219). The rule requiring normal communication conditions has no counterpart in the Austinian set, because of Austin's general attitude as regards what is 'normal', which according to him should not be defined positively (as fulfilling a finite set of conditions, which would never be exhaustive), but presumed by default (unless special conditions obtain). Moreover, while in Austin rules of the A and B forms apply to a speaker's invocation of a procedure, in Searle the invocation of the procedure is itself turned into a condition of successfulness of the procedure by requiring (in the essential condition)

---

and p. 148) and from his appeal to the same rules while discussing assertion as an illocutionary act (*ibid.*, pp. 136–138).

the speaker to intend to achieve the procedure's effect and (in the meaning-intention condition) to utter the words that are part of the procedure.[4]

Beyond the differences between the two philosophers, their accounts converge on granting the power to make the act null and void (and therefore suspending or 'making undone' its effect) (Sbisà 2007, pp. 465–466) to a subset of rules comprising, for Austin, rules of the forms A and B, and for Searle, all his rules but the sincerity rule. In their respective speech-act theoretical contexts, these rules are indeed such that success in the act's performance depends upon compliance with them. They are therefore meant as 'constitutive' in the clearest and strongest sense of the word.

Other rules that have been viewed as constitutive may not have the above-described property. I am referring in particular to Searle's sincerity condition (Searle 1969, p. 60), to Austin's rules (or rule templates) Γ1 and Γ2 (Austin 1962, p. 15 and pp. 39–41), and to the Knowledge Rule put forward by Williamson (2000, p. 243) as the norm of assertion.

According to Austin, the procedures for performing illocutionary acts specify the psychological state that the speaker invoking them should be in, but non-compliance with this kind of requirements is an abuse of the procedure which cannot make the act null and void (Austin 1962, p. 16). Likewise, Searle admits that an insincere promise may be a successful promise nevertheless: it does commit the speaker, even if she lacks the intention to do what she promises (Searle 1969, p. 62).[5] He agrees that an insincere promise is somewhat defective, but not in such a way as to hinder the promise from doing its job, namely, committing the speaker. Also rules of Austin's Γ2 kind, requiring appropriate subsequent conduct, do not make the act null and void in case of violation: it would be absurd to absolve breakers of promises and of other speech-act related commitments because of their very non-compliance. According to Williamson's norm of assertion, the speaker must have knowledge of what she asserts (Williamson 2000, p. 243). This means that whoever asserts something without knowing that things are so is thereby committing a violation and is

---

4 It is controversial whether Austin and Searle are externalist or internalist about the conditions for illocutionary act performance and which approach is preferable (for different readings and opposite evaluations, see Sbisà 2002; Harnish 2009). I would argue, however, that the essential condition and the meaning-intention condition at least introduce internalist requirements into Searle's set of constitutive rules, while Austin's rules of the A and B kinds only pose externalist requirements. I also find the externalist approach more suitable to dealing with constitutive rules, since in principle, their violation should be publicly detectable.

5 Searle does not thereby become an externalist. Even if the intention to do what one promises is not indispensable to making a successful promise, the intention to commit oneself to doing something remains such, since it is required by the essential condition.

subject to criticism. But Williamson grants the utterance to be an assertion nevertheless, and he is certainly right: also in those conditions, the speaker will be committed to the truth of the content of her utterance.

According to Williamson's understanding of constitutive rules, the decisive trait for a rule to be constitutive is whether it contributes to the definition of the act it applies to. Now, sincerity rules (Searle's sincerity condition, Austin's Γ1 rule) and Austin's consistency rule Γ2 are certainly part of the definitions of illocutionary act types. All these rules can be called 'constitutive', if by this it we mean that they contribute to defining illocutionary act types. But their violation is never a fatal flaw in the procedure of performing an illocutionary act token: it does not lead to suspending or annulling the illocutionary effect. So, an agent can well perform her illocutionary act successfully (insofar as its effect is concerned) without abiding by them. I will say that rules like these are constitutive in the weak sense, while only a subset of them, those fixing the requirements which must be complied with to ensure the success of the illocutionary act, are constitutive in the strong sense I prefer to use here.

Constitutive rules may interact or overlap with both linguistic rules and norms of politeness. They overlap with linguistic rules when they fix the utterance of certain words or of words in a certain syntactic construction as part of the procedure for performing illocutionary acts of a certain type. From the point of view of the rules of language, this amounts to assigning to a certain form of utterance, or to a certain word or expression, the role of an illocutionary indicator. As to politeness norms, they affect the performance of speech acts, just as they affect all interactional behaviour. For example, they may impose or recommend the use of indirect forms for the performance of illocutionary acts that might turn out to be 'face-threatening', such as (most famously) requests (Brown and Levinson 1987; for an overview of research on requests, see Walker 2013; for the role of face-work in social interaction, see Goffman 1967; 1971). When the indirect forms that are motivated by politeness become standard ways to perform a given type of illocutionary act in a given language and culture, it would be reasonable to say that they are now part of its 'accepted conventional procedure' (Austin 1962, p. 14): consider, for example, idiomatic formulas for requesting such as 'Would you mind ...?' or for apologizing such as 'Sorry'. Moreover, there are types of illocutionary acts whose function in social interaction is to cope with politeness requirements, repairing or preventing threat or damage to face, or fostering the participants' positive face. While on the one hand it is a norm of politeness (for example) that participants in a speech event of a certain kind should foster one another's positive face, on the other, in order for kinds of illocutionary acts which help to achieve this aim, such as wishes or congratulations, to be performed (or even to be merely available for performance), there must be constitutive rules for them.

3 Maxims

The second kind of speech act norms I would like to distinguish are maxims. They encode advice for optimal communicative behaviour from the point of view of the subjects involved. Since Grice makes reference to Kant, in introducing conversational maxims (albeit on a somewhat different topic; see Grice 1989, p. 26), it might be interesting to recall the use Kant made of maxims in his *Appendix to the Transcendental Dialectics*. There, Kant introduces maxims of Reason, sharply distinguished from the categories which are constitutive of judgment and therefore of knowledge, to express the guidelines that Reason follows in its attempts to optimize knowledge.

In the sense outlined above, Grice's conversational maxims stemming from the Cooperative Principle, and the Cooperative Principle itself (Grice 1989, pp. 26–27) are maxims. They serve the optimization of communicative behaviour in two main ways: when they directly inspire the speaker's utterances (see *ibid.*, p. 26) and when speaker and hearer rely on the assumption that they hold in projecting or deriving conversational implicatures (see *ibid.*, pp. 32–33). Among the rules or conditions specified by Searle and Austin, Searle's sincerity condition and Austin's rules Γ1 and Γ2, which (as I have already argued in Section 2) do not function as constitutive rules, can be taken to be maxims.

Maxims are regulative, not constitutive.[6] Contrary to a recent interpretation, which expresses a recurrent temptation (see Bermejo-Luque 2011), I do not take the Cooperative Principle to be 'constitutive of meaning'. In Grice's perspective one can well say something without abiding by the CP: this happens, for example, when a philosopher discussing perceptual knowledge says 'This post-box seems red to me' in circumstances in which she can see very clearly that it is red. Here there is truth-conditional meaning, but no cooperativity, at least in the standard sense in which ordinary conversation is cooperative. But I do not take the CP to be constitutive of conversation either.

---

6 Regulative rules are prescriptive. A referee has objected to my treatment of Grice's maxims as 'maxims' (in my sense), arguing that Grice's maxims are descriptive. But Grice conceives of the CP and the maxims specifying it that they formulate how it is rational to behave in verbal interaction, and therefore how participants in a conversation should behave (Grice 1989, p. 29). By the way, if conversational maxims were merely descriptive, then they would depict how speakers actually behave; but it is not the case that we always follow the maxims.

Conversation is not a rule-governed activity in the sense in which an activity such as a card game is rule-governed and even less in the sense in which acts such as commands, warnings, promises, apologies are governed by constitutive rules. It is a matter of fact that there are conversational exchanges: that people talk to each other is just a fact the occurrence of which does not depend on definitions and labels. Moreover, when a covert and non-repairable violation of a conversational maxims is discovered, the penalty for the speaker consists of criticism, damage to reputation, or loss of reliability, but does not include making the conversational episode 'null and void'. This does not make sense with conversations, since there is no single conventional effect to be associated with conversation as such (while there are conventional effects brought about by single conversational moves *qua* illocutionary acts). People actually and thoroughly not cooperating with one another cannot be said to have a conversation: they just talk past each other, which, again, is a matter of fact and not the effect of (or penalty for) non-compliance with rules.

The sincerity rule associated with illocutionary acts by Searle (1969; 1979) and the illocutionary type-specific versions of Austin's rule Γ1 are analogous in content (at least when applied to speech acts of the assertive family) to Grice's first maxim of Quality 'Do not say what you believe to be false' (Grice 1989, p. 27). That the sincerity rule cannot be constitutive in our strong sense, as are other speech act norms apparently belonging to the same set, is recognized, as reported above (in Section 2), both by Austin and Searle. Austin is explicit in distinguishing his A and B rules from his Γ rules, which read as follows (and again, are rule-templates rather than rules for specific illocutionary acts):

> Γ1:   where, as often, the procedure is designed for use by persons having certain thoughts, feelings, or intentions, or for the inauguration of certain consequential conduct on the part of any participant, then a person participating in and so invoking the procedure must in fact have those thoughts or feelings, and the participants must intend so to conduct themselves, and further
> Γ2:   must actually so conduct themselves subsequently. (Austin 1962, p. 15)

The main difference between the A and B rules and Γ rules is that failure to comply with the former may lead to failure to perform the act, while failure to comply with the latter generates defects that make the act liable to certain kinds of criticism (as an abuse of the procedure or as a performance followed by inconsistent behaviour). By calling the latter kind of rules 'maxims', I mean to imply that the procedure for achieving a certain conventional effect is optimally performed only if it complies with them too.

In Searle (1969, p. 60) the sincerity condition is included among necessary and sufficient conditions for the successful and non-defective performance of illocutionary acts. Apparently, according to Searle, this condition functions as a constitutive rule. So, on the one hand, the mental state that should accompany a certain illocutionary act is part of the very definition of that illocutionary act, but on the other, violating the sincerity rule does not undermine the performance of the illocutionary act: insincere assertion, deceptive promise, etc. are assertion, promise, etc. nevertheless. Sincerity therefore seems to be a requirement for perfection, which the sincerity norm advises the speaker to achieve. But the sincerity norm cannot be both a constitutive rule and a maxim. Searle's solution of the puzzle is to propose a reformulation of the sincerity condition that can work as a constitutive rule while allowing insincere promises to be successfully performed promises: for promises, he replaces the condition 'S intends to do A' with the condition 'S intends that the utterance of T will make him responsible for intending to do A' (Searle 1969, p. 62). An insincere speaker may comply with the reformulated condition, while she obviously does not comply with the original one. It should be noted that Grice's approach to sincerity norms is more radical, since in his theory all connections between sincerity and constitutive rules are severed. His super-maxim of Quality requires that the speaker should attempt to provide the addressee with good quality information, namely attempts to say something true (see Grice 1989, p. 27). The more specific maxim recommending sincerity is derived from this general one: indeed, if you say something you do not believe to be true, you are certainly not attempting to say something true. Being sincere, then, amounts to avoiding one kind of hurdle on one's way towards saying what is true.

Austin's Γ_2 rule has no direct counterpart among Grice's maxims and one may wonder whether we need it as a maxim, since subsequent behaviour is in general mandated, directly or indirectly, by the illocutionary effect of the performed speech act. I think it is reasonable to keep it among speech act maxims, however, as consistency with the deontic states assigned by the illocutionary act to the speaker is not automatic, but contributes to optimizing the performance of the speech act from the point of view of the participants.

In some respects, maxims of politeness such as 'Don't impose' or 'Show solidarity' (see Lakoff 1973), insofar as they apply to speech acts, may also be included in this group of speech act norms: they advise us to select, from among the alternative forms for performing a certain illocutionary act, the form which is most suitable to the face-wants in the situation.

4   Objective Requirements

A third kind of speech act norms is what I would like to call objective requirements. These are normative standards for 'accomplished utterances' (Austin
1962, pp. 140–141), or complete speech act tokens, which take into consideration both their force and their meaning. In proposing a characterization of
this kind of norms, I will start from a reassessment of what Austin says about
'correspondence to facts'.

As is known, Austin considers the idiom 'correspondence to facts' as significant but not to be taken too literally (Austin 1961, pp. 117–133). He does
not assume one-to-one correspondence between true propositions and
facts, nor does he posit a truth-maker for every sentence or proposition
(*ibid.*, p. 123). His theory of truth links statements (or assertions) to 'historical situations' in the world by means of 'demonstrative conventions', which
he conceives of as distinct and even opposed to the 'descriptive conventions'
in virtue of which sentences represent types of situation (*ibid.*, pp. 121–122).
Thus the 'historical situation' with regard to which the assertion is to be assessed is not identified by means of its descriptive characterization by the
sentence used in making the assertion. 'Correspondence to facts', therefore,
means – in the case of assertions – that the pertinent situation in the world,
demonstratively identified, is as the assertion says it is: that it is correct to
speak of it as the speaker has done, in the light of the facts, but also of certain elements of the context, among which are the speaker's goals in making
the assertion (Austin 1962, p. 145).

Austin considers 'It is true that *p*' and other formulations of the assessment
in the dimension of truth and falsity as giving an assessment of the overall
correctness of a statement, or other assertive speech act. I speak of 'overall'
correctness, because the assessment targets both the locutionary and the illocutionary dimension of the assertion: obviously, it is concerned with its meaning, but it also presupposes the felicitous performance of the act of asserting
(in our terms, the satisfaction of its constitutive rules; see Austin 1962, p. 138
and p. 145). It is (so to say) the 'total speech act' that has to be the 'right thing'
to say and therein do within the 'total speech situation' (cf. *ibid.*, p. 52 and
p. 148), with respect to the 'historical situation' referred to. And what makes it
the 'right thing', is not merely the participants' belief (or even justified belief),
but also, and primarily, how the world actually is.

Austin's theory of truth has been criticized by Strawson (1950) and others
(see Pitcher ed. 1964), mainly for not managing to avoid all the mistakes that
correspondence theories are liable to make. I shall not discuss this issue here,
nor shall I tackle the issue of the nature and functioning of what Austin calls

'demonstrative conventions', an aspect of his theory that he failed to fully develop, despite its being most central, and one which has often been misunderstood (see for example Johnson 1992; Vision 2004). What I am interested in here is the role Austin assigned to the assessment of speech acts as regards their 'correspondence to facts'.

Indeed, according to Austin, speech acts other than assertion or statement are also liable to be assessed in the dimension of 'correspondence with facts', that is, to use the terms adopted in this paper, have to comply with their objective requirements. He introduces the topic thus:

> Can we be sure that stating truly is a different *class* of assessment from arguing soundly, advising well, judging fairly, and blaming justifiably? Do these not have something to do in complicated ways with facts? (Austin 1962, p. 142)

Austin discusses briefly how this kind of assessment applies to acts of judgment (which he calls 'verdictives') such as estimating or pronouncing, acts of exposition (which he calls 'expositives') such as arguing and inferring, acts concerned with social behaviour (or 'behabitives') such as praise, blame and congratulations, and acts of exercising authority (or 'exercitives') such as warning and advising or even naming and appointing. In my opinion, developing his suggestions in a full-blown speech-act theoretical perspective would involve more effort in the direction of specifying how an assessment considering 'correspondence with facts' applies to speech acts of any kind of illocutionary force. For example, when we leave the field of cognitively oriented speech acts to which assertion or statement belong, evaluative terms other than 'true' and 'false' come in, and the objective requirements they embody differ from truth in ways that need to be further explored. Estimates and assessments (albeit 'verdictives', cf. Austin 1962, p. 153) are not so much 'true' as 'right' or 'fair': being right, or fair, is their way of being correct. In order to deem them right or wrong, fair or unfair, we have at least to consider: the speech situation, the situation in the world to which the speech act refers, the pertinent criteria of judgment and their application, possible application precedents and, finally, the aims for which the estimate or assessment was contributed. But we also have 'good' and 'bad' advice, 'merited' and 'unmerited' blame and (I would like to add) 'just' or 'unjust' orders. In each case what is at issue is not whether the speech act was felicitously performed (a matter of constitutive rules, in the sense of our Section 2), nor whether it was performed optimally in the subjective perspective of the participants (a matter of maxims, in the sense of our Section 3), but whether the speaker was right in performing that speech act for those aims in that context, given how things are in the world. A complete survey of forms of assessment of speech acts of all kinds of illocutionary forces might tell us whether and how speech acts of the various illocutionary classes have to 'correspond to facts' in order to comply with their standards of correctness.

The requirements or standards of overall correctness for a speech act can be called objective, since they are to be complied with objectively. In order for an assertion to be true, it does not matter what the speaker or the receiver believe, it does not matter even what its evaluator believes: it matters how the assertion, as made in a certain speech situation with a certain descriptive content, actually relates to the historical situation to which it refers. Truth and falsity (as well as other values concerning satisfaction or failure to satisfy the pertinent standard) are therefore 'mind-transcendent':[7] any of the participants in the speech situation might be wrong about whether a certain assertion is true or false, or a certain piece of advice good or bad, and so on. For Austin, certainly, a speech act always occurs in a context, and so does the assessment of a speech act according to its pertinent objective requirements (cf. Austin 1961, p. 127, 129). In taking the speech situation into account, such an assessment has to consider facts such as the ongoing activity, the participants' state of knowledge, and the aims of the speaker in issuing the speech act. In this process, the contextual character of the application of objective requirements does not undermine either their objectivity or the objective nature of the assessment: when evaluating correctness (in the case of assertions, truth), if the aims for which the speech act is performed have to be taken into consideration, this is precisely because it is in its speech situation that the speech act must meet, or fail to meet, its pertinent standard.[8] Disagreements among participants about how to 'objectively' assess the same speech act may also be taken to undermine the objective character of the requirements. But there is indeed no clash, because meeting the requirement at issue 'objectively' means merely that only one of the disagreeing participants (or at most one) can be right in her application of the relevant assessment criteria.

---

7   I am borrowing this word from Gauker (1998).

8   While Austin's discussion of the assessment of assertions such as 'France is hexagonal', 'Lord Raglan won the battle of Alma' or 'All swans are white' (Austin 1962, pp. 142–145) has been a source of inspiration for contextualists (e.g. Travis 2000; 2008; Carston 2002; Recanati 2004), it should be kept in mind that his original considerations focus on the context-dependency of truth-falsity assessments (or in Austin's terms, of assessments in the dimension of correspondence with facts), not on the context-dependency of expressed propositions.

5   **Three Examples**

Let us now exemplify the proposed three-fold distinction by applying it to a small sample of illocutionary act types: promise, advice, and congratulations.

(i)   Promise

(a) Constitutive rules:
  – the promised feat must be a future feat of the speaker or to be performed under the speaker's responsibility,
  – its performance must be in the powers of the speaker,
  – it must also be in the interest of the addressee, or at least be believed by speaker and addressee to be such,
  – some linguistic form must be used such as to make the act of promising recognizable: the explicit performative 'I promise that ...', a performative gloss ('That was a promise'), or words clarifying that the speaker is not simply expressing an intention but actually committing herself.

(b) Maxims:
  – the speaker must have the intention to perform the promised feat,
  – the speaker must behave consistently with the obligation she has undertaken (unless this becomes impossible for reasons beyond her control).

(c) Objective requirements:
  – the promise is objectively correct when the speaker was right in promising that addressee, in that situation, for those aims and with those expected consequences, to perform that feat, and the promise was, therefore, a righteous action.

Comments:

If it turns out that the feat mentioned in the utterance is not in the speaker's powers or is not to be performed under the speaker's responsibility, or that it cannot be performed in the future at all, the speech act cannot be a promise, even if it presents itself as a realization of the procedure of promising. But due to the general tendency to accept speech acts at their face value in default conditions, if it is merely uncertain whether it is or is not in the speaker's powers to perform the promised feat, the belief that it is so is tacitly accepted or 'accommodated' by the audience, thus letting the illocutionary act take effect.[9] Also the belief that the promised feat is in the interest of the addressee may

---

9 Constitutive rules, successful performance and the 'accommodation' phenomenon (Lewis 1979; Stalnaker 1999) are closely linked. Accommodation is discussed in Section 7.

be accommodated by members of the audience other than the addressee, provided the latter does not belie it. Compliance with the maxims is assumed by default if there is no reason to doubt the speaker's good faith. Of course, time will show whether the maxim concerning consistency is actually complied with. As to objective requirements, they apply to the accomplished promise as its standard of correctness, provided that the action of promising was actually performed. They are concerned both with its locutionary and illocutionary aspects, possibly also covering those perlocutionary effects that are reasonably expected. It should be noted that insincere promises would fail both compliance with the maxims and satisfaction of objective requirements (to the extent to which they are in fact misleading), while sincere promises, albeit complying with the maxims, may still fail to meet the objective requirements.

(ii)   Advice
   (a) Constitutive rules:
      – the speaker must have authority over the addressee with respect to the field of activities with which the piece of advice is concerned,
      – the speaker must have competence about the relevant features of the situation, especially those potentially relevant to the achievement of the addressee's goals,
      – it must be open to the addressee to choose one among various lines of conduct,
      – the speaker's words must be a realization of the procedure of giving advice, indicating a line of conduct or criteria for choosing it and clarifying that it is best suited to the addressee's goals, given the constraints and requirements of the situation,– when not clear enough from the situation (as when the speaker is officially in charge of giving advice to the addressee) or from the content of the speaker's utterance, some additional linguistic form must be used to make the act of advising recognizable, such as the explicit performative 'I advise ...' or a performative gloss ('This is my advice').
   (b) Maxims:
      – the speaker must believe that it will be good for the addressee, in view of his goals, to behave as advised,
      – the speaker must behave consistently with the piece of advice provided, for example neither hindering nor pre-empting the addressee's compliance with it.
   (c) Objective requirements:
      – the accomplished piece of advice is 'good' advice if it is apt to help the addressee to achieve or approximate his goals in a manner

conforming to the other possible constraints and requirements of
the situation.

Comments:

If it turns out that the speaker has no relevant authority or no relevant competence or that there is no point in advising since the addressee has no choice,
the speech act, even if it presents itself as a realization of the procedure of
giving advice, cannot be the giving of a piece of advice.

But in default conditions the speech act may be taken as successfully performed advice, accommodating the relevant beliefs about the speaker's competence and the availability to the addressee of more than one course of action.
The speaker's authority may also be accommodated, in informal settings at least.

Compliance with the first maxim is assumed by default and compliance
with the second is standardly expected. While we may assess a piece of advice
as 'good' or 'bad' already on the basis of our knowledge of the addressee's situation and our consequent expectations, whether or not it was 'good' advice will
often become clear over time.

(iii)   Congratulations

    (a)   Constitutive rules:

       – the addressee must be the author of a certain achievement,

       – the speaker must be in such a relationship to the addressee, that
         she has an obligation to recognize that achievement,

       – the words to be uttered must be suitable to fulfilling this obliga-
         tion: for example 'Congratulations on ...' or some phrase com-
         mending the addressee.

    (b)   Maxims:

       – the speaker must have a positive attitude towards the addressee's
         achievement,

       – the speaker must subsequently behave in ways consistent with
         the appreciation demonstrated.

    (c)   Objective requirements:

       – congratulations are objectively correct if they are, not merely so-
         cially expected, but actually merited.

Comments:

If it turns out that the alleged achievement of the addressee did not occur or
is something which the speaker should not be congratulating him on, the speech
act does not bring about the effect of an act of congratulating. But in default conditions, any audience of an act of congratulating not previously informed about
the achievement of the addressee will accommodate the belief that one such
achievement has occurred. The speaker's obligation to recognize the addressee's achievement also depends on the speaker putting herself in the position of

being so obliged, provided she is not kept from doing so for some specific reason. Compliance with the sincerity maxim is assumed (in default conditions), so that the act of congratulating may even be said to 'express' appreciation. But usually nobody cares about what the speaker really thinks of the addressee's achievement, because the point of congratulating lies more in social recognition than in actual appreciation. The consistency maxim licenses certain expectations of the audience, which may be confirmed or disconfirmed with time. As to objective requirements, there is a subtle difference between an act of congratulating being due and therefore appropriate, that is, conforming to its own constitutive rules, and the congratulations actually being actually deserved. Social conventions about what people should be congratulated on and the kind of relationship holding between speaker and addressee play a more important role in the former assessment than in the latter.

6   What about Assertion?

Since assertions too are speech acts and have illocutionary force, one should expect that the distinctions put forward in this paper apply to them too. We have no room here to tackle the issue of norms of assertion in depth, so I shall give just a few very informal hints of how things appear from the point of view of our distinction.

A plausible constitutive rule (in the sense adopted here) would be that the speaker must be in a position to make the assertion. I would consider as a separate constitutive rule the condition that the situation referred to must be one about which an assertion (with that purported content) can be made. While the latter rule appears to me unproblematic, the former gives rise to some problems. As to the 'position' required of the speaker, I am inclined to agree with Williamson (2000) that it should involve knowledge. Indeed, the best way to be in a position to make an assertion is to know how things are. In our framework, though, this has the undesired consequence that any time a speaker makes a sincere assertion which then turns out to be false, because she did not actually know how things were (but only thought she knew), she violates the constitutive rules of assertion and therefore has failed to make a real assertion, according to our definition of constitutive rules (her assertion is only apparently such, but fails to produce the expected binding and licensing effects). False assertions, however, are assertions nevertheless, in that they, at least, are binding for the speaker, and addressees acting upon them do so legitimately. In order to get out of the impasse, one can either follow Williamson and weaken one's conception of constitutive rule, or keep the stronger conception of constitutive rule and weaken the constitutive rules for assertion (cf. Maitra 2011, pp. 280–284). However, weakening knowledge into belief will not do. Belief in the truth of what is asserted is already the object of the maxim of sincerity for assertion, and we have already seen that sincerity rules cannot be constitutive in the strong sense. The only way to weaken the Knowledge Rule which is compatible with our framework is to take the speaker to be in a position to assert something when she (because of circumstances and personal competence) has publicly recognizable good chances to produce an objectively correct assertion, namely, an assertion that is true. One might even conceive of adopting an *ad hoc* technical sense of 'knowledge', to be used to refer to socially or intersubjectively ratified entitlement to make assertions, based for example on acquaintance with data, reasoning ability, recognized methodological competence in the specific field, thereby formulating knowledge for the use of the addressees (for a notion of knowledge so oriented, see Kusch 2002).

Maxims for optimal assertions are less problematic. They should require (at least) belief that what is asserted is true and subsequent behaviour (both verbal and non-verbal) consistent with the assertion made. Objective requirements, too, come as no surprise: assertions are evaluated in the dimension of truth and falsity. I would like to point out, however, that it is one thing for the uttered sentence to satisfy abstract truth-conditions, but quite another for the assertion as an action performed in specific circumstances to be the right speech act to be made. If an assertion is to be true as an assertion (and not as the expression of an opinion or guess), it must be true not by chance, but because it is made by a competent and therefore knowledgeable speaker upon evidence or reasons (as Ball (this volume), puts it, in asserting we incur an obligation to know the truth of the proposition). This takes us back once again to Williamson's Knowledge Rule. It might be said that the Knowledge Rule sets an objective requirement for assertions, alongside with the requirement of truth. One could also add that the Knowledge Rule may influence the maxims for optimal assertion, suggesting that these should include the recommendation that, in order to be fully sincere in asserting, the speaker should be willing to do everything reasonably within her power to make a true assertion. But all these are mere speculations in need of further discussion, and I shall therefore leave aside this topic now and return to themes concerning speech act norms in general.

7   Are There 'Rules of Accommodation'?

In discussing the examples in Section 5, we saw that the dependency of the performance of the illocutionary act (and of the achievement of its illocutionary effect) upon the fulfillment of the constitutive rules for the relevant illocutionary act type has also a reverse application in actual situations, since in default conditions, there is a general tendency to accept speech acts at their face value: this can be done only if the fulfilment of constitutive rules is tacitly accepted or 'accommodated' by the audience. In his well-known paper 'Scorekeeping in a language game', David Lewis (1979) describes this phenomenon and introduces a new kind of rules, which he calls 'rules of accommodation'. These rules have been introduced into speech-act theoretical investigations as norms that are applied by speakers and audience in producing and understanding speech acts (cf. for example McGowan 2004).

Lewis represents conversation as a game, the moves of which affect 'scores' marked on a 'scoreboard'. The 'kinematics' of the scores, their moving up and down, or entering and exiting from the scoreboard, may be seen as analogous to what other authors writing around the same time began to describe as 'context change' (Isard 1975; Ballmer 1978; Ballmer 1981; Gazdar 1981), as Lewis too mentions in a footnote. Indeed, Lewis includes among the abstract objects that constitute the scores presupposed propositions and deontic roles of the participants (the latter under the name of 'permissibility facts'), both components of the context of a speech act. What counts as correct play at each time depends on the scores (the context) at that time, and correct play makes the scores move (the context change). In addition to this, Lewis posits a tendency of the conversational score to evolve in ways that make whatever is done count as correct play. That is accommodation: a matter of context change again, but adapting the scores (the context) according to which a move is to be evaluated to that conversational move, rather than the other way around. As any move in a game and any change in the scores are described by Lewis as connected to rules, accommodation too is governed, according to him, by rules of accommodation, of the following form:

> If at time t something is said that requires component sn of conversational score to have a value in the range r if what is said is to be true, or otherwise acceptable; and if sn does not have a value in the range r just before t; and if such-and-such further conditions hold; then at t the score-component sn takes some value in the range r. (Lewis 1979, p. 347)

Lewis uses accommodation to describe both cases of context change such as those brought about by explicit performatives or formal permissions and prohibitions (which a speech-act theoretical consideration of language use would rather explain in terms of the conventional effects of illocutionary acts, as in Sbisà 1984; 2002), and cases in which, as Witek points out (2015a, p. 17), the context-changing process adjusts the source score of an act in order to make the act a 'binding and felicitous' illocution of a certain type. My issue here is not with the former cases (since I am assuming a speech-act theoretical, non-reductionist framework: see Witek's considerations in his 2015a, p. 20), but with the latter. And my concern is not whether to accept that accommodation phenomena exist: of course they do.[10] My concern is, instead, whether we need specific rules governing the accommodating context-changes, and whether these should be considered as speech act norms mandating those context-changes.

The framework within which Lewis theorizes about accommodation is influenced by the notion of language game and by the comparison between speech activities and games. It focuses on activities, as opposed to acts which are defined at least in part by their effects, and is therefore distinct from a speech-act theoretical framework which considers the speech act as part of a procedure designed to produce a conventional effect. Witek (2015a) has attempted to bring together the speech-act theoretical framework (and, with it, the context-change perspective) and Lewis' 'scorekeeping' analysis of conversation: he uses the scorekeeping metaphor to deal with the felicity conditions of illocutionary acts as well as with their illocutionary effects. Following Lewis, he distinguishes appropriateness rules (corresponding in part to constitutive rules as described in this paper, Section 2, and in part to what I have called maxims, Section 3), which govern the relationship between scores and moves, from kinematics rules which govern the relationship between moves and scores (and which in our terms are constitutive rules, cf. Section 2, since they establish what conventional effect is achieved by what procedure). He also admits of accommodation rules, which govern the context-changing process by adjusting the source score of an act in order to make the act a successful and appropriate illocution of a certain type (Witek 2015a). He focuses on the accommodation of those components of the score that correspond to the initial position of the speaker (her deontic role: competence, authority, state of debt, and the like), making them be such as required by the type of the illocutionary act that the speaker's utterance is designed to perform. Here is the form of accommodation rules as revised by Witek (2015a, p. 18):

If at time t speaker S makes a binding illocution I, and if the felicity of I requires Austinian personal presupposition p [that is, a certain deontic

---

10   I have myself made lengthy explorations of both informative or persuasive presuppositions (since Sbisà 1979) and the 'backwards effects' of illocutionary acts on the deontic roles of their speakers (since Sbisà and Fabbri 1981). See Sbisà 1984; 1999a; 1999b; 2006.

> role of the speaker] to be part of the illocutionary score relative to which
> *I* is evaluated, and if *p* is not part of the score just before time *t* at which
> I is made, then – ceteris paribus and within certain limits – *p* becomes
> part of the score at *t*.

While maintaining that the phenomenon at issue is quite real, that is, that
the initial deontic role of the speaker is in fact often retroactively adjusted in
correspondence to the recognition of her illocutionary act as successfully performed, I do not find Witek's reformulation wholly satisfactory. In adapting
Lewis's formulation, originally concerned with 'saying something' and its being 'true, or otherwise acceptable', to illocutionary acts and their conforming to
constitutive rules, it squeezes the dynamics of illocution in a way that renders
invisible the distinction between the issuing of an utterance and the making of
the illocutionary act (which amounts to the achievement of its conventional or
'binding' effect) as well as the role of the securing of uptake in the achievement
of the illocutionary effect. But leaving aside the details in the formulation of
the rule, why should there be such a rule at all?

Witek appears to assume, with Lewis, that since there is a change in accommodation too, there must be specific rules governing that change. But
while any change may be represented as a function (here, a function from non-
accommodated scores to accommodated scores), it is not the case that every
function should be expressed as a rule, or that anything expressed in the form
of a rule should act as a norm. In fact, I would argue that there is no need
for rules of accommodation, since the dynamics of illocution is enough to explain why the initial context is retroactively adjusted in certain cases. Once the
speaker secures uptake – either by uttering words unmistakably recognizable
as (part of) the performance of a certain illocutionary procedure, or by otherwise getting the audience to recognize it as such a performance – and unless
there is reason to question the satisfaction of one or more of the act's constitutive rules, the illocutionary effect is achieved and the deontic role required as
the initial position of the speaker is attributed to her as the grounds for her act.
No rule is needed to achieve the latter effect apart from the constitutive rules
governing the illocutionary act type in question.

Accommodation, then, is a peculiar way in which constitutive rules can be
made to function and not a phenomenon governed by specific rules of its own.
Such a peculiar way of functioning is governed by general principles, one of
which concerns pattern recognition (a pattern can well be recognized from
the presentation of some of its parts) and the other the by-default recognition
of other minds or subjects. These principles are not norms, but general characteristics of human cognition. It is indeed quite obvious that a pattern that

is partially presented may be completed by the observer if the part presented suffices to make it emerge. If the pattern is articulated in temporal terms, the presentation of its central and final parts will be completed by the initial one. As to the recognition of other minds or subjects and the attribution to them of mental states, meaning intentions, and actions, all these processes typically function on a default basis, *ceteris paribus* or in absence of defeaters.

Finally, even if one chose to keep track of the phenomena described above by formulating accommodation rules, these would not act as a new kind of speech act norms, since they would not posit conditions to be satisfied (beyond those already established by constitutive rules) nor advise or mandate appropriate behaviour (not already advised or mandated by the dynamics of illocution). Indeed, the motivation underlying accommodation phenomena lies in the fact that the rejection of the speaker's attempted illocutionary act as a misfire (or of her utterance as otherwise void, uncooperative, or inconsistent) would jeopardize the interactional relationship between the interlocutors, an undesirable outcome in many respects, both emotional and rational.

The dynamics of illocution is also enough to explain why there are cases in which accommodation affects the cognitive states of the interlocutors (presupposition accommodation changes the beliefs of the participants, not the facts) and cases in which it affects features of the actual world (albeit at the deontic or institutional level). The difference between these two kinds of accommodation – which Witek (2015a, pp. 20–21) refers to as 'subjective' and 'objective' accommodation – is more a question of the kinds of contextual elements to be accommodated than of the nature of the accommodation procedure. If the initial state to be accommodated is of a kind that can be introduced into the real world by (undefeated) intersubjective agreement, as are the deontic roles of agents, accommodation is – in absence of defeaters – 'objective'. If a defeating situation is the case, the speaker has no access to the accommodated deontic role, even against the beliefs of the participants (which are false). While informal leadership in a peer group can develop by accommodation (once members start accepting a given member's imperatives as orders: there are no defeaters in this situation), no accommodation can make a thief dressed like a policeman become a real policeman, even if some may be temporarily misled into believing that person to have actual authority to give certain kinds of orders. If the initial state to be accommodated is of a kind that cannot be introduced into the real world by (undefeated) intersubjective agreement, accommodation is 'subjective' (although one must admit that it remains objectively motivated, since what is needed to make the utterance felicitous is that the accommodated content is actually true). Think for example of the accommodation of the belief that I have a sister, as presupposed by the utterance of 'I cannot come to the meeting. I have to meet my sister at the airport': obviously, the accommodation does not make any non-existent sister of the speaker exist, but merely makes 'The speaker has got a sister' part of the common ground for that conversation. However, the utterance of 'I have to meet my sister at the airport' is really appropriate and makes a felicitous assertion (and, moreover, gives a felicitous account of the speaker's absence from the meeting) only if the speaker really has got a sister, while if she has no sister, the accommodated belief notwithstanding, the utterance is liable to be rejected as infelicitous.

8   Are Speech Act Norms Conventional?

The conventionality of speech acts is one of the oldest and the most debated issues in speech act theory (since at least Strawson 1964). I would also like to emphasize that it is made particularly complex by the difficulty to identify which notion of conventionality is really pertinent to speech acts, as well as by a basic uncertainty about what it is that is supposed to be either 'conventional' or 'non-conventional' in speech acts (the procedure for performing it? the illocutionary effect? cf. Sbisà 2007; 2009). I cannot discuss this issue thoroughly here: I would merely like to examine how it interacts with the three-fold distinction regarding speech act norms that has been argued for in this paper.

First of all, what does it mean for a norm to be 'conventional'? Some authors have made sharp distinctions between norms and conventions as if these were two mutually exclusive notions (cf. Pagin 2015, who does not take constitutive rules to be norms). I have already explained, though, why I prefer to use 'norms' as a general term for our field of inquiry, thereby encompassing certain rules that many have taken to be 'conventional'. So, let us assume that the question is legitimate. As to its possible answers, we may say that a norm is conventional when it is not inescapably imposed on us by some kind of natural or rational necessity, but when its normative powers as well as the choice of its content depend on social agreement (which may vary across times and cultures). This fits with the idea that the procedure by which an illocutionary act is performed may be 'conventional' (which would mean, then, that it is fixed by norms depending on social agreement). It may also fit with Millikan's notion of convention as the repetition of procedures motivated by reference to precedents, already applied to illocutionary acts (Millikan 1998; 2005; Witek 2015b; this volume), which suggests describing the relevant social agreement as agreement about the precedents and the repetition relation. It is also worth pointing out that there are norms, the observance or violation of which is related to achieving or not achieving the conventional effects of a speech act. We shall bear these aspects in mind in the rest of this section.

In consideration of our three-fold distinction between constitutive rules, maxims, and objective standards, I would suggest that constitutive rules can be taken to be conventional, while maxims and objective standards (even if they apply to conventional acts) cannot.

Constitutive rules (in the sense illustrated in Section 2) fix the requirements which must be complied with to ensure the success of the illocutionary act. Since success in performing the act depends upon compliance with constitutive rules, if something 'goes wrong' with them the performance may turn out to be ineffective and its alleged effect may be null and void. Now, the very liability to annulment manifested by the effects of illocutionary acts confirms their conventional nature, since only conventional (agreement-depending) states of affairs can be annulled or 'made undone'. But if we assume that only conventional means can bring about conventional effects (as Austin seems to think: cf. Austin 1962, p. 119, admitting of non-conventional means for perlocutionary effects only), then we see that the procedures for performing illocutionary acts must be conventional themselves. This means that the content of our constitutive rules will consist of procedures that are not determined by natural inclinations or rational motivations but are established by social agreement as repetitions of precedents. In this sense, constitutive rules can be taken to be conventional.

Some maintain that constitutive rules (also called 'constitutive norms') are not conventional: according to Williamson (2000, p. 239), they possess a necessary character which appears to exclude any potential choice (taken to be essential to conventionality). There is some truth in this remark. Once a set of constitutive rules for a certain act is fixed, nothing can be an act of that kind if it is not subject to those rules (and, in our framework, if it does not observe them). Thus the constitutive rules for a certain act actually impose upon all those who intend to perform acts of that kind. But one might not want to play that game. Or the social agreement upon that set of rules and its effect may change. Or it may not hold for a different social group.[11] Williamson himself seems to find the conventional view of constitutive rules compatible with his

---

11   Not all conceivable sets of constitutive rules are compatible with all cultural frameworks. Let us imagine a culture that does not believe people to be able to control their future behaviour and therefore take responsibility for future action: it would lack any procedure corresponding to our promise (while it might have weaker forms of commitment, say, expressing intention). Or let us imagine a strictly egalitarian society in which people in need of help would perform acts of request, but orders could not exist. Incidentally, anthropologists have sometimes noticed procedures in distant cultures that we lack (cf. for example Duranti 1992 on the Maaloo exchange in the Samoa Islands).

theory insofar as they are necessary only for the game or language they apply to: if conventions change, then that game or language turns into another (Williamson 2000, p. 266). What I would suggest is that the constitutive function, far from being incompatible with conventionality, presupposes it.

As to speech act norms other than constitutive rules, I agree with Pagin (2015) that they are not conventional. Certainly, the speech act norms which we have called 'maxims' (Section 3) are not compulsory mechanisms and people may observe them or not. But maxims such as those requiring sincerity or consistency (or specifying what sincerity or consistency should consist of with respect to a certain kind of illocutionary act) do not exist because of some arbitrary choice: people do not just agree on them. As Grice says (with reference to his maxims of conversational cooperation; see Grice 1989, p. 29), it is rational of speakers to follow them. Likewise, consistency is rationally mandated. Moreover, as we have seen, the violation of a maxim does not hinder the conventional effects of speech acts from being brought about.[12] Those speech act norms we have called objective requirements (Section 4) are also not conventional themselves, although they apply to performed speech acts (that is, executions of conventional procedures which achieve conventional effects). The point of a certain type of illocutionary act may be fixed by social agreement, but once it is fixed, the standard applying to it follows and the application of the standard must consider the actual performance in actual circumstances. It cannot therefore be a matter of convention, in any of the senses considered here, whether the function or point of a speech act of a certain kind is served well by a certain speech act token in certain circumstances.

9   Concluding Remarks

The picture of speech act norms we have outlined comprises three main kinds: constitutive rules, upon which the performance of illocutionary acts

---

12   One might object that norms of politeness, which have been assimilated to maxims (cf. for example Grice 1989, p. 28; Lakoff 1973), must be conventional because they change across cultures. I think that this is wrong. Not all politeness norms change with cultures (think of facework-related norms: Goffman 1967; 1971; Brown and Levinson 1987) and those that do change are either not speech act norms (and so our considerations about the sense in which a speech act norm may be conventional do not apply to them), or are indeed constitutive of some kind of a speech act. Think of those illocutionary acts whose point is to keep social relationships fair and smooth (such as greeting, thanking, apologizing, congratulating) or whose linguistic procedures come in varieties to concerned to varying extents with avoiding threat or damage to face.

depends; maxims, based on rational motivations, to be followed as requirements for perfection in order to perform a speech act optimally satisfactory in
the perspective of the participants; and objective requirements for the overall
correctness of the accomplished speech act with regard to the situation in the
world to which it relates. These three kinds of norms engender three different
sorts of penalty when not complied with. The penalty for the violation of constitutive rules is infelicity, which may lead to failure in performing the act and
therefore in bringing about its illocutionary effect. The penalty for failing to
observe maxims never leads to the annulment of the performed act, but consists of blame and disrepute. The penalty for not meeting the objective requirements has both an interactional and an objective side. The former consists of
the negative assessment of the speech act as not being the right thing to say
and do in the circumstances, and of the speaker as responsible for making a
'wrong' speech act. The latter consists of the mere fact that the speech act is
unfit to contribute to the achievement of the goals of the speaker or possibly
of other participants in that situation.

Of the three kinds of norms, only constitutive rules can be said to be conventional, since they establish procedures that are repeatable and recognizable from one occasion to another and whose function (bringing about
changes in the deontic roles of the participants) is only exercised against a
background of social agreement. That our distinction is three-fold, however,
has a consequence for the received picture of the relation between speech
acts and conventions. In place of the received image of a group of 'conventional' speech acts distinct from a group of 'non-conventional' ones, one
may conceive of all speech acts as conventional for certain aspects and non-
conventional for others.

Clearly, the examples presented in Sections 5 and 6 of how our three-fold
distinction may apply to some speech act types are a very limited test of its
potential as a descriptive framework and organizer of intuitions and doubts.
I am confident, however, that it can provide fruitful and principled ways of
organizing discussion about types of illocutionary act as well as about the illocutionary forces of speech act tokens, towards a fuller understanding of the
dynamics of illocution.

Bibliography

Austin, J.L. (1961). *Philosophical papers.* Oxford: Oxford University Press.
Austin, J.L. (1962). *How to do things with words.* Oxford: Oxford University Press.

Ball, B. (this volume). Commitment and Obligation in Speech Act Theory. In. M. Witek and I. Witczak-Plisiecka (eds.), *Normativity and Variety of Speech Actions*, pp. 51–65. Leiden: Brill (*Poznań Studies in the Philosophy of the Sciences and the Humanities* 112).

Ballmer, T.T. (1978). *Logical Grammar: with Special Consideration of Topics in Context Change*. Amsterdam: North-Holland.

Ballmer, T.T. (1981). Context change and its consequences for a theory of natural language. In: H. Parret, M. Sbisà, J.Verschueren (eds.), *Possibilities and Limitations of Pragmatics*, pp. 17–55. Amsterdam: John Benjamins.

Bermejo-Luque, L. (2011). *Giving Reasons: a Linguistic-Pragmatic Approach to Argumentation theory*. Berlin: Springer.

Brown, P. and S. Levinson (1987). *Politeness. Universals in language use*. Cambridge: Cambridge University Press.

Carston, R. (2002). *Thoughts and Utterances*. Oxford: Blackwell.

Duranti, A. (1992). *Etnografia del parlare quotidiano*. Roma: Carocci.

Gauker, C. (1998). What is a context of utterance? *Philosophical Studies* 91, 149–172.

Gazdar, G. (1981). Speech act assignment. In: A.K. Joshi, B.L.Webber, I.A. Sag (eds.), *Elements of Discourse Understanding*, pp. 64–83. Cambridge: Cambridge University Press.

Goffman, E. (1967). *Interaction ritual: Essays on face-to-face behavior*. Garden City, N.Y.: Doubleday.

Goffman, E. (1971). *Relations in public*. Basic Books: New York.

Grice, H.P. (1989). *Studies in the Way of Words*. Cambridge, Mass.: Harvard University Press.

Harnish, R.M. (2009). Internalism and Externalism in Speech Act Theory. *Lodz Papers in Pragmatics* 5 (1), 9–31. DOI: 10.2478/v10016-009-0001-2

Isard, S. (1975). Changing the Context. In E. Keenan (ed.), *Formal Semantics of Natural Language*, pp. 287–296. Cambridge: Cambridge University Press.

Johnson, L.E. (1992). *Focusing on truth*. London: Routledge.

Kusch, M. (2002). *Knowledge on agreement*. Oxford: Oxford University Press.

Lakoff, R.T. (1973). The logic of politeness; or, minding your p's and q's. In. C. Corum, T. Cedric Smith-Stark, & A. Weiser (eds.), *Papers from the Ninth Regional Meeting of the Chicago Linguistic Society*, pp. 292–305. Chicago Ill.: University of Chicago.

Lewis, D. (1979). Scorekeeping in a language game. *Journal of Philosophical Logic* 8, 339–359.

Maitra, I. (2011). Assertion, norms and games. In: J. Brown and H. Cappelen (eds.), *Assertion. New philosophical essays*, pp. 277–296. Oxford: Oxford University Press.

McGowan, M.K. (2004). Conversational exercitives: something else we do with our words. *Linguistics & Philosophy* 27, 93–111.

Millikan, R.G. (1998). Proper function and convention in speech acts. In: L.E. Kahn (ed.), *The Philosophy of P. F. Strawson*, pp. 25–43. Chicago, Ill.: Open Court.

Millikan, R.G. (2005). *Language. A biological model.* Oxford: Oxford University Press.

Pagin, P. (2015). Assertion. *The Stanford Encyclopedia of Philosophy* (Spring 2015 Edition), Edward N. Zalta (ed.), URL = <http://plato.stanford.edu/archives/spr2015/entries/assertion/> (last accessed: 13 May 2017).

Pitcher, G. (ed.) (1964). *Truth.* Englewood Cliffs, N.J.: Prentice-Hall.

Recanati, F. (2004). *Literal meaning.* Oxford: Oxford University Press.

Sbisà, M. (1979). Perlocuzione e presupposizioni. In: F. Albano Leoni & M.R. Pigliasco (eds.), *Retorica e scienze del linguaggio*, pp. 37–60. Roma: Bulzoni.

Sbisà, M. (1984). On illocutionary types. *Journal of Pragmatics* 8, 93–112.

Sbisà, M. (1999a). Ideology and the persuasive use of presupposition. In J. Verschueren (ed.), *Language and ideology. Selected papers from the 6th International Pragmatics Conference*, pp. 492–509. Antwerp: International Pragmatics Association.

Sbisà, M. (1999b). Presupposition, implicature and context in text understanding. In P. Bouquet, L. Serafini, P. Brézillon, M. Benerecetti, F. Castellani (eds.), *Modeling and Using Context*, pp. 324–338. Berlin, Springer.

Sbisà, M. (2002). Speech acts in context. *Language & Communication* 22, 421–436.

Sbisà, M. (2006). Communicating citizenship in verbal interaction: Principles of a speech act oriented discourse analysis. In H. Hausendorf, A. Bora (eds.), *Analysing citizenship talk*, pp. 151–180. Amsterdam: John Benjamins.

Sbisà, M. (2007). How to read Austin. *Pragmatics* 17 (3), 461–473. DOI: 10.1075/prag.17.3.06sbi

Sbisà, M. (2009). Uptake and conventionality in illocution. *Lodz Papers in Pragmatics* 5 (1), 33–52. DOI: 10.2478/v10016-009-0003-0

Sbisà, M. and P. Fabbri (1981). Models (?) for a pragmatic analysis. *Journal of Pragmatics* 4, 301–319.

Searle, J.R. (1969). *Speech acts.* Cambridge: Cambridge University Press.

Searle, J.R. (1979). *Expression and meaning.* Cambridge: Cambridge University Press.

Stalnaker, R. (1999). *Context and Content.* Oxford: Oxford University Press.

Strawson, P.F. (1950). Truth. In: *Proceedings of the Aristotelian Society*, Suppl. Vol. 24, 129–56.

Strawson, P.F. (1964). Intention and convention in speech acts. *The Philosophical Review* 73, 439–460.

Travis, C.S. (2000). *Unshadowed Thought: Representation in Thought and Language.* Cambridge Mass.: Harvard University Press.

Travis, C.S. (2008). *Occasion sensitivity. Selected essays.* Oxford: Oxford University Press.

Vision, G. (2004). *Veritas. The correspondence theory and its critics.* Cambridge, Mass.: The MIT Press.

Walker, T. (2013). Requests. In: M. Sbisà and K. Turner (eds.), *Pragmatics of speech actions*, pp. 445–466. Berlin: Mouton de Gruyter.

Williamson, T. (2000) *Knowledge and its limits.* Oxford: Oxford University Press.

Witek, M. (2015a). Mechanisms of illocutionary games. *Language & Communication* 42, 11–22.

Witek, M. (2015b). An interactional account of illocutionary practice. *Language Sciences* 47, 43–55.

Witek, M. (this volume). Coordination and Norms in Illocutionary Interaction. In. M. Witek and I. Witczak-Plisiecka (eds.), *Normativity and Variety of Speech Actions*, pp. 66–97. Leiden: Brill (*Poznań Studies in the Philosophy of the Sciences and the Humanities* 112).

Wittgenstein, L. (1953). *Philosophische Untersuchungen/Philosophical Investigations*. Ed. by Elizabeth Anscombe and Rush Rhees. With English translation. Oxford: Blackwell.

CHAPTER 2

Commitment and Obligation in Speech Act Theory

Brian Ball

Abstract

This paper aims to illuminate the notions of commitment and obligation, as well as their explanatory role, in the theory of speech acts. I begin (Section 2) by arguing in support of the view that assertion involves a commitment to the truth; and, building on Williamson's (2000) account of this act, I suggest that we can understand such commitment in terms of an obligation to ensure. I then argue (Section 3) that this foundationalist account of the commitment involved in assertion is preferable to the discursive coherentism of Brandom (1983). Next (Section 4), I propose that MacFarlane's (2011) taxonomy of views of the nature of assertion should be simplified, so that there is just a broad division into those that understand the act in descriptive, vs those that understand it in normative, terms. And finally, I show (Section 5) how we can understand the normative view I favour through a comparison with Stalnaker's (1999) descriptive account of assertion which, I hope, reveals the role played by obligation in the characterization of this act.

1   Introduction

It is often said that to make an assertion is to commit to the truth of the proposition asserted: thus, Searle, for instance, says 'an assertion is a (very special kind of) commitment to the truth of a proposition' (Searle 1969, p. 29).[1] I believe that this claim is correct. It is not immediately clear, however, just what it amounts to: what exactly is involved in undertaking the special kind of commitment to truth that Searle speaks of? Various theorists have made attempts to answer this question, and to explain the notion of commitment involved. My own view is that to undertake a commitment is to incur an obligation to ensure: and so to commit to the truth of a proposition is to incur an obligation

---

1   Thanks to Maciej Witek for organizing the workshop on *Speech Acts in Theory and Practice* in December 2013 (University of Szczecin, Poland) which served as the impetus for this paper, and for his contributions as editor of this volume. Thanks also to the audience at that workshop, and to the referees for this journal for useful feedback.

to ensure its truth. Following Williamson (2000) I will suggest, moreover, that one ensures the truth of a proposition in the manner relevant to assertion *epistemically*, by knowing it.

In what follows I will briefly motivate the thought that assertion involves a commitment to truth, and spell out in more detail a general notion of commitment that can be applied in the context of speech act theory. Next, I will consider what kind of commitment is involved in assertion: in particular, I will argue that we should prefer Williamson's (2000) epistemic foundationalism over Brandom's (1983) discursive coherentism. I will then distinguish two ways of thinking about illocutionary speech acts (such as assertion): on one, these speech acts can be understood independently of such normative notions as commitment; on the other these notions play a central role. In the process I will criticize MacFarlane's (2011) four category taxonomy of views. Finally, I will show how we can modify Stalnaker's (1999) famous model of assertion, which is descriptive in character, to yield a more plausible normative account.

2   Commitment and Obligation

Following Searle (1969) and others, I have said that assertion involves undertaking a commitment. But why should we believe this? My reasoning is simple. Assertions can be retracted. But assertions can only be retracted if they involve undertaking a commitment. So, assertions involve undertaking a commitment.[2]

I take it that the first premise of this argument is uncontroversial. The major premise, therefore, is the second. In order to see that it is true, we should consider the nature of the act of retraction. So, what is retraction? 'To retract an assertion', as MacFarlane notes, 'is to "take it back," rendering it "null and void."' (MacFarlane 2011, p. 83) But what does this mean? Not that to retract an assertion is to undo it in the sense of bringing it about that the assertion was never made! Rather, something other than the assertion itself is undone, or cancelled. That something is the result of the assertion, the commitment.

The key point here concerns the timing. The commitment to the truth of the proposition asserted begins at the time of the assertion *and then lasts indefinitely*. When an assertion is retracted, one does not make it the case that one was *never* committed to the truth of the proposition in question; one simply makes it the case that one is *no longer* so committed. Accordingly, there must

---

2   The argument here is a refinement of one hinted at by MacFarlane (2011).

be, not only the *act* of asserting (which, let's say, occurs at *t*), but also the state of being committed (which exists for a period of time beginning at *t*). If at *t'* one retracts an assertion that *p* made at *t*, one undoes one's commitment *from t' on-wards*: one *ceases* to be committed to the truth of *p*; one does not make it the case that one was not so committed from *t* (to *t'*). This is only possible if the act of asserting brings about a state distinct from that act – a state which I have been suggesting is one of commitment. Any adequate theory of assertion (and, I would suggest, some other speech acts) must recognize the existence of this state (though, of course, they may differ on how to characterize it).

So far we have seen reason to believe that making an assertion involves un-dertaking a commitment. But what is a commitment? What is meant by saying that a commitment is undertaken? I suggest that in undertaking a commit-ment one incurs an obligation. More specifically, to commit to something is to incur an obligation to ensure it.

Consider promising, for instance. Suppose I promise I will meet you for din-ner. Then I incur an obligation to ensure that I do so. How can I ensure that I meet you for dinner? By so acting as to bring it about that I do. My action ensures the result. That result is the state of affairs that I promised. I fulfil the obligation that I incurred in promising by ensuring through action that the promised outcome (i.e. the outcome to which I committed) occurs.[3]

Some computer scientists have a generalized notion of an action: they say that when an agent *α* so acts as to guarantee the outcome *that p*, *α sees to it* that *p*.[4] It is, I think, no accident that the logical grammar of this notion is the same as that of the propositional attitudes: the phrase 'sees to it', like 'believes' or 'desires' is, as Prior put it, 'a predicate at one end and a connective at the other;' (Prior 1971, p. 19) that is, just like the attitude expressions it takes a noun and a sentence (well, complement clause) to make a sentence. This is no accident because the propositional attitudes are, paradigmatically at least, the results of cognitive actions: to judge that *p*, for instance, is to act cognitively on the proposition that *p*,[5] with the result that one believes that p; and, of course, if all goes well, this belief will constitute knowledge that *p*. Accordingly, it seems to me that when we commit to the truth of a proposition by asserting it, we incur

---

3 Things may seem to be a little trickier when I promise to do something, i.e. to perform some action. For then what I need to ensure is my performance of the action in question. Does this require a meta-action? I don't think so. Suppose, for instance, that I promise not only that there will be cake at the party, but that I will bake it. Then by baking the cake and bringing it to the party, I ensure through my actions that I have baked a cake and brought it to the party. No additional action is required.

4 See Horty (2001) for an excellent book length use of this approach.

5 I do not intend to suggest that these acts are voluntary.

an obligation to so act (or better, to have so acted) cognitively as to ensure its truth. And we can see to it that a proposition is true, cognitively, by knowing it.[6] Thus, I suggest that when we assert that p, we incur an obligation to know that p. Of course, others have suggested that the obligations we incur in performing the speech act of assertion are different ones than this. In the next section I argue that they are mistaken.

3   Epistemic Foundationalism and Discursive Coherentism

Brandom thinks that assertion is best understood (partly) in terms of the notion of commitment: thus, he says that '[i]n asserting a sentence one ... commits oneself to it'. (Brandom 1983, p. 640) Of course, this claim mistakenly takes sentences, rather than propositions, to be the objects of assertion: what one asserts, when one makes an assertion, is something which might be expressed by a different sentence in a different context (or indeed language), and which might not be expressed by the same sentence in a different context; and this is so even if one asserts it *by* uttering a sentence which expresses it (in one's context). As a result of this error, Brandom also misidentifies the object of commitment here: obviously, one's commitment is to the proposition one expresses, not to the sentence which one uses to express it. Clearly, if a speaker says that she is hungry by uttering the sentence 'I am hungry', she need not defend that *sentence* against those who says that they are not hungry by uttering its negation; nor, indeed, if she has eaten in the intervening time, need she defend the sentence anymore.

But let us set these points aside: what is of more immediate interest is how Brandom thinks the commitment undertaken in asserting something is honoured. What is it that one becomes obliged to do, or responsible for doing, when one asserts that p? According to Brandom, one must (in effect) provide independent evidence for p in the form of further assertions, if one's assertion is challenged. But this can't be right in general. Suppose that one asserts that

---

6   How so? Well, to ensure the truth of a proposition is to do something which makes that proposition not only true, but *safely* true – i.e. true in nearby possible worlds. Thus, when I (so act as to) intentionally bring it about that p, p is (typically) not only true in the actual world, it is also true in nearby worlds where things go slightly differently (but not so differently as to disrupt the success of my action and the fulfillment of my intention); and thus I ensure that p is true. Similarly, when I so act cognitively as to ensure that p is true (by properly judging that p, thereby activating knowledge that p), not only will p in fact be true, it will also be true in nearby worlds where things go slightly differently (but not so differently as to disrupt the success of my cognitive act).

there is a Goldfinch in the yard; and suppose this assertion is challenged. One might, perhaps, provide some independent evidence in support of this claim, maybe by noting that one can *see* that there is a Goldfinch in the yard. But what if this in turn is challenged? It seems clear that one is entitled to make the assertion in question (one need not retract it, for instance): but it is far from obvious that there is a further assertion one might make that would serve to justify this claim. The thesis that knowledge is what licenses assertion, by contrast, copes well with this case. Since one knows that one sees that there is a Goldfinch in the yard, one is entitled to assert that one sees that there is. The fact that one cannot provide further, independent evidence for this claim does not impugn one's right to make it: after all, some propositions must be evidentially basic, on pain of regress or circularity; but we might still want to transmit our knowledge of these propositions to others.

Brandom also thinks that a full account of the speech act of assertion must take note of the entitlements an assertion proffers. In particular, Brandom thinks that when one asserts that p, others become entitled to assert p (as well as its immediate consequences). But this is not, in general, true. Suppose S lies, thereby asserting something false – let's say, the proposition p. Is S's hearer H thereby entitled to assert p? Clearly not. If he does, and his audience A relies on his word, believing what he has said, she will err: accordingly, if A comes to recognize that p is false she is within her rights to rebuke H; for he has made an unwarranted assertion, one which he is not entitled to make. Of course, H might pass the buck, blaming S for the falsity of his assertion; and A might accept the fact that S told H that p as an excuse for H's having asserted this falsehood. But this just confirms the point: it is only wrong-doing that can be excused; so if H is to be exculpated in this way, he must have done something wrong in asserting p. In short, H's assertion was unwarranted, and illegitimate: he was not entitled to make it, even if he was blameless in having done so.

It is important to recognize that blamelessness is not entitlement. We can see this by contrasting the above case with the following one. Suppose S asserts p. Working as a translator, H utters a sentence in another language which means that p. A hears H's utterance and understands that p. If p is false in this case, A should not rebuke H: for H did not assert p; accordingly, he was never responsible for ensuring the truth of p in the first place. By contrast, in our original case, H *was* responsible for ensuring p's truth: for even though S misled him by telling him that p, H re-iterated this assertion; he was accordingly committed to the truth of p, and obliged to ensure it. While it might be harsh for A to blame H in this case, we need not regard it as irrational (for given that H was not entitled, there is an open question whether he was blameless); whereas in the translator case, A should certainly *not* shoot the messenger, H, who is not responsible (ultimately or otherwise) for ensuring the truth of p (and therefore *clearly* blameless).[7]

'In asserting a claim', says Brandom, 'one ... authorizes further assertions [and] commits oneself to vindicate the original claim, showing that one is entitled to make it'. (Brandom 1983, p. 641) We have seen reasons to think that both components of this claim are mistaken. Perhaps, with the addition of epicycles, the phenomena can be captured within this approach.[8] It seems to me, however, that we do better to abandon Brandom's discursive account of assertoric entitlement, which descends ultimately into a kind of coherentism about justification; instead, we should endorse a foundationalist epistemic position, recognizing that one is entitled to assert a proposition if and only if one knows it. In the final section I develop this Williamsonian alternative further; but first, an interlude on the taxonomy of speech acts.

4   Descriptive and Normative Accounts of Speech Acts

MacFarlane thinks 'there are four broad categories' of views of the nature of assertion, namely:

1.   To assert is to express an attitude.
2.   To assert is to make a move defined by its constitutive rules.
3.   To assert is to propose to add information to the conversational common ground.
4.   To assert is to undertake a commitment. (MacFarlane 2011, p. 80)

This taxonomy of positions may be arrived at by means of two cross-cutting distinctions. The first distinction is that between views (such as the second and fourth) on which we can understand assertion only in normative terms, on the one hand, and those (such as the first and third) on the other hand,

---

7   Brandom says, "[a]n assertion in force [that is, one which has not been overturned] licenses others to re-assert the original claim (and to assert its immediate consequences) *deferring to the author of the original assertion the justificatory responsibility which would otherwise thereby be undertaken.*" (Brandom 1983, p. 642) It is unclear, however, whether one who defers responsibility to another in this way is nonetheless responsible.

8   Brandom recognizes that '[i]t is only assertions one is entitled to make that can serve to entitle others to its inferential consequences;" (Brandom 1983, p. 641) and this might be thought to help with the second problem encountered above. I agree: as we shall see, it is only in normal cases that one is entitled to assert what one is told. Brandom also acknowledges that "[t]here are cases in which it is inappropriate to issue a justificatory challenge to an assertor;" (*ibid.*, p. 643) but he suggests these are to be understood as "parasitic on a paradigm in which justificatory responsibility is undertaken." (*ibid.*, p. 643). This might help with the first kind of problem case discussed above; though in this case I am less optimistic.

on which assertion can be characterized in wholly descriptive, non-normative terms. The second distinction aims to differentiate positions (such as the first and second) on which we can understand assertion by looking 'upstream' to the conditions of the production of the speech act, and those (such as the third and fourth) on which we must look 'downstream' to its effects.

It seems to me, however, that this second distinction is largely illusory, being at best one of degree, or emphasis, not one of kind. Consider first the descriptive views. According to Bach and Harnish (1979) to assert a proposition is to express a belief in that proposition, as well as an intention that one's hearer believe it, where to express an attitude is to reflexively intend one's audience to take one's utterance as a reason to think one has it. It is, I think, an oversimplification to regard this as an entirely speaker-oriented account of assertion: for it is clear that the intentions one must have in order to assert, on this view, are hearer-directed; the intentions in question are intentions to bring about certain effects in the hearer. And it is for this reason that theorists sympathetic to this approach have wondered whether, if one has the relevant intentions, but they are not recognized, one has succeeded in making an assertion.

At the same time, if we consider the third view, Stalnaker's (1999) account of assertion, we see that it is said (by MacFarlane) to characterize this speech act in terms of its 'essential effect'. Yet the effect in question is the alteration of the conversational common ground, which is in turn defined by the various interlocutors' attitudes *prior* to the performance of the act. We cannot understand Stalnaker's view of assertion if we ignore the conditions upstream from the assertion, any more than we can understand Bach and Harnish's approach without looking to the intended effects of this speech act.

Moreover, I will argue that something similar can be said in the case of the normative views of types 2 and 4. To begin with, Searle, who is rightly described as having a commitment view (i.e. one of the fourth kind), *also* clearly thinks that speech is governed by constitutive rules; indeed, an entire section of his (1969) book *Speech Acts* is devoted to making this point. Furthermore, MacFarlane himself concedes that '[i]n principle, the two approaches [can] be combined', (MacFarlane 2011, p. 91); and he suggests Alston (2000) as a theorist who does so combine them. My own view is that Williamson's insights are best understood from such a combined perspective. The upshot of the considerations to be adduced will be that, as I have suggested elsewhere (Ball 2014), there are just two (broad) kinds of views about the essences of illocutionary speech acts such as assertion: in particular, on one they are *natural kinds*, and we can give an account of their essences in purely descriptive terms; on the other we must employ normative terminology in characterizing them, and they are what I accordingly called *normative kinds*. To see this, however, in the next section I will contrast the descriptive approach of Stalnaker with William-son's normative account.

5   Language Games and the Very Idea of a Normative Kind

Williamson (2000) advocates a view of MacFarlane's second type, on which assertion is individuated by its constitutive rules. In fact, Williamson thinks there is just one such rule, *the knowledge rule*:

> (KR) One must: assert *p* only if one knows *p*.

MacFarlane also considers views of this general kind on which there is some other single constitutive rule (such as the truth rule, or the reasonable belief rule, the details of which need not detain us here); he then says, ';[i]t is not clear to me whether any of the proponents of these accounts intend them as explications of the illocutionary force of assertion'. (MacFarlane 2011, p. 85). The problem, for MacFarlane, seems to be that these rules do not appear to be very informative. Let me try to draw out the nature of this concern, before responding to it.

It is common for authors who take speech acts to be governed by consti-tutive rules to draw an analogy with the moves in a game.[9] Let us pursue that analogy.

Castling is a move in chess which appears to have what Williamson would call a constitutive norm: one cannot (legitimately) castle if either one's king or one's rook has moved previously.[10] In fact, we can re-write this castling rule in a form exactly analogous to the knowledge rule:

> (CR) One must: castle only if neither one's king nor one's rook has moved previously.

Notice, however, that the rules of chess also appear to say what castling *is* quite independently of this rule: according to Wikipedia, '[c]astling consists of mov-ing the king two squares towards a rook on the player's first rank, then moving the rook onto the square over which the king crossed'. The constitutive norm governing castling does not appear to individuate that move. There seem to be

---

9   See, for instance, Searle (1969), Lewis (1979), and Williamson (2000).
10   There are also other conditions on castling; I ignore them here.

other possible moves subject to the same restrictions:[11] for example, one might have the rule that the king moves next to his rook, and then the rook moves to the other side of the king.[12] So if the constitutive norm governing castling doesn't individuate it, how can the knowledge rule individuate assertion? If constitutive norms can't individuate, then it is not clear that the notion of a normative kind is even coherent, and the Williamsonian account of assertion is in trouble.[13]

This concern can be raised in a more general form. Don't we need to know what an act *is* independently of knowing when it *may* be performed? Actions are events;[14] and events, in turn, are changes in states of affairs. Thus, in order to know what an action is, it seems we must know at least what change it effectuates; or at least, we must know what change it is supposed to effectuate – for actions are arguably differentiated from other events by having intended outcomes, goals, or purposes. If so, then the need for an account of what change an act is supposed to produce is even more pressing; for effectuating that change is, presumably, the purpose of that act, and therefore essential to it (*qua* type). Thus, what we want to know is: What are the dynamics of assertion?

There is, I think, a response to this concern which can be made on the normative theorist's behalf. Suppose that we could not define the game board in chess independently of the permissible moves. Then perhaps castling would be individuated by the constitutive norm governing it, CR. In particular, the two possible moves subject to the restrictions on castling that I have discussed are differentiated by their differing outcomes (the positions of the king and the rook in the queen's side versions of the moves). If those two outcomes could not be distinguished, then arguably there would be just one move subject to the norm in question. Maybe the proponent of speech acts as normative kinds

---

11   Conversely, it seems that this same move might be subject to other restrictions. This suggests that if CR is constitutive of something it is not castling (the move) but chess (the game). In fact, though, it will be turn out to be (partially) constitutive of both, as we shall see.

12   This is the same as castling on the king's side, but differs from it on the queen's side.

13   Hindriks (2007) is puzzled by the idea of a kind whose essence is (exclusively) normative, and he objects to Williamson's account of assertion on these grounds. He makes this point, however, through an inexact analogy between language and games: in particular, he compares assertion – which is akin to a move – to the bishop, which is, of course, a piece. MacFarlane (2011), on the other hand, draws the analogy pursued here between assertion and castling. He does not press the concern that KR does not individuate the act of assertion: but he does say that "one could know [the castling rule] and have *no idea* how to move the pieces in such a way as to castle;" (MacFarlane 2011, p. 86) this suggests his concern is much like the one pressed in the main text.

14   See Davidson (1967).

can claim similarly that the positions on the game board in a conversation cannot be distinguished independently of the permissible moves such as assertion itself. It will be worth exploring this possibility; to do so I shall develop the analogy between linguistic activities and games.

If language is like a game then it seems natural to suppose that the players are the speakers and hearers in a given conversation, and the pieces are the propositions on which they act.[15] The game states, or configurations, are defined by the relations the players stand in to the propositions. The moves are changes to these game states, i.e. to the relations players stand in to the propositions. Finally, the board consists of the collection of all possible game states.

There are two ways of developing this thought. According to the first, the relations between players and propositions which serve to define the game states are descriptive in nature; according to the second, they are normative. In what follows I first consider descriptive accounts, raising a concern about all such approaches. This will serve to motivate the second approach, and allow me to articulate a coherent account of what it would be for assertion to be a normative kind.

Stalnaker (1999) provides the most precise and explicit descriptive account of language games involving assertion in the philosophical literature. On his view, the *context set* is defined as the set of possible worlds compatible with the (shared) *presuppositions* of the various conversational participants. Working in this framework, we can then define the game board as the collection of possible context sets involving those players.[16] Since presupposition can be understood independently of assertion and other speech acts,[17] assertion can be defined by the transitions it effects on the game board: assertion is that move

---

15 One might think that the pieces are certain linguistic items rather than what those items express. I will not explore this possibility here, for the reasons given above in connection with Brandom's account of the object of assertion.

16 Stalnaker says, "[o]ne may think of a ... conversation as a game where the ... context set is the playing field." (Stalnaker 1999, p. 88) If a field is to outdoor sports what a board is to board games, this conflicts with my suggestion. Instead we should regard the context set as a configuration of the playing field, something akin to the fact that the players on one team in a soccer game have formed a wall, when a free kick is about to be taken. Such a configuration of the game board/playing field of course leaves players a range of options regarding what they may legitimately do next – e.g. try to shoot past the wall, or pass to a teammate – just as Stalnaker was (presumably) hoping to suggest through his analogy.

17 In fact, Stalnaker has given a number of accounts of the attitude of presupposition (Stalnaker 1973; 1999; 2002); on one of them it turns out to be a disposition to act in certain ways in speech situations. But the point could be made even more clearly if we simply replaced shared presupposition with common knowledge, or – as Stalnaker himself has sometimes been inclined to do – with common belief.

in which one adds the content of the act to the presuppositions. Since Stal-naker takes propositions to be sets of possible worlds[18] we can put this claim another way: the effect of an assertion that p on a context c is to yield a new context $c' = c \cap p$.

Stalnaker makes a number of controversial assumptions: for instance, he maintains that the attitude which serves to define the context set is trans-parent[19] and mutually held amongst conversational participants; more fun-damentally, he holds that propositions are unstructured sets of possible worlds.[20] Yet either of these assumptions might be given up without compro-mising the descriptive character of the account of language games on offer; what is crucial is that the effect of an assertion is to bring about a change in the attitudes of conversationalists. Nevertheless, whatever attitude is taken by the descriptive theorist to be affected by assertion, it seems that this effect will not be universal: it will not occur in all cases of assertion. If hearer knowledge is said to be produced by assertions, we need only reflect on the fact that false statements are sometimes made. If belief is said to be induced, we need only recognize that some lies are obvious, and that hearers will not accept them. Making the relevant attitudes mutual merely exacerbates the problem: liars do not believe, and therefore do not know, what they assert. Indeed, it is not even the case that assertion always produces in hearers the attitude of pre-supposition – that is, of acting, for the sake of discussion, as if one takes for granted (Stalnaker 1973, p. 448); for as Stalnaker recognizes (1999, p. 86–87), a hearer may reject what is asserted, and when he or she does so, the proposi-tion in question is not presupposed, despite having been asserted. It seems, then, that there is no change in the descriptive psychological relations that conversationalists bear to propositions which is universally brought about as the effect of an assertion.

Perhaps, then, assertions have irreducibly normative effects. As MacFarlane points out, '[b]oth Stalnaker's view and … Brandom's view … are influenced by … Lewis' suggestion (1979) that we can think of speech acts in terms of the way they alter a shared "conversational score." Stalnaker takes the score to be the common ground of accepted propositions; Brandom takes it to be a

---

18   Of course, we can all agree that propositions *determine* sets of worlds.
19   According to Stalnaker, presupposition obeys both positive introspection (if one presup-poses that p then one presupposes that one presupposes that p), and negative introspec-tion (if one does not presuppose that p, then one presupposes that one does not presup-pose that p). Hawthorne and Magidor (2009) have argued that this assumption is false, and that its being so raises serious problems for Stalnaker's theory of assertion.
20   See for instance Soames (1987).

collection of normative statuses'. (MacFarlane 2011, p. 88) We have seen that there are problems, however, with the way in which Brandom develops this thought; if Williamson's view can be developed in this way, however, this will serve to demonstrate that MacFarlane's claim that 'while the constitutive-rules approach looks at "upstream" norms – norms for *making* assertions – the commitment approach looks at "downstream" norms – the normative *effects* of making assertions' (MacFarlane 2011, p. 91) is mistaken, and there is just one kind of view here on which speech acts are normative kinds. In what follows I undertake to do just this.

Williamson appears to endorse the thought that there is just one (universal normative) effect of assertion. 'To make an assertion', he says, 'is to confer a responsibility (on oneself) for the truth of its content; to satisfy the rule of assertion, by having the requisite knowledge, is to discharge that responsibility, by epistemically ensuring the truth of the content'. (Williamson 2000, p. 269) This suggests that he thinks that the effect of an assertion that p is, just as I have claimed, that the speaker becomes obliged to know that p – that is, to ensure, by knowing, that p is the case.

The knowledge rule may, however, appear inadequate on its own to establish that this is the effect of an assertion. Williamson stresses that the modal expression 'must' takes wide scope over the conditional expression 'only if' in KR. This suggests that he has in mind to formalize the knowledge rule within modal logic as $\Box(Asp \to Ksp)$. But this formula, together with Asp does not entail $\Box Ksp$ in normal modal logics. The reason is that there can be $\neg Asp$ worlds accessible from Asp worlds, and some of them may also be $\neg Ksp$ worlds. Williamson's account of assertion, on which it is defined by the knowledge rule, therefore appears to be incomplete.[21]

What is needed, if we are to solve this problem, is an account of the accessibility relation for the box operator of constitutive normative necessity. Suppose, then, that the worlds accessible from w at t are those which comply with the knowledge rule and in which exactly the same moves of the language game have been made as in w up to t. Since assertion is such a move, all the facts

<hr />

21   MacFarlane says, "[o]ne might object that the ... castling rule ... is incomplete." (MacFarlane 2011, p. 86). Strangely, however, he does not pursue this objection in connection with the knowledge rule, suggesting instead that Williamson might overcome the problem by noting that assertion is what Austin (1962/1975) called a 'constative', rather than a 'performative' speech act, and that it is therefore to be expected that it has no constitutive effect(s). This suggestion seems to me to be misguided: better to pursue the response given here.

concerning who has asserted what in w up to t must be matched in accessible worlds; but knowledge is not such a move, and so the knowledge facts need not match those in w at t. Accordingly, after S asserts that p in w, the only worlds accessible from w will be ones in which the knowledge rule is adhered to and in which S has asserted that p; these, of course, will all be worlds in which S knows that p, and so 'S must know that p' will be true in w at that time t.[22]

On this approach, KR does individuate assertion – and indeed is constitutive of this act – though it only does so in terms of the characteristic deontic 'must' of the language game, which is in turn defined partly in terms of assertion. That is, the move (assertion) and the game to which it belongs (indefinitely iterated assertion, together, perhaps, with retraction)[23] are defined in terms of each other. This is not an illegitimate vicious circularity: each is simply essentially related to the other. On this reading, Williamson's account of assertion is not so much incomplete as inexplicit: a great deal of information is packed into the deontic modal expression occurring in KR; in particular, the dynamics of assertion is built into it.

I have provided a model of assertion based on Williamson's normative account of the essence of this act; so there is clearly no incoherence somehow embedded in the very notion of a normative kind. We do not need to know what an act is independently of when it may be performed; for it may in part be constituted by the rules governing its correct performance. In such cases of rule governed behaviour, Searle was right: the rules in question make possible

---

22   We might compare this with an approach, modelled on von Fintel and Heim's (2011, p. 60) 'naïve' suggestion for the accessibility relation for a deontic modal, on which the worlds that are accessible from w at time t are those in which the rules of the game are conformed to and *everything whatsoever* up to t is as in w. Although this will have the effect that 'S knows that p' will be true in every world accessible from one in which S asserts that p, it will also have the consequence that whenever an improper assertion is made everything is required – the reason being, of course, that no worlds will be accessible. This is counterintuitive, and yet it might be defended on the grounds that our intuitions on the matter are clouded by our ignorance: since we don't *know* that the assertion is improper, we don't *regard* everything as mandatory; yet the fact remains that it *is*. Moreover, it is worth noting that on the proposal considered in the main text this difficulty will arise, though in a less acute form: for whenever two propositions are asserted, the knowing of both of which is impossible, no worlds will be accessible. This may happen if, e.g. S asserts that p but also asserts that S does not know that p; interestingly, it may also happen if S asserts that p but someone else asserts that not p, or that S does not know that p – though in such cases it is less clear who is responsible for the messy situation. I suspect that the desire to avoid such cul-de-sacs in which everything is required is what motivates the practice of retracting assertions.

23   See the previous footnote for some relevant considerations.

'new forms of behavior' (1969: 33); forms of behaviour whose effects could not be described independently of (the obligations incurred by) the rules.

6   Conclusion

I have argued that those who claim that assertion involves a commitment to the truth are right, for only by accepting this claim can we account for the phenomenon of retraction; and I have suggested that we can understand undertaking a commitment as incurring an obligation to ensure (Section 2). Next, I argued that this understanding of the commitment involved in assertion, which has a foundationalist character, is superior to the discursive coherentist alternative proposed by Brandom (Section 3). I then suggested that MacFarlane's four-fold taxonomy of accounts of assertion should be simplified, so that there is only a broad division between descriptive and normative views (Section 4). And finally, I argued that a normative account, on which in asserting we incur an obligation to know the truth of the proposition asserted, is both fully intelligible and superior to a purely descriptive account (Section 5). The upshot, I hope, is an illumination of the role of commitment and obligation in speech act theory.

Bibliography

Alston, W. (2000). *Illocutionary Acts and Sentence Meaning.* Ithaca, NY: Cornell University Press.

Austin, J.L. (1962/1975). *How to Do Things with Words.* Oxford: Oxford University Press.

Bach, K. and R.M. Harnish (1979). *Linguistic Communication and Speech Acts.* Cambridge, Mass.: MIT Press.

Ball, B. (2014). Speech Acts: Natural or Normative Kinds? *Mind and Language* 29 (3), 336–350.

Brandom, R. (1983). Asserting. *Nous* 17 (4), 637–650.

Davidson, D. (1967). The Logical Form of Action Sentences. In: N. Rescher (ed.), *The Logic of Decision and Action*, pp. 104–112. Pittsburgh, PA: University of Pittsburgh Press.

Von Fintel K. and I. Heim (2011). *Intensional Semantics.* MIT 2011 Spring Edition. http://web.mit.edu/fintel/fintel-heim-intensional.pdf (last accessed: 4 May 2017).

Hawthorne. J. and O. Magidor (2009). Assertion, Context, and Epistemic Accessibility. *Mind* 118 (470), 377–397.

Hindriks, F. (2007). The Status of the Knowledge Account of Assertion. *Linguistics and Philosophy* 30 (3), 393–406.

Horty, J. (2001). *Agency and Deontic Logic*. Oxford: Oxford University Press.

Lewis, D. (1979). Scorekeeping in a Language Game. *Journal of Philosophical Logic* 8 (1), 339–359.

MacFarlane, J. (2011). What is Assertion? In: J. Brown and H. Cappelen (eds.), *Assertion*, pp. 79–96. Oxford: Oxford University Press.

Priori, A.N. (1971). *Objects of Thought*. Oxford: Clarendon Press.

Searle, J.R. (1969). *Speech Acts*. Cambridge: Cambridge University Press.

Soames S. (1987). Direct Reference, Propositional Attitudes, and Semantic Content. *Philosophical Topics* 15 (1), 47–87.

Stalnaker, R. (1973). Presuppositions. *Journal of Philosophical Logic* 2 (4), 447–457.

Stalnaker, R. (1999). *Context and Content*. Oxford: Oxford University Press.

Stalnaker, R. (2002). Common Ground. *Linguistics and Philosophy* 25 (5–6), 701–721.

Williamson, T. (2000). *Knowledge and Its Limits*. Oxford: Oxford University Press.

CHAPTER 3

Coordination and Norms in Illocutionary Interaction

Maciej Witek

Abstract

My aim in this paper is to develop a model of the coordinative function of language conventions and, next, use it to account for the normative aspect of illocutionary practice. After discussing the current state of the philosophical debate on the nature of speech acts, I present an interactional account of illocutionary practice (Witek 2015a), which results from integrating Ruth G. Millikan's (1998; 2005) biological model of language conventions within the framework of Austin's (1975) theory of speech acts. Next, I elaborate on Millikan's idea that the proper function of illocutionary conventions is coordinative and put forth a hypothesis according to which conventional patterns of linguistic interaction have been selected for the roles they play in producing and maintaining mental coordination between interacting agents. Finally, I use the resulting model of coordination to develop a naturalistic account of the so-called sincerity norms. Focusing my analysis on assertions and directives, I argue that the normative character of sincerity rules can be accounted for in terms of Normal conditions for proper functioning of speech acts understood as cooperative intentional signs in Millikan's (2004) sense; I also discuss the possibility of providing a naturalistic account of the normative effects of illocutionary acts.

1   Introduction: Three Accounts of the Nature of Illocutionary Acts

According to Gerald Gazdar, 'a speech act is a function from contexts into contexts.'[1] (Gazdar 1981, p. 68) In a similar vein, Marina Sbisà claims that speech

---

1   I gratefully acknowledge the support of the Polish National Science Centre through research grant No. 2011/03/B/HS1/ 00917 for the preparation of this work. An earlier version of this paper has been presented at the workshop *Speech Acts in Theory and Practice* in December 2013 (University of Szczecin, Poland). I would like to thank the participants of this workshop for the valuable comments and discussion, especially Brian Ball, Anita Fetzer, Kepa Korta, Marcin Matczak, Marina Sbisà, and Iwona Witczak-Plisiecka. I am also very grateful to the two anonymous reviewers for their helpful remarks that significantly improved this paper.

acts are 'context-changing social actions,' (Sbisà 2002, p. 421) thereby capturing a central idea behind John L. Austin's conception of linguistic practice. In *How to Do Things with Words*, Austin put forth a hypothesis according to which most of our utterances are speech acts that can be typed by reference to the effects that they have on the context of their production: *locutionary* acts create linguistic representations of states of the world, *illocutionary* acts affect the domain of conventional facts, whereas *perlocutionary* acts 'produce certain consequential effects upon the feelings, thoughts, or actions of the audience, or of the speaker, or of other persons.' (Austin 1975, p. 101) It is worth stressing that locutionary, illocutionary and perlocutionary acts normally have no independent existence: they are abstract aspects of what Austin called 'the total speech act in the total speech situation.'(*ibid*, p. 147) We distinguish them, however, to account for the three types of effects—representational, conventional, and consequential, respectively—that our utterances can have on our social environment.

In this paper I focus on the illocutionary aspect of linguistic interaction. Following Austin, I assume, first, that to issue an illocutionary act is to utter a sentence with 'a certain (conventional) force' (Austin 1975, p. 109)—e.g., with the force of informing, warning, ordering, requesting, promising, offering, and so on—and, next, that the *force* or *type-identity* of the act is to be defined by reference to how it affects the context in which it is made. According to Austin, the issuing of a felicitous illocutionary act involves the production of the following three effects: (e_1) the *securing of uptake* on the part of the audience, which normally 'amounts to bringing about the understanding of the meaning and of the force of the locution,' (Austin 1975, p. 117), (e_2) the *taking of effect*, *i.e.*, the bringing about of normative facts construed as the rights and commitments of interacting agents, and (e_3) the *inviting of a response or sequel, e.g.*, the response of obedience, if the act is an order, or that of fulfilment, if the act is a promise. It remains to be examined, however, which one of these three effects plays a central role in determining the force of an act (for an extensive discussion of this issue, see Witek 2013).

According to the *intentionalist* or *Gricean approach* (Strawson 1964; Bach and Harnish 1979; Harnish 2005), most illocutionary act types—*e.g.*, statements, warnings, requests, promises, offers, and so on—are communicative rather than conventional and as such are to be defined by reference to Gricean intentions with which they are made. More specifically, the proponents of the Gricean approach maintain that to make a communicative illocutionary act is to utter a sentence with the intention to induce a certain response on the part of the hearer by getting him to recognize *this* intention; in other words, the success of the act—*i.e.*, the fulfilment of its force-determining intention—necessarily *involves* (Strawson 1964) or even *consists in* (Bach and Harnish 1979) the achievement of the effect of the (e_1) type, *i.e.*, the securing of uptake on the part of the hearer. They also claim that the force of the act depends on the response that the speaker intends to produce. The proponents of the *institutionalist approach* (Searle 1969; 1979; Alston 2000; Williamson 1996; García-Carpintero 2004; Sbisà 1992; 2002; 2009; 2013; this volume; Ball 2014a; 2014b; this volume), by contrast, claim that illocutionary acts are to be classified by reference to their normative effects of the (e_2) type: every felicitous assertion takes effect by bringing about the speaker's commitment to the truth of the proposition she asserts,[2] every binding directive act, in turn, takes effect by creating the hearer's commitment to comply with what he is told, and so on. As Marina Sbisà puts it, the normative effect of an illocutionary act is conventional in that 'it comes into being by being agreed upon by the relevant members of a social group.' (Sbisà 2009, p. 49) Finally, according to the *interactional approach* (Millikan 1984; 1998; 2004; 2005; Witek 2015a; Corredor this volume), the force of an act should be defined in terms of its interactional effect of the (e_3) type.[3] For example, Ruth G. Millikan claims that speech acts are conventional moves 'classified by conventional outcomes.' (Millikan 2005, p. 151) Roughly speaking, the conventional outcome of an act can be identified with the response that it invites 'by convention,' (Austin 1975: 117) where the Austinian phrase 'by convention' can be explicated as 'in accordance with a pattern of cooperative interaction that the speaker and the hearer jointly reproduce'. More specifically, every pattern of the type under discussion consists of two complementary elements: the speaker's part, which involves her uttering a certain linguistic form (*e.g.*, an indicative or imperative sentence), and the hearer's part, which consists in his cooperative response to what the speaker says (*e.g.*, in believing or complying with what he is told, respectively).

---

2 See Ball this volume for an extensive discussion of the role the notions of commitment and obligation play in speech-act theoretic accounts of assertion.

3 It is instructive to note that what Cristina Corredor calls in her contribution to this volume the 'interactionalist view of communication' combines elements of the institutionalist and interactional approaches presented above. She defines the interactionalist view as claiming that 'the characteristic conventional effect of illocutionary acts is to create, cancel or change deontic states of affairs in the domain of commitments, obligations, rights, entitlements, and the like that articulate the intersubjective relations of the interactants in the ongoing interaction. This view is thus internally related to a normative conception of communication. Conversations are considered to be forms of joint action, in which the interactants negotiate meaning to eventually agree upon the fact that a particular speech act has been performed, thus bringing about its conventional effect in virtue of this very agreement.' (Corredor this volume, p. 140–141)

In my view, it is the interactional model that provides the best understanding of the mechanisms of illocutionary practice and the essence of its constituent moves. Most crucially, it does justice to the idea that illocutionary acts necessarily form parts of joint activities and 'have their origins in social practices.' (Clark 1996, p. 139) In other words, it allows for what Sbisà (1992; 2002) takes to be Austin's basic insight into the nature of linguistic practice, *i.e.*, his recognition of the indispensably social and bilateral character of speech acts construed of as constitutive parts of discourse (see Fetzer 2013; this volume). According to the interactional model illocutionary acts form a subclass of what Millikan calls *cooperative intentional signs*:

> Cooperative intentional signs are produced by systems designed to make natural signs for use by cooperating interpreting systems. That is, the sign-maker system and the sign-using system must have evolved or been designed to function symbiotically. Cooperating intentional sign-makers must be designed to cooperate with interpreting systems that have been designed, in turn, to cooperate with them. (Millikan 2004, p. 73)

Illocutionary acts *qua* cooperative intentional signs, then, are produced and interpreted by agents who, as part of their adaptation to their social environment, are disposed to cooperate with each other in accordance with certain conventional patterns of interaction:

> Speakers in the language community are adapted to an environment in which hearers are responding, sufficiently often, to the forms speakers produce in ways that reinforce these speaker productions. And the hearers in the community are adapted to conditions under which speakers, sufficiently often, produce these language forms in circumstances such that making conventional responses to them aids hearers. (Millikan 2004, p. 105)

One can ask why it is beneficial for speakers and hearers to reproduce conventional patterns of verbal interaction or, to put it in Millikan's (1984; 2004; 2005) technical terms, what is their *proper function* or *proper purpose, i.e.*, the function that is responsible for their continuous and stable use. According to Millikan (1998), the proper function of language conventions is coordinative: conventional patterns of speaker-hearer interaction proliferate because they help achieve coordination between conversing agents. In my view, this answer is true as far as it goes. I would like to go further, however, and consider what type of coordination problem language conventions are designed to solve. My hypothesis is that the proper function of conventional patterns of verbal interaction is to help achieve *mental coordination* between conversing agents, *i.e.*, to help them produce and maintain a preferred correspondence between their individual representations of their shared mental states: beliefs, desires, intentions, expectations, and so on.

One can also ask whether the interactional approach can be used to account for the normative aspect of illocutionary interaction or, more specifically, whether it provides a sufficient basis for explaining two facts: firstly, that speech acts are subject to norms and, secondly, that they produce normative states of affairs characterizable in terms of rights and commitments (for a discussion of the latter see Witek 2015c). The proponents of the interactional model can no longer take these facts to be explanatorily basic. In my view, however, they can allow for them by developing a naturalistic account of the normative aspect of linguistic interaction. My second hypothesis in the present paper is that at least some illocutionary norms—i.e., the so-called sincerity norms—can be accounted for in terms of Normal[4] conditions for the proper functioning of illocutionary acts *qua* cooperative intentional signs.

The paper goes as follows. In section 2, I outline the interactional model of illocutionary practice. In particular, I draw a distinction between primary and secondary conventional patterns and claim that they operate locally rather than globally, *i.e.*, that they constitute the structure of local language games or activity types in Levinson's (1979) sense. In section 3, I consider the coordinative function of conventional patterns of verbal interaction and claim that it consists in producing mental coordination between conversing agents. Next, in section 4, I use the resulting model of coordination to explain the normative aspect of illocutionary practice. More specifically, I argue that the normative character of the so-called sincerity rules—*e.g.*, 'one must: assert that p only if one believes that p'—can be accounted for in terms of Normal conditions for proper functioning of conventional patterns. I also make a few remarks as to how one can use the interactional model to account for normative effects of illocutionary acts, focusing my analysis on two types of illocutionary force: assertive and directive.

2   An Outline of the Interactional Model of Illocutionary Practice

The interactional account of illocutionary practice builds on Ruth G. Millikan's biological model of language (Millikan 1984; 1998; 2004; 2005), whose

---

4   Following Millikan (2005), I use the term 'Normal' with capital 'N' to distinguish 'Normal conditions' in Millikan's technical sense from 'normal conditions' in the statistical sense.

underlying assumption is that we can univocally attribute *proper functions* or *purposes* to items such as genes, organs, biological mechanisms, behavioural dispositions, linguistic devices, speech acts and conventional patterns of linguistic interaction. Roughly speaking, a function *F* of item *A* is its *proper function* or *proper purpose* if '*A* originated as a 'reproduction' (to give one example, as a copy of a copy) of some prior item or items that, *due* in part to possession of the properties reproduced, have actually performed *F* in the past, and *A* exists because (causally historically because) of this or these performances.' (Millikan 1989, p. 28; cf. Matczak 2016; this volume). In short, *F* is the proper function of items or traits of a certain type if it is causally responsible for their continuous reproduction and proliferation. For example, a hammer that I keep in my office is usually used as a paperweight. Sometimes I use it as a temporary rest for my projector, whose original bracket is broken. Very seldom I use this hammer for driving nails. In short, the hammer under discussion performs at least three different functions, *i.e.*, it is used as a paperweight, as a temporary rest for my projector, and as a tool for driving nails. Note, however, that only the last one is its *proper* function. It does not matter that the hammer in question is seldom used for driving nails. What matters is that it has been produced as a copy of other hammers because they, due to their possession of the properties reproduced, have been used as tools for driving nails. In general, an individual item can have many different uses, but only some of them correspond to its proper purpose or function.

According to Millikan, we can also attribute proper functions to linguistic devices, speech acts, and speaker-hearer patterns of verbal interaction. She claims that the proper function of a sentence—as well as the proper purpose of the act made in uttering it—is to evoke a certain cooperative response on the part of the hearer (Millikan 2005). For example, the proper function or purpose of indicative sentence '*p*' is to induce the belief that *p* in the hearers' minds. Generally, indicative sentences have been designed as conventional tools for inducing beliefs. Imperative sentences, in turn, have been selected for their use in getting hearers to do what they are told. Consistently, the proper function of a speech act is to evoke the hearer's cooperative response. For example, the proper function of an assertion is to get the hearer to believe what the speaker asserts, whereas the proper function of a directive act is to get the hearer to do what he is told. If the acts are literal and direct, their proper functions coincide with the conventional purposes of the sentences by means of which they are performed (for a discussion of this issue see Millikan 1984, esp. Chapter 3; 2005). Next, the proper purpose of a speaker-hearer pattern—which involves the speaker's utterance of a certain linguistic form and the hearer's cooperative response to it—is to help achieve coordination between communicating agents (Millikan 1998). For example, the proper function of any pattern that involves the speaker's utterance of an indicative or imperative sentence and the hearer's cooperative response—*i.e.*, the hearer's believing or complying with what he is told, respectively—is to help achieve coordination between the speaker and the hearer.

In summary, conventional linguistic devices and speaker-hearer patterns of interaction were selected for their cooperative and coordinative functions, respectively; what makes them *conventional*, in turn, is the fact that their forms are to some extent arbitrary or, more precisely, have been reproduced due to the weight of their cultural precedents rather than due to their capacity to perform their functions. According to Millikan (1998), a behaviour is conventional if its form (*i*) has been reproduced from previous behaviours and (*ii*) is arbitrary relative to its function, *i.e.*, proliferates due to the importance of its cultural precedents rather than due to its capacity to perform its function. The performance of an illocutionary act, then, consists in reproducing the speaker's part of a speaker-hearer pattern by uttering an appropriate linguistic form; the force of the act thereby produced depends on what counts as the hearer's complementary portion of the pattern or, in other words, on what I call the conventionally determined *interactional effect* of the act. The effect can be likened to a response or sequel that the act invites 'by convention' (Austin 1975, p. 117), where the Austinian phrase 'by convention' is explicated along the Millikanian lines, *i.e.*, in terms of speaker-hearer patterns of verbal interaction.

In short, the interactional model of illocutionary practice results from integrating elements of Millikan's model of language conventions within the theoretical framework of Austin's speech act theory. Besides drawing on the general concept of speaker-hearer conventional patterns, it identifies and explicates two other ideas that seem to be inherent to Millikan's original theory.

Firstly, the interactional model distinguishes between two types of cooperative responses—*primary* and *secondary*—that a speech act can conventionally elicit or, in other words, between the act's *primary interactional effect* and its *secondary interactional effects*. For example, the primary interactional effect of a directive act made in uttering sentence 'Do *A*!' is the hearer's complying with what he or she is told. Undoubtedly, the occurrence of this effect is partly responsible for the continuous reproduction of the sentence in question and the proliferation of the practice of using it to make directive speech acts: if hearers systematically refused to comply with what they were told, the form would be eventually abandoned by speakers. Nevertheless, one can be regarded as cooperating with one's interlocutor even though one fails to produce the primary interactional effect of the interlocutor's act. Rather than directly complying with what he is told, the addressee of a directive act can provide the speaker with information or clues from which she can elaborate a plan to achieve the conversational goal behind her utterance. For example, the addressee of the utterance of 'Give me something to eat!' can respond *either* by giving the speaker something to eat—e.g., a ham sandwich—thereby producing the primary interactional effect of the speaker's act, *or* by uttering the sentence 'Go to the dining room! There are a few toasts on the table', thereby producing one of the secondary effects available in this type of verbal interaction. In the former case, the addressee can be described as completing the *primary pattern* of interaction invoked by the speaker, whereas in the latter case he can be regarded as completing one of the *secondary patterns* associated with the primary one. In both cases, however, he behaves cooperatively. The crucial point here is that conversational cooperation goes beyond straightforward trust (in the case of assertions) and compliance (in the case of directives). To allow for this fact, however, we need the distinction between primary and secondary interactional effects and the corresponding contrast between primary and secondary speaker-hearer patterns. The force of an act depends on what counts as its primary interactional effect; we refer to its secondary effects in order to explain those forms of cooperation that cannot be described as cases of straightforward trust or compliance.

Secondly, the interactional account claims that the patterns in question operate locally rather than globally; more specifically, they can be grouped into coherent systems constituting different local semiotic systems (Millikan 2004) or, as Stephen C. Levinson would put it, different activity types conceived of as 'goal-defined, socially constituted, bounded events with *constraints* on participants, setting, and so on, but above all on the kinds of allowable contributions.' (Levinson 1979, p. 368). The interactional account, then, is *not* committed to a traditional version of the literal force hypothesis, according to which the indicative mood encodes the force of making a statement, the imperative mood encodes the force of issuing a command, and the interrogative mood encodes the force of asking a question (for a discussion of this hypothesis, see Gazdar 1981, p. 74); depending on the type of the language game that is currently being played, rather, one can use an indicative sentence to make a statement, a request, a command, a promise, a permission, and so on.

In my view, the above-mentioned tenets of the interactional account provide a sufficient basis for examining two different though closely interconnected issues: the coordinative function of speaker-hearer patterns (Section 3) and the normative aspect of illocutionary practice (Section 4).

3   Conventional Patterns and Their Coordinative Function

According to Millikan, the proper function of speaker-hearer patterns is to help achieve coordination among conversing agents. It is not clear, however, what type of coordination they are designed to produce and maintain. In this section I put forth a hypothesis according to which language conventions proliferate because they help achieve *mental coordination*. Following Richmond H. Thomason, I assume that the participants in a conversation 'are working together to build a shared date structure [henceforth, SDS]' (Thomason 1990, p. 339) construed of as a set of their shared beliefs, desires, intentions, expectations. As Thomason has noted, however, there is no 'literally shared memory' (*ibid.*); normally, the participants in a dialogue build their own representations of their SDS and assume by default—*i.e.*, unless there is a reason to think otherwise—that they match or coincide with each other. Producing and maintaining mental coordination between the conversing agents, then, consists in keeping their own representations of SDS sufficiently aligned or, in other words, in achieving a *preferred correspondence* between what the agents take to be their shared beliefs, desires, intentions, expectations, and so on.

In what follows, I examine the structure of speaker-hearer patterns (in Subsection 3.1), thereby setting the stage for the discussion of their coordinative proper function (in Subsection 3.2).

3.1   *The Structure of Speaker-Hearer Patterns*

Consider John and Mary who are looking at guests coming to Linda's wedding party. John says:

(1)   The man with a purple tie is Linda's cousin.

Mary responds by forming the belief that the man with a purple tie is Linda's cousin. The second event takes place in a university canteen. Tom, who is about to pay, realizes that he has no cash in his wallet and says to Peter:

(2)   Lend me 10 euros.

Peter responds by opening his wallet and handing Tom a 10 euro bill. Consider, thirdly, a father who is sitting at a kitchen table reading a newspaper. His daughter, Hanna, runs into the kitchen and shouts sentence (3a); the father responds by uttering sentence (3b).

(3)   a.   I am hungry!
        b.   There is a piece of pizza in the fridge.

The three events discussed above can be described in terms of one agent's initiating and the other's completing the reproduction of a certain speaker-hearer coordinative pattern. Consider the wedding scenario first. Let us assume that the reproduction begins with (i_1) John's belief that the man with a purple tie is Linda's cousin, moves through (ii_1) his utterance of sentence (1), and ends with (iii_1) Mary's forming the belief that the man with a purple tie is Linda's cousin. Next, let us assume that Tom and Peter are engaged in reproducing a speaker-hearer pattern that involves four components: (i_2) Tom's having a desire that Peter lends him 10 euros, (ii_2) his utterance of sentence (2), (iii_2) Peter's forming an intention to lend Tom 10 euros, and (iv_2) his handing Tom a 10 euro bill. In the kitchen scenario, in turn, the reproduction involves (i_3) Hanna's desire to get something to eat, (ii_3) her uttering sentence (3a), (iii_3) the father's forming the desire that Hanna gets something to eat, and (iv_3) his uttering sentence (3b).

In general, the three patterns under discussion have roughly the same structure with the exception that the pattern reproduced by John and Mary involves no response at the behavioural level. This common structure can be represented as a sequence of the following four elements:

(i)   a certain mental state of the speaker;
(ii)   the speaker's utterance of a certain linguistic form in a context;
(iii) the hearer's forming a mental state that stands in a preferred correspondence relation to the speaker state specified in (i);
(iv)   the hearer's practical response to the speaker's utterance (ii).

A central tenet of the interactional account is that making a speech act consists in producing component (ii) of a certain speaker-hearer pattern; the force of the act thereby performed depends on what counts as its interactional effect or, more precisely, on what counts as its *primary* interactional effect. This effect is to be identified with the hearer's cooperative response that is determined by the primary pattern invoked by the speaker. In the wedding scenario, for example, by forming the belief that the man with a purple tie is Linda's cousin, Mary completes the reproduction of the primary pattern invoked by John's utterance of indicative sentence (1). Similarly, Peter's handing Tom a 10 euro bill completes the reproduction of the pattern invoked by Tom's utterance of imperative sentence (2). In short, the two acts under discussion succeed in bringing about their primary interactional effects. It is worth noting, however, that the primary effect of John's act is Mary's mental state, whereas the primary effect of Tom's utterance is Peter's publicly observable action. The hearer's cooperative response to the speaker's utterance can therefore occur either at the level of belief formation or at the level of practical responses, depending on whether the utterance has the force of making an assertion or that of making a directive act. In uttering imperative sentence (2), Tom makes a directive act, whereas John's utterance of indicative sentence (1) has the force of making an assertion. Generally speaking, assertions invite *by convention* the response of trust, whereas directive acts invite *by convention* the response of compliance or doing what one is told. It is instructive to stress, however, that 'by convention' as used here means 'in agreement with primary speaker-hearer patterns'.

The primary interactional effect of an utterance is a second act on the part of the hearer. Its performance completes the cooperative function of the speaker's act. In some cases, however, a hearer can be justifiably regarded as cooperating with the speaker even though he fails to respond in agreement with the primary pattern that she invokes. This is exactly what takes place in the kitchen scenario: instead of giving his daughter something to eat, the father utters sentence (3b). Still, this response is cooperative. Although the father fails to comply with Hanna's directive act, he adopts conversational goal (i_3) behind her utterance—*i.e.*, he takes it to be desirable that Hanna gets something to eat—and utters sentence (3b). The function of this utterance is to help Hanna elaborate a plan to achieve goal (i_3) behind her utterance of (3a). As Nicolas Asher and Alex Lascarides (2001; 2003) would put it, the act made in uttering (3b) is relational. More precisely, it is a rhetorical relation of *Plan Elaboration* represented by means of the formula '*Plan-Elab*(3a, 3b)' meaning 'the act made in uttering (3b) has the force of *Plan Elaboration* with respect to the act made in uttering (3a)'. Viewed from the perspective of the interactional model, this formula stands for a secondary speaker-hearer pattern reproduced by Hanna and her father; consistently, the father's utterance of sentence (3b) can be regarded as a secondary interactional effect of Hanna's directive act. This effect is *interactional*, because it can be justifiably described as the father's *cooperative* reaction to Hanna's request: the felicity of the relational act of *Plan-Elab*(α, β) presupposes that the speaker of β adopts the conversational goal behind utterance α; it is *secondary*, because it cannot be described as a case of straightforward trust or compliance. It is worth stressing, however, that it is secondary *with respect to* what would count as the primary effect of Hanna's utterance, *i.e.*, with respect to the father's giving his daughter something to eat. Note, namely, that what these two responses—*i.e.*, the primary and the secondary— have in common is that their performances presuppose adoption (iii_3) of the same conversational goal (i_3). Nevertheless, the phrases 'primary effect' and 'secondary effect' differ in the roles they play in our theorising about linguistic practice. We employ the former to define types of speech acts and to explain their stability by reference to their cooperative proper functions;[5] we use the latter, in turn, to account for those cases of conversational cooperation that cannot be described in terms of straightforward trust or compliance.

---

5 For a discussion of the stabilizing aspect of Millikanian proper functions, see Matczak (this volume), p. 189.

Discussing the kitchen scenario I have tacitly assumed that in uttering sentence (3a) Hanna performs a conventional and direct request; more specifically, I have taken her utterance to constitute component (*ii*) of a primary pattern whose force-determining component (*iv*)—i.e., the primary interactional effect—consists in the addressee's giving the speaker something to eat. One can object, however, that this assumption fails to provide an adequate description of that talk exchange. One can claim, namely, that in uttering sentence (3a) Hanna performs two illocutionary acts: she makes a direct and conventional statement to the effect that she is hungry and, in doing this, she indirectly and non-conventionally asks for something to eat; the force of making a statement is direct and conventional, because it fits the one encoded by the indicative mood of sentence (3b); the force of making a request, in turn, is indirect and non-conventional, because it is communicated at the level of what is conversationally implicated (for a discussion of a similar example, see Bach 1987, p. 73). To strengthen this Gricean reading of the kitchen scenario, one can consider its slightly modified version in which the father precedes his utterance of (3b) with the utterance of sentence (4):

(4)   That's strange. You have just had lunch.

One can maintain, namely, that in uttering (4) the father makes a comment on Hanna's direct statement, whereas in uttering (3b) he responds to her indirect request. In other words the utterance of (3a) seems to function as a reference point for two rhetorical relations: *Comment*(3a, 4) and *Plan-Elab*(3a, 3b): the former exploits Hanna's direct contribution to the kitchen dialogue, whereas the latter exploits what she communicates at the level of conversational implicature.

In my view, however, Hanna's utterance of (3a) can be regarded *either* as a direct and conventional statement, *or* as a direct and conventional request, *or* as two direct and conventional acts—a statement and a request—made in one utterance. The actual force of this utterance depends on the type of the game that Hanna and her father are playing. I assume that game or activity types can be represented as coherent systems of speaker-hearer patterns that put constraints 'on the kinds of allowable contributions.' (Levinson 1979, p. 368) If in uttering sentence (3a) Hanna invites her father to play an information-exchange game, then her act is to be regarded as a direct statement and as such responded by the utterance of (4); this move is an allowable contribution in the game or, in other words, the rhetorical relation of *Comment* is one of the secondary speaker-hearer patterns that the players are allowed to reproduce. If, by contrast, in uttering sentence (3a) Hanna invites her father to play an instruction-exchange game, then her utterance should be regarded as constituting a direct request and as such can be responded either by direct compliance (*i.e.*, the father's giving Hanna something to eat) or by the father's producing one of the secondary effects that are allowable in this game (*e.g.*, by his uttering sentence (3b) with the relational force of *Plan Elaboration*). In some cases, however, Hanna's initiating utterance can be regarded as an invitation to play both the information-exchange and the instruction-exchange games. If this is the case, her act can be legitimately regarded as both a direct statement and as a direct request and, as the corollary of this, felicitously responded by uttering (4) followed by (3b).

In short, speaker-hearer patterns operate locally rather than globally and make up coherent systems representing different game types. To accept this idea is to reject a classical formulation of the literal force hypothesis, according to which the indicative mood encodes the force of making a statement, the imperative mood encodes the force of issuing a command, and the interrogative mood encodes the force of asking a question. As a matter of fact, sentences of the forms (3a) can be used to make moves in different games and, as the corollary of this, to initiate the reproduction of different speaker-hearer patterns. If uttered by a patient examined by her physician, the pheme token thereby produced constitutes a direct act of informing; no wonder, since medical examination is an information-exchange game. If, by contrast, it is uttered by a child who speaks to her father, it constitutes a direct request. Finally, if pheme (3a) is produced by my colleague who enters my office in lunch time, it constitutes a direct suggestion that I should take a break and go to the canteen. These three speech situations contribute to one phatic type or—as Millikan (2005; cf. Witek 2015b) would put it, to one phatic lineage—which is a collection of past uses of pheme (3a). The lineage criss-crosses different illocutionary lineages or, more precisely, different game types within which its constituent pheme tokens function as different illocutionary acts.

3.2   *The Function of Speaker-Hearer Patterns*

According to Millikan, 'all that is required for a [speaker-hearer] convention to survive, to be repeated and passed on, is to succeed in coordinating the interests of speakers and hearers some critical proportion of the time, weighting the value of coordination success against the disvalue of failures.' (Millikan 2008, p. 88) The proper function of a speaker-hearer pattern, then, is to help achieve coordination between participants in a dialogue.

My aim in this subsection is to elaborate on the above-mentioned idea by considering the relationship between three types of coordination problems that speaker-hearer patterns can be seen as designed to solve: task-specific, signalling, and mental. In particular, I argue that the *focused* proper function of language conventions is to ensure what I call *mental* coordination: even though a given speaker-hearer pattern serves various task-specific purposes on different occasions, they all converge and depend on its function to produce and maintain a preferred correspondence between the mental states of the conversing agents. The distinction between the focused proper function of a device and its further proper functions comes from Millikan (1984, pp. 34–38), who explicates it by discussing a number of examples; for instance, she claims that a 'brake pedal has as a focused function to slow or stop the car, further functions of that slowing or stopping may have being alternative and diverse.' (Millikan 1984, p. 36)

Task-specific coordination problems can be defined by reference to the various goals that are accepted and shared by the interacting agents on different occasions. Let us consider, for example, two engineers whose common aim is to defuse a pair of interconnected bombs located in different rooms. Each bomb has a colourful tangle of wires under its cover. To perform their task successfully, however, the engineers have to achieve coordination between their complementary contributions to their joint activity, *e.g.*, to simultaneously cut wires of the same colour. In short, they face a task-specific coordination problem, which can be solved by means of a speaker-hearer pattern that involves one of the engineers saying 'The red one, now!' and the other engineer cutting the red wire in his bomb (let us assume that they communicate by phone). Other examples of joint activities that may generate task-specific coordination problems are group hunting, playing a basketball match, carrying a heavy sofa upstairs, repairing a car, and so on. Some of these problems can be solved with the help of linguistic devices or, more specifically, by reproducing appropriate speaker-hearer patterns. The reproduction begins with component (*i*), *i.e.*, the speaker's mental state whose content is appropriately related to the speaker's contribution to the activity—*e.g.*, with the first engineer's intention to cut the red wire in her bomb—and ends with component (*iv*), *i.e.*, the hearer's cooperative response that stands in a preferred correspondence relation to the speaker's contribution; the coordination thereby produced ensures the achievement of the task-specific goal that is commonly accepted by interacting agents.

Each signalling problem, in turn, involves two agents: a signaller and a responder. The signaller, unlike the responder, has a perceptual access to certain states of affairs. The responder, however, is supposed to respond to the states in accordance with a certain correspondence rule. More specifically, the common aim of the signaller and the responder is to ensure a preferred correspondence *between* the states of affairs that the signaller can see *and* the actions performed by the responder. This aim can be achieved only if there is a coordination between what Lewis (2002, p 122) called (*a*) the *contingency plan* followed by the signaller and (*b*) the *contingency plan* followed by the responder.

The signaller's contingency plan consists of rules in accordance with which she translates the states she is aware of into the signals that the responder can perceive; by analogy, the responder's contingency plan consists of rules in accordance with which he translates the signals produced by the signaller into responses that are preferred in the light of the accepted correspondence rule. The plans can be coordinated by a *signaller-responder pattern* whose structure involves the signaller's perceptual state, the signal she produces, and the responder's preferred response.

If the coordination between the contingency plans is achieved, the responder's perception is in a sense *extended*: in practice, he takes the signals produced by his partner to be perceptually available symptoms of the states that they stand for (for a discussion of this idea, see McDowell 1980; Millikan 2004, pp. 113–125). Consider, following Millikan (1989, p. 288; cf. Matczak this volume, p. 187), a beaver hitting the water with its tail to produce a splashing sound that signals the presence of a predator in its vicinity; other beavers, even though they cannot see or hear the predator, respond to this signal by flying out and looking for places to hide.[6] In this case, the coordination between the contingency plan followed by the signaller and that followed by the responder is ensured by natural selection or learning: the plans make up a signaller-responder pattern that is in a sense *built in* the structure of the beavers' minds. Another example of solving a signalling problem is the International Code of Signals that consists of two complementary contingency plans: one of the form 'if in such-and-such predicament, hoist such-and-such flags,' (Lewis 2002, p. 125) and the other of the form 'if a ship hoists such-and-such flags, act as would be appropriate on the assumption that it is in such-and-such predicament.' (*ibid*) This time, the plans are coordinated by a convention created by agreement. The convention, let us note, can be represented as a lineage of signaller-responder interactions.

In summary, signalling problems can be solved with the help of conventional or non-conventional signaller-responder patterns. At the current stage of analysis it does not matter what is the mechanism whereby the patterns

6 I assume that splashing sounds produced by beavers are not only symptoms, but also signals. One of the reviewers has suggested that it would be useful to consider the functioning of this and other examples of animal signalling systems—which seem to be evolutionary precursors of human illocutionary practices—in terms of the distinction between symptoms and criteria (Navarro-Reyes 2010). I am very grateful to the reviewer for this suggestion. Let me add that another possibililty would be to employ the conceptual framework of the evolutionary biology of communication—built around such notions as *cues, signals, indices*, and *handicaps*—adopted and developed by Mitchell S. Green (2009; forthcoming). However, for the sake of keeping this paper within reasonable limits, I leave discussing this topic for another occasion.

perform their coordination function; in particular, we can leave it as an open question whether it involves expressing and recognising Gricean reflexive intentions. What matters is that the signaller is disposed to translate his perceptual states into signals in accordance with her part of a certain signalling pattern and the responder is disposed to react to the signals produced by the signaller in accordance with his part of the pattern.

Quite often interacting agents are interested in achieving signalling coordination because they are interested in solving certain task-specific coordination problems. In other words, the *focal* proper function of a signalling patter is to coordinate the agents' contingency plans, whereas its various *further* proper functions consist in helping them achieve their task-specific goals. This is true of the patterns that make up the International Code of Signals as well as of the pattern reproduced by engineers involved in defusing a pair of bombs. Note, namely, that the utterance of 'The red one, now!' made by one of the engineers can be regarded as a signal that stands for what she is currently doing and thereby 'extends' the other engineer's perception. Reproducing the pattern that involves the utterance of 'The red one, now!', the engineers solve a certain signalling problem, *i.e.*, they ensure a preferred correspondence between their contingency plans. In doing this, they solve a corresponding task-specific coordination problem: they ensure a preferred correspondence between their complementary contributions to their joint action and, as a result, succeed in defusing a pair of interconnected bombs. By analogy, one may ask what is the task-specific coordination problem that John and Mary want to solve by reproducing the pattern involving the utterance of (1). I am inclined to say that there is no such problem in particular: apart from letting Mary know who the man with a purple ties is, there seems to be no ulterior motive behind John's utterance.

It is instructive to note, however, that the reproduction of the pattern that involves steps from (i_1) to (iii_1) results in a partial overlap between John's mental states and Mary's mental states or, more accurately, it updates their representations of their SDS (*i.e.*, their shared data structure) with the same piece of information. In other words, the reproduction of the pattern in question is a self-manifest event that results in a preferred correspondence between John's and Mary's representations of their SDS: John and Mary have information that this event takes place, it indicates to each of them that they both have information that this event takes place, and it indicates to both John and Mary that they both believe that the man with a purple tie is Linda's cousin.[7]

---

7   I model my analysis of updating the representations of SDS on Herbert H. Clark's definition
    of a *basis* for a piece of common ground; see Clark 1996, p. 99.

Generally speaking, even though a reproduction of a given speaker-hearer pattern solves no particular task-specific coordination problem, it results in what I call *mental coordination*. The *focused* proper function of speaker-hearer patterns, then, is to help achieve mental coordination between the conversing agent, that is to say, to produce a preferred correspondence between their representations of the SDS. Normally, the participants in a conversation are interested in making their representations of the SDS aligned or coinciding with each other, because they are interested in building a comprehensive basis for solving any task-specific coordination problem that they happen to face. In other words, any belief that the interacting agents jointly represent as shared is a potential coordination device that can be consumed in the future. The richer the stock of the assumptions they jointly represent as shared, the greater the number of particular task-specific coordination problems that they can immediately solve. Therefore, it is beneficial for the conversing agents to cooperate on producing a preferred correspondence between their representations of the SDS; in other words, it is beneficial for them to cooperate on producing and maintaining mental coordination. All that is required for a speaker-hearer conventional pattern to proliferate, then, is to succeed in achieving mental coordination between speakers and hearers 'some critical proportion of the time, weighting the value of coordination success against the disvalue of failures.' (Millikan 2008, p. 88)

So far I have limited my discussion to assertions. It can easily be extended, however, to include cases of directives and other types of illocutionary forces. For instance, one can argue that the reproduction of the pattern that involves the utterance of sentence (2)—see the canteen scenario discussed in subsection 3.1.—results in a partial overlap between Tom's mental states and Peter's mental states; namely, it updates their representations of their SDS—i.e., Tom's representation of what he (Tom) takes to be their shared mental states and Peter's representation of what he (Peter) takes to be their shared states—with the desire that Peter lends Tom 10 euros. By analogy, let us consider the kitchen scenario discussed in subsection 3.1. Recall that the pattern that goes through Hanna's utterance of (3a) and her father's utterance of (3b) involves, as its hidden element, the father's adopting the desire that Hanna gets something to eat, *i.e.*, his adoption of the conversational goal behind her utterance. In other words, the reproduction of this pattern results in enhancing mental coordination between Hanna and her father: the desire in question becomes part of their individual representations of their SDS and as such can be used as a basis for solving further coordination problems that they happen to face. It is also instructive to note that the pattern under discussion is secondary: even though the father fails to produce the primary interactional effect of Hanna's speech act, he adopts the conversational goal behind her utterance and, as the corollary of this, responds cooperatively by performing the act of *Plan Elaboration*. In sum, the *focal* proper function of the secondary pattern seems to be the same as the *focal* function of its corresponding primary pattern, *i.e.*, the one that involves Hanna's utterance of (3a) and her father's giving her something to eat. One can argue, namely, that these two conventions has been selected for their use in enhancing mental coordination among the conversing agents or, more precisely, in contributing the desire in question to the set of mental states that they jointly represent as shared.

Millikan seems to assume that language conventions consist of signaller-responder patterns whose proper function is to solve particular and current task-specific problems. Nevertheless, quite often we speak to others without any particular aim or motive apart from sharing our mental states—beliefs, desires, intentions, expectations, and so on—with others; that is to say, rather than aiming at solving a particular task-specific coordination problem, our objective is merely to enhance mental coordination among the members of our community. One way to do this is to invite our interlocutors to reproduce certain speaker-hearer patterns.

4   The Normative Aspect of Illocutionary Practice

Illocutionary practice has a characteristic normative aspect that distinguishes it from other forms of human activity. Roughly speaking, speech acts construed as moves made in an illocutionary game *are subject to* norms and *produce* normative effects (see Witek 2015c). More specifically, they are subject to sincerity norms, one example of which is the famous knowledge rule for assertive acts discussed by Williamson (1996; cf. Green 2009; Ball 2014a; 2014b; this volume, esp. pp. 5–9), according to which one is only to assert what one knows; on its weaker version it says that one is only to assert what one believes.[8] Illocutionary acts produce normative effects in that they bring about changes in the domain of the commitments and rights of conversing agents. For instance, a felicitous assertion *takes effect*—see the discussion of effects of the (e_2) type in Section 1—by creating the speaker's commitment to the truth of what she says as well as the hearer's right to include the asserted proposition into his belief system; by analogy, a binding order results in the speaker's being entitled to expect the hearer to perform a certain action as well as in the hearer's being committed to perform the action. In short, there are at least two normative

---

8   For a discussion of the idea of weakening the knowledge rule, see Sbisà this volume, esp. pp. 27–28.

elements involved in the practice of performing illocutionary acts: sincerity norms and act-produced normative states of affairs; the former govern the practice, whereas the latter are brought about by its constituent moves and contribute to the construction of the institutional reality (see Searle 2005).

In what follows I attempt to account for the normative aspect of illocutionary practice within the framework of the interactional model presented in Sections 2 and 3. It should be stressed that I limit my analysis to two types of illocutionary force: assertive and directive. In subsection 4.1, I focus on two sincerity rules—the *belief rule* and the *desire rule*—and put forth a hypothesis according to which their normativity can be explained in terms of Normal conditions for proper functioning of assertive and directive acts, respectively. Next, in section 4.2, I examine the possibility of providing a naturalistic account of the normative effects of illocutionary acts.

4.1   *The Normative Character of Sincerity Rules*
My aim in this subsection is to consider the sincerity rules and the role that they play in illocutionary practice. More specifically, I focus on two rules to which assertive and directive acts are subject:

> (BR) One must: assert that p only if one believes that p.
> (DR) One must: order the hearer to do A only if one desires the hearer to do A.

According to some theorists (Williamson 1996; Green 2009; Ball 2014a; 2014b), the sincerity rules *constitutively* govern the practice of making illocutionary acts;[9] for instance, (BR) is constitutive of assertion—construed of as a speech act type—in that it governs every performance of this act. In my view, what constitutes illocutionary practice are primary and secondary speaker-hearer patterns that make up coherent sets representing different activity types. In saying this, however, I do not want to eliminate the normative aspect of speech acts. Although I am reluctant to call (BR) and (DR) *constitutive rules*, I take their normativity to be a genuine phenomenon that calls for explanation. In what

---

9 According to Sbisà (this volume, p. 28 ff.) sincerity rules are constitutive in a weak sense of this term or, in other words, are 'weakly constitutive:' the violation of a weakly constitutive rule does not result in the nullification of the speaker's act, but subjects her to certain forms of criticisms, e.g., it exposes her to accusations of being insincere or inconsistent. In general, a given rule is *weakly* constitutive for a certain act only if it contributes to the definition of the type to which the act belongs, but the non-compliance with it does not annul the act's normative effects. By contrast, to say that a given rule is *strongly* constitutive in Sbisà's sense is to assume that its violation results in making the speaker's purported act void and null.

follows, then, I assume that illocutionary acts are subject to sincerity norms. In particular, I assume that assertions are subject to (BR) and directives are subject to (DR). I claim, however, that the observed normative character of (BR) and (DR) can be accounted for within the framework of the interactional model.

My argument consists of two main claims: (C_1) that a Normal condition for proper functioning of an illocutionary act is that the act is sincere, and (C_2) that speakers obligation to perform sincere illocutions—*e.g.*, their obligation to act in accordance with rules (BR) and (DR)—is derived from their more general responsibility for providing normal conditions for proper functioning of the practice of interpreting speech acts.

To support claim (C_1), I argue that illocutionary acts form a type of *cooperative intentional signs* in Millikan's sense. Generally speaking, every cooperative intentional sign stands 'midway between two systems that have been designed to cooperate with one another:' (Millikan 2004, p. 73) a *sign-producer*, whose proper function is to produce signs that represent world affairs by a required semantic mapping function—which can be likened to a preferred contingency plan in Lewis' sense (see Lewis 2002: 122 and the discussion in Subsection 3.2 above)—and a *sign-consumer*, whose job is to translate the signs produced by the first system into responses that are beneficial to both of them. Depending on a particular case, the systems in question may be either two separate organisms or two parts of one organism. To illustrate the former possibility, recall the beaver who produces a splashing sound to signal the presence of a predator and the other beavers who respond to this signal by flying out and looking for places to hide (see the discussion in Subsection 3.2 above): the signalling beaver is a sign-producer, the other beavers are sign-consumers, and the splashing sound is a cooperative intentional sign. The latter eventuality can be illustrated by a cooperating pair of two mental systems that are parts of one organisms: a *perceptual system* or *predator-recognition module*, whose proper job is to produce percepts representing predators, and an *executive system*, whose job is to translate these percepts into appropriate behavioural reactions of the organism. By analogy, in what follows I distinguish between two aspects or parts of human illocutionary competence: the illocution-producer and the illocution-consumer. More specifically, I assume that that illocution-producing mechanisms in speakers and illocution-consuming mechanisms in hearers have been designed to function symbiotically in accordance with appropriate speaker-hearer patterns whose proper function is to help achieve mental co-ordination among the conversing agents. I argue that a Normal condition for proper functioning of the illocution-consuming system is the sincerity of the act it responds to: if the act was insincere, the hearer's cooperative response to it would not result in mental coordination between him and the speaker, *i.e.*, it would not contribute to the achievement of the proper purpose of the pattern that is currently being reproduced. To support claim (C_2), in turn, I assume—following Brian Ball—that 'speakers always have (some, possible overridden) reason to do what is [N]ormal.' (Ball 2014a, p. 16) More specifically, I account for the normative character of sincerity rules (BR) and (DR) by reference to speakers' general responsibility for providing conditions necessary for the stability of the illocutionary practice they participate in.

Before I get into the details, let me say a word on the notion of *Normal conditions*, which plays a key role in my argument.[10] Following Millikan (1984, p. 33–34), I use the phrase 'Normal conditions' with a capital 'N' to distinguish Normal conditions in her technical sense from Normal conditions in an ordinary sense: the former, unlike the latter, do not have to be average conditions. Roughly speaking, in the case of devices that have been selected for performing a certain function, normal conditions for their proper functioning 'are the conditions to which the device that performs the proper function is (…) adapted.' (Millikan 1984, p. 34) According to Millikan, the term 'Normal' applies to both explanations and conditions:

> A 'normal explanation' explains the performance of a particular function, telling how it was (typically) historically performed on those (perhaps rare) occasions when it was properly performed. Normal explanations do not tell, say, why it has been common for a function to be performed; they are not statistical explanations. They cover only past times of actual performance, showing how these performances were entailed by natural law, given certain conditions, coupled with the dispositions and structures of the relevant functional devices. In the second instance, 'normal' applies to conditions. A 'normal condition for performance of a function' is a condition, the presence of which must be mentioned in giving a full normal explanation for performance of that function. (Millikan 1989, pp. 284–285)

For example, a Normal condition for the proper functioning of a rabbit's behavioural disposition to run away every time it hears a soft noise is that the noise is caused by a predator. In my view, if the rabbit reacts to a noise that

---

10   An alternative account of the normative character of sincerity rules in terms of Normal conditions comes from Brian Ball (2014a; 2014b). A detailed discussion of Ball's proposal goes beyond the scope of the present paper. My main objection to his account is that he seems to ignore Millikan's distinction between normal and proper functioning of a trait (see, for instance, Millikan 2004, p. 76), which plays a key role in my argument.

is not produced by a predator, this disposition functions properly, though not Normally.[11] A Normal condition of a sign-consuming system, in turn, is that the sign it responds to is true in accordance with an appropriate semantic-mapping function (for a discussion of this idea, see Millikan 2004, esp. Chapter 6).

According to Millikan, the 'term 'normal' should be read normatively, historically, and *relative to specific function.*' (Millikan 1989, p. 284, my emphasis—M.W.) Recall that on the interactional model, the proper function of speaker-hearer patterns is to help achieve *mental coordination* between interacting agents or, more accurately, to produce and maintain a preferred overlap between their representations of the SDS. The proper function of a speech act, in turn, is to produce its interactional effect or, in other words, to evoke a cooperative response on the part of the hearer. More specifically, as far as its role in producing mental coordination is concerned, a speech act of type F functions properly only if it succeeds in inducing a mental state of type M in the hearer's mind. The force of the act depends on what counts as its conventionally determined interactional effect, where 'conventionally' means 'in accordance with a speaker-hearer pattern that is currently being reproduced'. For example, the cooperative proper function of an assertion that p is to get the hearer to believe that p, and the cooperative proper function of a request to do A is to get the hearer to desire to do A. (For the sake of generality I assume that the interactional effect of a directive act occurs at the level of mental states formation rather than at that of practical responses.) My claim in this subsection is that these functions are performed Normally—or, more accurately, in Normal conditions—if the acts are sincere. Recall that the proper function of an illocutionary act is to evoke the hearer's cooperative response. In other words, the proper function of the hearer's illocution-producing mechanism is to translate the speaker's act into an appropriate mental state: a belief, if the act is an assertion, or a desire, if the act is a directive. The response is beneficial for both the speaker and the hearer, however, if it contributes to the achievement of mental coordination between them. That is to say, the proper function of an illocutionary act *qua* a cooperative intentional sign is to evoke a certain mental state on the part of the hearer and *thereby* enhance the overlap between the interacting agents' representations of the SDS.

To justify my point, let me begin with considering a signalling pattern whose reproduction requires two complementary contributions: one by the signaller and the other by the responder. The signaller's contribution consists in

---

11   Of course it can be said to function 'normally' in the non-technical sense of this word.

translating her perceptual states into observable signals in accordance with her contingency plan, whereas the responder's contribution consists in translating the signals into his actions in accordance with his contingency plan. The proper function of the whole pattern, in turn, is to coordinate these two plans and, as a result, to ensure a preferred correspondence between the states that the signaller can perceive and the actions performed by the responder.

In short, the signalling coordination is achieved if the signaller and the responder do their jobs properly. The signaller's job is to produce signals that are true in accordance with her contingency plan. The responder's job, in turn, is to perform actions that are appropriate in the light of his contingency plan. Viewed from the perspective of Millikan's teleosemantic theory (Millikan 2004, p. 76), the Normal condition for proper functioning of the responder's contribution is that the signal he consumes—*i.e.*, the signal that he translates into his action—is true in accordance with the signaller's contingency plan. It does not matter how it is produced; rather, what is required for the responder to do his job properly and Normally is that the signal that he consumes is true. If it were not true, then the responder's job, despite being done properly, would fail to ensure the preferred correspondence between the states that the signaller can perceive and the actions performed by the responder.

It is worth noting that the responder's job coincides in content with what can be called the signal's proper function: it is to evoke a preferred action on the part of the responder. Therefore, the claim that the Normal condition for proper functioning of the responder's contribution is the truth of the signal that he consumes can be paraphrased by saying that the truth of the signal is the Normal condition for its proper functioning.

As Millikan puts it, it 'is always possible that a trait should cause some proper effect, an effect it was selected for, by accident in some cases;' (Millikan 2004, p. 69) to survive, however, the trait is supposed to perform its proper function in the Normal way often enough. One can add that the proper functioning of the trait is supposed to involve, at least in some cases, mechanisms and conditions that are Normal; otherwise the trait is likely to die out. Let us call this idea the *principle of Normal functioning*. It is worth noting that this principle behaves like a norm: although often violated, it cannot be regularly disobeyed. Consider, for example, the idea that signals whose production is designed to contribute to the solution of signalling problems—by getting responders to perform appropriate actions—are supposed to be true. Undoubtedly, this principle is like a norm: if it were systematically disobeyed, the signals would no longer be followed by the responders and the whole pattern would eventually die out.

Consider, by analogy, a speaker-hearer pattern whose function is to ensure mental coordination between two agents: a speaker and a hearer. Roughly speaking, the proper effect of its reproduction is a preferred overlap between the speaker's representation of the SDS and the hearer's representation of the SDS. The reproduction of the pattern requires two complementary contributions: one by the speaker and the other by the hearer. The speaker's contribution involves (i) the speaker's having state M and (ii) her uttering an appropriate sentence. The hearer's contribution, in turn, consists in his responding to utterance (ii) by (iii) forming a corresponding state M'. If the act performed in making utterance (ii) is an assertion, states M and M' are beliefs that are equivalent with respect to their contents; if the act has a directive force, in turn, states M and M' are desires to the effect that the hearer performs certain action A.

Let us focus on illocutionary acts made in utterances (ii) and consider Normal conditions for their proper functioning. Recall that the reproduction of a speaker-hearer pattern results in mental coordination if the speaker and the hearer do their jobs properly. The speaker's job—or, more accurately, the function of the speaker's illocution-producing mechanism—is to make a sincere illocution, whereas the hearer's job—or, in other words, the function of the hearer's illocution-consuming mechanism—is to respond to the act by forming an appropriate mental state, where 'appropriate' means 'corresponding to the state expressed by the speaker in accordance with a preferred correspondence rule'. Doing his job properly, the hearer contributes to the achievement of mental coordination between him and the speaker. One of the Normal conditions for proper functioning of the hearer's contribution is that the illocution produced by the speaker is sincere. To say this, however, is to assume that the sincerity of an illocution is a Normal condition for its proper functioning and, for the same reasons, is a Normal condition for the proper functioning of the hearer's illocution-consuming mechanisms. The proper function of the speaker's illocutionary act, namely, is equivalent in content with the proper function of the hearer's contribution to the reproduction of the pattern they reproduce: it is to evoke a cooperative response on the part of the hearer.

According to the principle of Normal functioning, the proper functioning of a trait is supposed to involve, at least in some cases, mechanisms and conditions that are Normal; otherwise the trait is likely to die out. For example, properly functioning illocutionary acts *qua* cooperative intentional signs—*i.e.*, acts that succeed in getting hearers to form appropriate mental states and thereby enhance the overlap between the interacting agents' representations of the SDS—are supposed to be sincere. In particular, one is supposed to assert only what one believes, and one is supposed to tell one's interlocutor only what one desires him or her to do. The point is that insincere illocutions that succeed in getting the hearer to form appropriate mental states—*i.e.*, illocutions that are insincere though interactionally effective—cannot be regarded as performing their proper function in a Normal way. In other words, although they function properly, they cannot be regarded as functioning Normally. For an illocutionary act to function properly is for it to be interactionally effective, *i.e.*, to succeed in evoking its interactional effect. To function normally, however, the interactionally effective act is supposed to produce a preferred correspondence between the mental states of the speaker and the hearer or, more accurately, to enhance the overlap between their representations of the sds; in short, next to being interactionally effective, it is supposed to be sincere. In saying this I do not want to claim that all *Normal* or, in other words, *sincere* illocutions are interactionally effective. As a matter of fact, illocutionary acts can be insincere and interactionally effective, sincere and interactionally effective, and sincere and interactionally ineffective. My point is that the sincerity of an illocutionary act is a Normal condition for its proper functioning, *i.e.*, a condition under which the act succeeds in producing mental coordination provided it succeeds in getting the hearer to form an appropriate mental state. An illocutionary act *qua* a cooperative intentional sign functions properly only if it produces its interactional effect; it performs its proper function in a Normal way, in turn, only if its production contributes to the *complete* reproduction of a speaker-hearer pattern whose structure involves elements from (*i*) to (*v*).

In summary, rules (BR) and (DR) behave like norms: despite the fact that they are often violated, they cannot systematically be disobeyed; if they were, the practice of making assertive and directive acts would be seriously destabilized and eventually such acts would die out. The crucial point is that if most of our illocutionary acts were insincere, then, even if they were interactionally effective, they would fail to produce mental coordination; in other words, the hearers' trust and compliance would no longer be adaptive attitudes.[12]

---

12   One of the reviewers has noted that the principle of Normal functioning seems to be insufficient to ground a stronger normative feature of sincerity rules. Namely, he or she claims that my description of Normal conditions for proper functioning of illocutionary acts does not provide a sufficient basis for explaining why exceptions to sincerity rules are necessarily wrongings; in particular, the fact that the practice of making assertions would not exist if people were not sincere often enough *does not* allow us to explain why every single case of insincerity is an act of wronging. I am very grateful to the reviewer for drawing my attention to this gap in my account. It seems to me, however, that it can be bridged by arguing that speakers' general responsibility for the stability of their illocutionary practices entails their responsibility for providing Normal conditions for proper functioning of their illocutionary acts or, more specifically, their responsibility for acting in accordance with sincerity rules. However, for the sake of keeping this paper within reasonable bounds, I leave a more detailed elaboration of this argument for another occasion.

Some theorists take sincerity norms to be constitutive of our linguistic practice (Williamson 1996; Green 2009; Ball 2014a; 2014b). Consistently, they assume that rules such as (BR) and (DR) should be cited in any adequate account of the function and nature of illocutionary acts. For example, Mitchell S. Green refers to sincerity norms to explain how it is possible for illocutionary acts to express mental states. He assumes that illocutionary acts are handicaps: signals 'that can only be faked with great difficulty as a result of being costly to produce;' (Green 2009, pp. 150–151) they are costly to produce because in performing a speech act that allows for Moorean absurdity, the speaker makes himself or herself subject to loss of credibility. As the corollary of this—Green claims—speech acts express the states that they signal as handicaps. In my view, however, it is the normativity of sincerity rules that poses a real challenge to the naturalistic model of linguistic practice. The capacity of speech acts to express psychological states, it seems, can be accounted for in terms of speaker-hearer conventional patterns and the role they play in coordinating joint actions. The normativity of sincerity rules, in turn, can be explained in terms of Normal conditions for proper functioning of illocutionary acts *qua* cooperative intentional signs.

4.2 The Normative Effects of Illocutionary Acts

Following Austin (1975), Sbisà (1992; 2002; 2009; 2013) and Searle (1969; 1979; 2005), I assume that making a move in an illocutionary game involves bringing about a change in the normative domain of the rights and commitments of interacting agents (see also Witek 2015c). In other words, a successful illocutionary act takes effect 'in certain ways, as distinguished from producing consequences in the sense of bringing about states of affairs in the 'normal' way, *i.e.*, changes in the natural course of events.' (Austin 1975, p. 117) According to the institutionalist approach (see Section 1), illocutionary acts should be typed in terms of their normative 'effects and explained by reference to constitutive rules of the form '*X* counts as *Y* in context *C*', where '*X*' stands for the utterance of a certain linguistic form and '*Y*' is the normative effect of the act performed in uttering *X*. For example, the utterance of 'I promise I will do *A*' 'counts as the undertaking of an obligation to do *A*.' (Searle 1969, p. 63) On the interactional model of speech acts, however, normative effects—construed as rights, entitlements, obligations and commitments—are no longer regarded as definitionally and explanatorily basic entities. In saying this, however, I do not want to eliminate them from an adequate picture of our linguistic practice. Quite the contrary, I take them to be real states of affairs that call for explanation in terms of interactional effects.

My aim in this subsection is to consider whether the interactional model can accommodate the normative effects of illocutionary acts. My tentative answer is that it can. Even though a detailed justification of this claim goes beyond the scope of the present paper, I would like to set the stage for a future discussion by making three general points.

Firstly, sincerity rules can be spelled out in terms of the commitments of the participants in an illocutionary game. For example, rather than saying that a speaker who asserts that p must believe that p, one can say that in asserting that p the speaker undertakes the commitment to have the belief that p or, in other words, makes herself responsible for having this belief (see Searle 1969, p. 62). This observation, however, does not support the view that sincerity norms can be reduced to act-produced norms. What it suggests, rather, is that the mechanisms responsible for bringing about at least some of the normative effects of speech acts involve the operation of sincerity norms and that the latter function as rules governing illocutionary practice.

Secondly, it seems that the normative effects of any illocutionary contribution to a language game can be spelled out in terms of the constraints that its performance puts on the types of moves that the players are allowed or obliged to make. In *How To Do Things with Words* Austin suggested that the performance of a binding illocutionary act makes certain subsequent actions allowable, mandatory or forbidden. For example, a binding act of naming a ship the *Queen Elizabeth* takes effect by making it the case that 'referring to [the ship] as the *Generalissimo Stalin* will be out of order.' (Austin 1975, p. 117) By analogy, a binding assertion takes effect by committing the speaker to the truth of what he asserts and giving the hearer the right to adopt the asserted proposition into her belief system. Let us consider, for instance, the wedding scenario discussed in subsection 3.1. In uttering sentence (1) John makes a binding assertion that creates two normative states of affairs: John's commitment to the truth of the proposition that the man with a purple tie is Linda's cousin and Mary's right to accept this proposition as part of her belief system. My hypothesis is that these two states can be unpacked and spelled out in terms of subsequent moves that John and Mary can or should make[13] *provided they want to continue the game* initiated by John's opening remark. In other words, the normativity of these effects is *conditional* with regard to whether John and Mary are interested in continuing this game in accordance with its constitutive patterns. If they are, then at every stage of their interaction they are supposed to contribute to the reproduction of the primary and secondary patterns that were invoked or activated by previous contributions. For example, to say that John's assertion made in uttering sentence (1) brings about Mary's certain rights is to say that

13   In this respect, I follow Brandom's (1983) discursive coherentism, which is critically discussed by Brian Ball in Section 3 of his contribution to this volume (see Ball this volume).

Mary, provided she is interested in continuing the game, can *either* produce the primary effect of John's act (*i.e.*, to form the belief that the man with a purple tie is Linda's cousin) *or* respond in agreement with one of the secondary patterns available at this stage of the interaction, *e.g.*, she can *challenge* John's assertion by saying 'How do you know?',[14] *reject* his opinion by saying 'No, he is not!', or merely *comment* on it by saying 'That's interesting.' (Note that the last response is not at odds with Mary's producing the primary effect of John's act.) To say that in uttering (1) John undertakes the commitment to the truth of the proposition that he asserts, in turn, is to say that he is supposed to justify this proposition in case it is challenged, or withdraw his assertion if Mary supports her rejection with convincing reasons. In general, my hypothesis is that the commitments and rights produced by moves made in an illocutionary game are, firstly, conditional with regard to whether the players are supposed to continue the game and, secondly, explicable in terms of the speaker-hearer patterns that are constitutive of the game.

Thirdly, the *total normative effect* of an illocutionary act has two aspects: one described in terms of rights and entitlements and the other defined in terms of commitments and obligations. For example, a felicitous assertion creates the *speaker's commitment* to the truth of the asserted proposition and the *hearer's rights* to accept this proposition as part of his belief system, whereas a binding order results in the *hearer's commitment* to do what he is told and the *speaker's right* to expect the hearer to comply. In short, the difference between the two forces under consideration—*i.e.*, the assertive and the directive one—can be described in terms of the distribution of rights and commitments among interacting agents: assertions commit speakers and give rights to hearers, whereas directives commit hearers and give rights to speakers.

In my view the asymmetry in question can be explained within the framework of the interactional model presented in Section 2. Let us recall that the

---

14   As one of the reviewers has aptly pointed out, not all assertions give the hearer the right to ask the speaker for evidence or reasons for what she asserts: for instance, self-ascriptions of many mental states—e.g., utterances of 'I feel cold' or 'I believe that he will win the election'—typicaly do not entitle hearers to ask 'How do you know?' It is possible to argue, however, that at least some utterances that involve self-reference and self-ascription of mental states perform a special function in a language game and as such cannot be counted as mere assertions. For example, the function of what Jaszczolt and Witek (2018) call *de se* utterances—i.e., utterances that involve referring to oneself *qua* the self—is to present a *discourse-constituted perspective* one takes on oneself in the speech situation one finds onself in, which corresponds to the role one plays in a language game (e.g., a professional whose experience entitles him or her to give advice on certain matters, perceiving subject whose feelings or experiences ground his or her opinion at issue, and so on); for an extensive discussion of this topic, see Jaszczolt and Witek 2018.

proper function of speaker-hearer patterns is to produce mental coordination between interacting agents. Let us take it for granted that participants in an interactional event are seriously interested in enhancing their representations of the SDS with representations of states whose propositional contents are *either* true *or* are likely to become true; the point is that false shared beliefs fail to constitute an adequate basis for successful interaction. With this assumption in mind let us consider the wedding scenario again. It is *up to* John rather than to Mary whether the proposition that the man with a purple tie is Linda's cousin is true. Therefore, it is John, not Mary, who is responsible for the truth of the statement. Consider, by analogy, the canteen scenario. It is *up to* Peter rather than to Tom whether the proposition that Tom gets 10 euros is true. Hence, it is Peter, not Tom, who is committed to seeing to it that the proposition is true.

5   Conclusions

The interactional account of illocutionary practice results from elaborating Austin's observation that 'many illocutionary acts invite by convention a response or sequel' (Austin 1975, p. 117) within the framework of Millikan's (1998; 2005) biological model of language. In this paper I have proposed an elaboration of Millikan's claim to the effect that the proper function of language conventions is to help achieve coordination between conversing agent. In Section 3, I have argued that the proper purpose of illocutionary conventions—construed of as complex patterns of speaker-hearer interaction—is to produce and maintain mental coordination between the speaker and the hearer. Next, in Section 4, I used the resulting model of mental coordination to develop a naturalistic explanation of the normative aspect of linguistic activity: firstly, I accounted for the normative character of sincerity rules in terms of Normal conditions for proper functioning of speech acts and, secondly, discussed the possibility of constructing a naturalistic explanation of the normative states of affairs brought about by moves made in illocutionary games.

Bibliography

Alston, W.P. (2000). *Illocutionary Acts and Sentence Meaning.* Ithaca and London: Cornell University Press.

Asher, N. and Lascarides, A. (2001). Indirect Speech Acts. *Synthese* 128, 183–228.

Asher, N. and Lascarides, A. (2003). *Logics of Conversation.* Cambridge: Cambridge University Press.

Austin, J.L. (1975). *How to Do Things with Words*. Oxford: The Clarendon Press.

Bach, K. (1987). *Thought and Reference*. Oxford: Clarendon Press.

Bach K. and Harnish R.M. (1979). *Linguistic Communication and Speech Acts*. Cambridge, Mass.: MIT Press.

Ball, B. (2014a). On the Normativity of Speech Acts. In P. Stalmaszczyk (ed.), *Semantics and Beyond. Philosophical and Linguistic Inquiries*, pp. 9–26. Berlin/Boston: De Gruyter.

Ball, B. (2014b). Speech Acts: Natural or Normative Kinds? The Case of Assertion. *Mind & Language* 29 (3), 336–350.

Ball. B. (this volume). Commitment and Obligation in Speech Act Theory. In. M. Witek and I. Witczak-Plisiecka (eds.), *Normativity and Variety of Speech Actions*, pp. 51–65. Leiden: Brill (*Poznań Studies in the Philosophy of the Sciences and the Humanities* 112).

Brandom, R. (1983). Asserting. *Nous* 17 (4), 637–650.

Clark, H.H. (1996). *Using language*. Cambridge: Cambridge University Press.

Corredor, C. (this volume). The dynamics of conversation: fixing the force in irony. A case study. In. M. Witek and I. Witczak-Plisiecka (eds.), *Normativity and Variety of Speech Actions*, pp. 140–158. Leiden: Brill (*Poznań Studies in the Philosophy of the Sciences and the Humanities* 112).

Fetzer, A. (2013). The structuring of discourse. In. M. Sbisà and K. Turner (eds.), *Pragmatics of Speech Actions*, pp. 685–711. Berlin/Boston: De Gruyter Mouton.

Fetzer, A. (this volume). Speech acts in discourse. In. M. Witek and I. Witczak-Plisiecka (eds.), *Normativity and Variety of Speech Actions*, pp. 101–121. Leiden: Brill (*Poznań Studies in the Philosophy of the Sciences and the Humanities* 112).

García-Carpintero, M. (2001). Gricean Rational Reconstruction and the Semantics/Pragmatics Distinction. *Synthese* 128, 93–131.

García-Carpintero, M. (2004). Assertion and the Semantics of Force-Makers. In: C. Bianchi (ed.), *The Semantics/Pragmatics Distinction*, pp. 133–166. Stanford: CSLI Publications.

Gazdar, G. (1981). Speech act assignment. In A.K. Joshi, B.L. Webber and I.A. Sag (eds.), *Elements of Discourse Understanding*, pp. 64–83. Cambridge: Cambridge University Press.

Green, M.S. (2009). Speech Acts, the Handicap Principle and the Expression of Psychological States. *Mind & Language* 24, 139–163.

Green, M.S. (forthcoming). Organic Meaning: An Approach to Communication with Minimal Appeal to Minds. In A. Capone (ed.), *Further Advances in Pragmatics and Philosophy*. Dordrecht: Springer.

Harnish, R.M. (2005). Commitments and Speech Acts. *Philosophica* 75, 11–41.

Jaszczolt, K.M. and M. Witek (2018). Expressing the Self: From Types of *De Se* to Speech-Act-Types. In M. Huang and K. Jaszczolt (eds.), *Expressing the Self: Cultural Diversity and Cognitive Universals*. Oxford: Oxford University Press, pp. 187–221.

Lewis, D. (2002). *Convention: A Philosophical Study*. Oxford: Blackwell Publishers.

Levinson, S.C. (1979). Activity types and language. *Linguistics* 17, 365–399.

Matczak, M. (2016). Does Legal Interpretation Need Paul Grice? Reflections on Lepore and Stone's *Imagination and Convention*. *Polish Journal of Philosophy* 10 (1), 67–87.

Matczak, M. (this volume). A theory that beats the theory? Lineages, the growth of signs, and dynamic legal interpretation. In. M. Witek and I. Witczak-Plisiecka (eds.), *Normativity and Variety of Speech Actions*, pp. 180–205. Leiden: Brill (*Poznań Studies in the Philosophy of the Sciences and the Humanities* 112).

McDowell, J. (1980). Meaning, Communication, and Knowledge. In Z. van Straaten (ed.), *Philosophical Subjects: Essays Presented to P.F. Strawson*, pp. 117–139. Oxford: Clarendon Press.

Millikan, R.G. (1984). *Language, Thought and Other Biological Categories*. Cambridge, Mass.: MIT Press.

Millikan, R.G. (1989). Biosemantics. *The Journal of Philosophy* 86, 281–297.

Millikan, R.G. (1998). Language Conventions Made Simple. *The Journal of Philosophy* 95, 161–180.

Millikan, R.G. (2004). *Varieties of Meaning*. Cambridge, Mass.: MIT Press.

Millikan, R.G. (2005). *Language: A Biological Model*. Oxford: Oxford University Press.

Millikan, R.G. (2008). A Difference of Some Consequence Between Conventions and Rules. *Topoi* 27, 87–99.

Navarro-Reyes, J. (2010). Speech Acts, Criteria and Intentions. *Lodz Papers in Pragmatics* 6 (1), 145–170.

Sbisà, M. (1992). Speech Acts, Effects and Responses. In. J. Searle et al., *(On) Searle on Conversation*, pp. 101–112. Amsterdam/Philadelphia: John Benjamins Publishing Company.

Sbisà, M. (2002). Speech acts in context. *Language & Communication* 22, 421–436.

Sbisà, M. (2009). Uptake and Conventionality in Illocution. *Lodz Papers in Pragmatics* 5 (1), 33–52.

Sbisà, M. (2013). Locution, illocution, perlocution. In. M. Sbisà and K. Turner (eds.), *Pragmatics of Speech Actions*, pp. 25–76. Berlin/Boston: De Gruyter Mouton.

Sbisà, M. (this volume). Varieties of speech act norms. In. M. Witek and I. Witczak-Plisiecka (eds.), *Normativity and Variety of Speech Actions*, pp. 23–50. Leiden: Brill (*Poznań Studies in the Philosophy of the Sciences and the Humanities* 112).

Searle, J.R. (1969). *Speech Acts: An Essay in the Philosophy of Language*. Cambridge, Mass.: Cambridge University Press.

Searle, J.R. (1979). *Expression and Meaning*. Cambridge: Cambridge University Press.

Searle, J.R. (2005). What is an institution? *Journal of Institutional Economics* 1, 1–22.

Strawson, P.F. (1964). Intention and Convention in Speech Acts. *The Philosophical Review* 73, 439–460.

Thomason, R. (1990). Accommodation, Meaning, and Implicature: Interdisciplinary Foundations for Pragmatics. In P.R. Cohen, J. Morgan, and M.E. Pollack (eds.),

Intentions in Communication, pp. 325–363. Cambridge, Mass.: MIT Press, London, England: A Bradford Book.

Williamson, T. (1996). Knowing and Asserting. *The Philosophical Review* 105, 489–523.

Witek, M. (2009). Scepticism About Reflexive Intentions Refuted. *Lodz Papers in Pragmatics* 5 (1), 69–83.

Witek, M. (2013). Three Approaches to the Study of Speech Acts. *Dialogue and Universalism* 23 (1), 129–142.

Witek, M. (2015a). An Interactional Account of Illocutionary Practice. *Language Sciences* 47, 43–55.

Witek, M. (2015b). Linguistic Underdeterminacy: A View from Speech Act Theory. *Journal of Pragmatics* 76, 15–29.

Witek, M. (2015c). Mechanisms of Illocutionary Games. *Language & Communication* 42, 11–22.

PART 2

Varieties of Speech Actions

∵

CHAPTER 4

Speech Acts in Discourse

Anita Fetzer

Abstract

This paper analyses speech acts in discourse, differentiating between the nature of the connectedness between speech act and discourse on the one hand, and discourse and context on the other. It suggests that the explicit accommodation of the strategic use of language provides a bridging point between the two, with utterances being constitutive parts of speech acts, and of discourse. Another bridging point lies in the conceptualization of speech act from a parts-whole perspective as the relational construct of discursive contribution with fuzzy boundaries based on the pragma-discursive premises of (1) cooperation and shared intentionality, (2) process and product, and (3) adjacency and sequentiality.

1   Introduction

It is impossible to conceptualize speech acts without the explicit accommodation of context, and it seems impossible to conceptualize speech acts in context without the explicit accommodation of discourse. Speech acts are situated in social context (cf. e.g., Mey 2011; Sbisà 2002a), they need the constitutive parts of linguistic context (e.g., grammatical constructions, lexicon, co-text) for production and interpretation, as is reflected in felicity conditions, in particular those of the utterance act (alternatively, the locutionary act) and its constitutive parts, and they need cognitive context (e.g., inferential processes and mental representations) for their production and interpretation.

Discourse is composed of linguistic context, and it needs cognitive context to account for discourse processing, grounding and discourse coherence. Discourse is embedded in social context and at the same time contains social context. While speech act and context, and discourse and context are connected intrinsically with context containing both speech act and discourse, and context being contained in speech acts and discourses, the nature of their connectedness remains controversial with respect to a number of questions regarding e.g., granularity and function, leading to the following questions, which are at the heart of this paper:

- Is discourse primarily descriptive and, for this reason, not relevant to speech act theory?
- Is the concept of discourse incompatible with speech act theory?
- Does discourse constitute some kind of macro speech act composed of concatenated micro speech acts (cf. e.g., Moeschler 2002; van Dijk 1980; Sbisà 2002b)? And is discourse only one macro speech act, or is it a combination of both micro and macro speech acts?

To answer these questions, the concept of discourse is going to be examined, accounting for its premises, the relationship between quantity and quality, and its status as process and product, as is done in section 2. Section 3 concentrates on the situatedness of speech acts in context and in discourse, considering the doubly contextual status of speech acts in discourse and its consequences for discursive sequencing. To account for their multifarious contextual references, this paper suggests to differentiate between classical speech acts, as put forward in speech act theory, and more peripheral speech acts, such as expositives, as discussed in Austin (1976). The refined conceptualization of speech act as doubly contextual, and as classical and more peripheral is captured by the discourse unit of discursive contribution.

2   Discourse

Discourse is one of those concepts which is frequently used across different research paradigms but hardly ever defined or made explicit; and neither is it generally delimited from another key concept: context. Discourse has been used synonymously with text, denoting longer stretches of written and spoken language, including other semiotic codes. It has been used to refer to both theoretical construct and its instantiation in context, i.e. type and token, and it has been used to refer to the semantic representation of concatenated propositions with the – more or less explicit – premise that any stretch of linearized propositions or sentences is discourse.

Discourse semantics, like text-linguistics, adopts a primarily discourse-internal perspective, examining discursive constraints, e.g., initial position, left dislocation, the right frontier or rhetorical distance, discursive move, or discourse relation (e.g., Asher and Lascarides 2003; Kühnlein, Benz and Sidner 2010). In conversation analysis (e.g., Schegloff 1995) and (Critical) discourse analysis (e.g., Schiffrin 1987; van Dijk 2008) participants produce and interpret utterances in discourse, and these utterances are generally conceived of as communicative actions or as social actions constituting discursive sequences. The questions of how utterances constitute social action (or: communicative action), and whether one utterance constitutes one social/communicative action have not been addressed explicitly in the paradigms. However, the important methodological issue whether discourse, as concerned with texts and their production and interpretation in context, belongs to semantics, or whether it is pragmatic in nature and therefore concerned with communicative action and the performance of speech acts in and through discursive units and sequences still needs to be addressed in more explicit terms (but cf., e.g., Sbisà 1991; 2002a b; Mey 2001; Fetzer 2004; 2013; Witczak-Plisiecka 2013; and Witek 2015a; 2015b; this volume). In spite of the controversial issues discussed above, there is general agreement about a quantity-based definition of discourse as well as on its multilayeredness.

If discourse analysis goes beyond a discourse-internal perspective concerned with the connectedness of propositions and their sequential ordering as regards discourse linearization and adopts a pragmatic perspective instead, as this paper suggests, it needs to account for the fundamental question of how discourse constitutes communicative action and what status the fundamental premises of rationality, intentionality and cooperation have.

As for rationality, the production and interpretation of discourse adhere to rational principles, i.e. inductive, deductive and abductive reasoning, with producer and recipient being accountable for their discourse, i.e. the discourse-as-a-whole as well as its constitutive parts. In any discourse, rationality is presupposed by default and only referred to or made explicit when communicative infelicities surface. For instance, in a communicative setting, in which participant B responds to an invitation to a cup of tea (A: 'Would you like a cup of tea?') by saying 'I thought you'd never ask', B ratifies A's invitation and has the intention of accepting it; s/he could have also accepted it by using the standard response 'yes, please'. If participant A is not familiar with the idiomatic meaning of 'I thought you'd never ask' and expresses their bewilderment either verbally by saying 'How do you mean?' or non-verbally by frowning, participant B can account for their particularized encoding of the acceptance by providing an explanation, such as 'this is an Irish phrase for saying 'yes, please''.

As for intentionality of communicative action, discourse is assigned the status of some kind of macro speech act with content and force (see van Dijk 1980), and intentionality of communicative action also holds by default. Analogously to a speech act, discourse is constrained by discourse-general and discourse-particularized felicity conditions, and is produced and interpreted accordingly. What is more, discourse is also some kind of communicative unit, in and through which communicative action is performed. For this reason, discourse requires the explicit accommodation of form and sub-forms with more or less fuzzy boundaries (or containers, to employ the conduit metaphor, Reddy 1979). Like a speech act, discourse provides the user, who is a rational and intentional agent by default, with the means to perform some larger-scale communicative action, which may be followed up by other larger-scale communicative action or discourse. Analogously to the taxonomy of speech acts as representative, directive, commissive, expressive and declaration (Searle 1983), discourse may be classified in accordance with possible prime communicative function, for instance narrative, argumentative, descriptive or instructional, as has been suggested by Werlich (1975) for text-types, or information-seeking, persuasive, narrative, descriptive or declarative. Discourse, and this applies in particular to its constitutive sub-discourses, can be composed of various sub-types with different communicative functions. For the communicative exchange (invitation/acceptance) examined above, an invitation is not generally produced out of some larger-scale discourse but rather is a constitutive part of that discourse, for instance some kind of dinner party or academic/business meeting. Irrespective of the larger discursive form, the sub-form of invitation needs to be produced in accordance with discourse-general felicity conditions as regards cognitive-context, social-context and linguistic-context conditions, and in accordance with discourse-particularized felicity conditions as part of an opening section addressing the participants' face-wants. The acceptance encoded with 'I thought you'd never ask' was intended to be in accordance with the discursive felicity conditions, but was not fully in accordance with the linguistic-context felicity conditions, as it required further negotiation. For this reason, the generalized boundary expected after the adjacency pair invitation/acceptance-rejection was expanded to accommodate a follow-up which accounted for the particularized encoding of the acceptance.

As for cooperation, discourse is produced and interpreted in accordance with the Gricean CP, the maxims and implicatures (Grice 1975), which has been adapted the larger scale projects, for instance the macro validity claim (cf. Fetzer 2000, for the larger-scale project of political interview), and also holds by default. As is the case with (micro) conversational contributions, participants produce and interpret discourse in accordance with the CP. However, they may also exploit one or more maxims to get in implicatures and communicate implicated meaning, which needs to be retrieved by their co-participants; they may violate maxims or they may opt out. For instance, the intended invitation '('would you like a cup of tea?') and its ratification by either acceptance or rejection may be expanded by B introducing 'tea' as a discourse topic and elaborating on it.

Discourse analysis addresses a number of key questions, such as the structure of discourse and linearization, discourse relations, cohesion and coherence.

The relevant questions for the investigation of speech acts in discourse are (1) granularity, i.e. what counts as unit of investigation: clause, sentence, proposition, utterance, speech act or some other kind of discourse unit, and (2) connectedness between discourse-as-a-whole and its constitutive parts. The most fundamental question to the analysis of speech acts in discourse is whether to proceed from a linguistic unit (clause, sentence, proposition or utterance) or from the pragmatic unit of speech act. Since utterance and speech act are no discursive categories as such, they do not automatically classify as appropriate units of investigation. The Gricean framework uses 'conversational contribution' as a unit of investigation, and as the CP is also one of the basic foundations of discourse, as this paper suggests, the discourse-pragmatic unit of discursive contribution is proposed as a unit of analysis. Discursive contributions are relational by definition, relating adjacently positioned discursive contributions, relating discursive contributions with other discursive contributions and with discourse-as-whole. For this reason, discursive contributions are indexical, expressing anaphoric, cataphoric and exophoric reference. Moreover, in a pragmatic account of discourse, the constitutive parts of discourse, i.e. discursive contributions, have illocutionary force. If discourse is approached from a bottom-up perspective, utterances need to be mapped on the unit of analysis, discursive contribution, realizing illocutionary force, propositional content and textual meaning. If discourse is analysed as a theoretical construct, discursive contribution needs to be filled with one or more utterances encoding illocutionary force, propositional content and textual meaning.

Speech acts are usually parts of larger plans, to use Bach's terminology (1990), and that is why there are no independent illocutionary acts and thus no independent locutionary (or propositional) acts. Rather, speech acts are doubly contextual, to adopt ethnomethodological terminology (Heritage 1984), referring to prior speech acts as constitutive parts of larger plans, for instance an invitation, and to succeeding speech acts, for instance an acceptance or rejection, as constitutive parts of larger plans. From a discourse perspective, there are no independent discursive contributions either, and even if a discourse is composed of one discursive contribution only, as is the case with written warnings, that particular type of discourse is part of a larger discourse, that is a discourse in which participants refer to that warning and act accordingly. Analogously to the argument above, discursive contributions are constitutive parts of discourse, relating discursive contributions at various levels of the discourse. Moreover, discursive contributions are also doubly contextual: they contextualize prior discursive contributions as the linguistic realization of what has been meant and pave the ground for the linguistic realization of the discursive contribution to follow, i.e. how the discourse is to continue. Adapting Bach's argument to discourse, discursive contributions have illocutionary force and propositional content. Apart from that, discursive contributions need to contain textual meaning (Hasan and Halliday 1987), which signifies the nature of the connectedness of a contribution with its discursive context in a more or less explicit manner. The term 'textual meaning is adopted from Systemic Functional Grammar (Halliday 1994), which is a discourse grammar *par excellence*. It is based on three metafunctions which are the foundation of a clause: the interpersonal metafunction operates on the level of exchange, the textual metafunction operates on the level of texture, and the ideational metafunction is concerned with semantics. Both interpersonal and textual metafunctions are non-propositional. Textual meaning is generally encoded by discourse connectives, pronouns and proforms, and adverbials with a cohesive function.

2.1   *Quantity Meets Quality*

While there is generally no disagreement about a quantity-anchored conception of discourse as 'language patterns above the sentence', (Widdowson 2004, p. 3), the question of granularity as regards the basic unit of investigation of the constitutive parts of discourse, that is the discourse unit, remains controversial. While text-linguistics- and discourse-semantics-based approaches assign the syntactic unit of sentence the status of a basic discursive unit (e.g., De Beaugrande and Dressler 1981), functional paradigms (e.g., Givón 1993) consider the clause as the basic discursive unit. In spite of these differences, all approaches share – more or less explicitly –the premise that discourse is a parts-whole configuration in which the whole is more than the sum of its constitutive parts (cf. Fetzer 2013). In various pragmatic approaches to discourse, the unit of investigation is the utterance, which may realize a speech act, as in the speech-act-theoretic paradigm, or a move, as in discourse-grammar paradigms (e.g., Moeschler 2002; Roulet 1991). To account for the parts-whole configuration of discourse, the unit of discursive contribution is suggested with the constitutive parts of illocutionary force, for instance invitation and acceptance/rejection, as discussed above, propositional content, e.g. reference to participant and object, e.g., speaker, addressee and cup, predication, e.g., have, and textual meaning, for instance pronouns or discourse markers.

The rather general definition of discourse as 'language patterns above the sentence' has been qualified by Widdowson (2004) himself, making explicit potential implications and arguing that the definition 'would seem to imply that discourse is sentence writ large: quantitatively different but qualitatively the same phenomenon. It would follow, too, of course, that you cannot have discourse *below* the sentence'. (Widdowson 2004, p. 3; original emphasis)

And there is another fallacy in the purely quantity-based definition. If 'the difference between sentence and discourse is not a matter of kind but only of degree, then they are presumably assumed to signal the same kind of meaning. If sentence meaning is intrinsically encoded, that is to say, a semantic property of the language itself, then so is discourse meaning'. (*ibid.*) Hence, a felicitous analysis of discourse and discourse meaning needs to go beyond the code model of language and analyze communication accordingly. Discourse meaning is thus encoded and implicated on the level of discursive contribution, and the meaning of the whole, that is discourse, is more than the sum of the meaning of its constitutive parts, be that separate sentences, utterances or speech acts. Against this background, discourse analysis 'has to do not with what texts mean, but with what might be meant by them, and what they are taken to mean. In this view there is no 'understanding' of texts as a semantic process, separate from, and prior to, a pragmatic 'evaluation' which brings context into play' (Widdowson 2004, p. 35). Widdowson (2004, p. 8) draws the conclusion that discourse is 'the pragmatic process of meaning negotiation'. While Widdowson stresses the constitutive factor of negotiation of meaning in discourse, which may span across the whole discourse, Mey highlights its context-dependence: 'Discourse is different from *text* in that it embodies more than just a collection of sentences; discourse is what makes the text, and what makes it context-bound'. (Mey 2001, p. 190; original emphasis)

Discourse is fundamentally concerned with the nature of the connectedness between parts and wholes, and is for this reason a relational construct *par excellence*, relating its constitutive parts locally as well as globally with regard to their connectedness to the discourse-as-a-whole. Discourse is thus both: quantity captured by the number of its constitutive parts, and quality, as is captured by the nature of their connectedness.

Qualitatively oriented discourse studies share the assumption that discourse comes in with the presumption of being coherent (cf. Bublitz, Lenk and Ventola 1999; Gernsbacher and Givón 1995; Chafe 1994), and it is not the 'language patterns above the sentence' and their semantic wellformedness which make them cohere but rather participants who negotiate the meaning of discursive units and of the discourse-as-a-whole, thus construing discourse coherence. Hence, discourse coherence does not lie in the discourse itself but rather in participants' minds and therefore is a socio-cognitive construct. Discourse coherence is connected intrinsically with cohesion and cohesive ties and thus with textual meaning (Hasan and Halliday 1987), viz. linguistic items which express the nature of the connectedness between its constitutive parts and the whole.

The structuring of discourse is based – more or less explicitly – on the premise of discourse coherence. The construal of discourse coherence is informed by discourse relations, which are conceived of as cognitive constructs (Maier, Hofmockel and Fetzer, 2016). In functional grammar, discourse coherence feeds on coherence strands (Givón 1993), that is referential continuity, temporal continuity, spatial continuity and action continuity. In discourse grammar, discourse coherence additionally considers the more general constraints of adjacency and dovetailedness (Fetzer and Speyer 2012; Speyer and Fetzer 2014), as well as the delimiting frame of discourse genre, which Thibault (2003, p. 44) describes as follows:

> genres are types. But they are types in a rather peculiar way. Genres do not specify the lexicogrammatical resources of word, phrase, clause, and so on. Instead, they specify the *typical* [original emphasis] ways in which these are combined and deployed so as to enact the typical semiotic action formations of a given community.

Connected intrinsically with the '*typical* ways' of doing things with words in a discourse genre – or in an activity type, in Levinson's parlance (1979, p. 370) – are inferential schemata:

> ... there is another important and related fact, in many ways the mirror image of the constraints on contributions, namely the fact that for each and every clearly demarcated activity there is a set of *inferential schemata* [original emphasis]. These schemata are tied to (derived from, if one likes) the structural properties of the activity in question.

The communicative value of discursive contributions is expressed in these '*typical* ways' of doing things with words in discourse genres, for instance accepting invitations by saying 'yes please' or 'I thought you'd never ask', and the corresponding '*inferential schemata*' feed on the discursive constraints discussed above.

2.2   *Process and Product*

Discourse has been described as a multifarious and multilayered construct, which is almost impossible to delimit (cf. Fetzer 2013; 2014). It has been defined as quantitatively larger than the sentence, and is thus composed of a number of concatenated sentences/clauses/utterances/propositions. The linearization of the constitutive units of discourse allows for multiple combinations, whose ordering is constrained by the producer's communicative goals and by the corresponding discourse genre. While the constitutive units of discourse can be analyzed as grammatical or ungrammatical, true or false, or felicitous or infelicitous, their ordering cannot be classified along those lines. This is because discourse is a parts-whole configuration in which the meaning of the whole is more than the sum of its separate parts. If the ordering of the parts changes, so does the meaning of the whole.

The analysis of discourse is thus fundamentally concerned with the nature of the connectedness between parts and wholes, and with their sequential organization. To account for the dynamics of discourse and for its status as both process and product, bottom-up and top-down perspectives are needed: the former concentrate on local discursive domains, and the latter on discourse-as-a-whole. Discursive contributions are linearized in discourse, and their production and interpretation requires their contextualization, i.e. they need to be produced in accordance with the pragmatic constraints discussed above as well as with their particularization as discourse-genre-specific constraints. For instance, a question asked by an interviewer in a political interview, such as 'Do you agree with X' does not count as a yes/no-question in that particular genre but rather as a request to voice an opinion and comment on X. A discursive contribution thus needs to be realized and interpreted in accordance with the local constraints, accommodating appropriate linguistic realization of propositional content, an explicit or implicit linguistic realization of illocutionary force and of textual meaning as regards the signaling of coherence strands and/or discourse connectives. At the same time, the discursive contribution paves the ground for the contribution to follow, signifying how the discourse is intended to proceed. A discursive contribution which does not 'fit' 'the current stage at which it occurs, by the accepted purpose or direction', (Grice 1975, p. 45) for instance answering the above question in terms of the opinion of the politician's ally or of their family (e.g., 'the press says X', 'X has an outstanding reputation' or 'it's not a question of agreeing or disagreeing with X'), comes in with the presumption of 'fitting' the stage where it occurs, of being coherent at a deeper level, and is interpreted accordingly. Its interpretation and making it cohere locally may, however, require the recontextualization of prior discourse as having been too narrow in scope or as having been inappropriate, for instance.

To capture the dynamics of discourse, the discursive function of anaphoric, cataphoric and exophoric reference and their context-change potential are connected explicitly with the particular parts of the discourse they are anchored to, with the parts of the discourse they ground, and with discourse-as-a-whole. Discourse analysis accounts explicitly for this sort of dynamic accommodation, through which new information is accommodated, stored, updated

and possibly changed in the communicators' (socio)cognitive constructs of individual and collective discourse (or dialogue) common ground (Fetzer 2004).
Thomason (1990) refers to the product of accommodation as conversational
record, and Clark (1996) refers to it as personal common ground, distinguishing it from more general cultural common ground.

A dynamic conceptualization of discourse can no longer avoid the question whether discourse constitutes communicative action. Not only Widdowson argues for an affirmative answer by saying that he identifies 'a text not
by its linguistic extent but by its social intent'. (Widdowson 2004, p.8) This is
because the 'meaning of words in texts is always subordinated to a discourse
purpose: we read into them what we want to get out of them. (...) The very
social nature of communication is bound to be based on an assumption of cooperation whereby the focus of attention on meaning will be regulated'. (Widdowson 2004, p. 86)

Discourse purpose is a pragmatic concept, which is dialectically related
to the pragmatic premise of intentionality of communicative action (Cohen,
Morgan and Pollack 1990; Levinson 1995; Searle 1983), and is made manifest in
the speech-act-theoretic operationalization 'X counts as Y in context C' with
felicity conditions as context categories (Sbisà 2002a), which, if adapted to the
contextual constraints and requirements of discourse, result in 'X counts as Y
in discourse D in context C'. Analogously to the felicity conditions of a (micro)
speech act, the felicity conditions for discourse are classified as preparatory
conditions, which are specifications of the context of the (macro) illocutionary
act, which can be realized implicitly or explicitly in discourse. Essential conditions and propositional-content conditions are specifications of direction of
fit, which can also be realized explicitly or implicitly in discourse by indicating
how the discourse is intended to proceed. Micro and macro speech acts 'both
rely on, and actively create, the situation in which they are realized'. (Mey 2001,
p. 219) They have cognitive effects regarding meaning and force, and they have
social effects regarding the assignment of obligations and force. Both micro
and macro speech acts count as context-changers. Speech acts in discourse
are doubly contextual and therefore do not only change context, but also carry
context.

The intentionality of discourse requires the accommodation of context
within a discursive contribution as well as the context embedding a discursive
contribution. What is more, intentionality of communicative action in discourse presupposes iterability of communicative action in discourse and thus
the differentiation between type, i.e. the type of macro communicative action
performed through discourse genre, and token, i.e. its linguistic realization in
accordance with typical ways how this is done.

3   Speech Acts and Discourse

Speaking a language, according to Searle, means formulating utterance acts and performing propositional and illocutionary acts: 'Thus, in performing different utterance acts, a speaker may perform the same propositional and illocutionary acts. (...) Utterance acts consist simply in uttering strings of words. Illocutionary and propositional acts consist characteristically in uttering words in sentences in certain contexts, under certain conditions and with certain intentions'. (Searle 1969, pp. 24–25) What is important to a discourse-based analysis of speech acts is the reference to 'certain contexts', 'certain conditions' and 'certain intentions', as contexts and conditions capture linguistic and extra-linguistic information, and they are constitutive parts of discourse (Fetzer 2010).

In Austin's frame of reference (Austin 1976), a speech act is composed of the constitutive acts of locution, illocution and perlocution, and their respective sub-acts, viz. phonetic act, phatic act, and rhetic act. Locution and illocution are defined by conventions, and perlocution is defined as achieving non-conventional effects. Departing from the constitutive parts of discourse, that is utterances, a trivial conclusion drawn for discourse-as-a-whole is that discourse is necessarily composed of utterances. If discourse was composed of speech acts, it would need to be composed of locutionary acts comprising phonetic, phatic and rhetic acts, determining sense and reference, and of illocutionary acts. There seems to be evidence in favour of the assumption that discourse contains speech acts, since discourse may indeed contain assertions, directives and promises, to name but a few. But is the conclusion that discourse contains concatenated speech acts valid?

Illocutions manifest themselves in the speaker's intention to achieve a certain effect: 'An effect must be achieved on the audience if the illocutionary act is to be carried out. (...) Generally the effect amounts to bringing about the understanding of the meaning and of the force of the locution'. (Austin 1976, pp. 116–117) Thus, speech acts are intended to achieve and secure uptake: in a micro frame of reference, they are intended to achieve the interlocutor's uptake. In a macro frame of reference, they are also intended to achieve the interlocutor's uptake with respect to the discourse-as-a-whole, and they are intended to achieve the interlocutor's uptake with respect to the speech act as a constitutive part of the discourse: 'Moreover, communicative (illocutionary) intentions generally are accompanied by perlocutionary intentions, and individual utterances are usually parts of larger plans. So it is plausible to suppose that identifying a speaker's perlocutionary intentions and broader plans is often relevant to identifying his communicative intention'. (Bach 1990, p. 397) It is at the stage from discursive parts to the discursive whole that the intention to perform some perlocutionary act (by means of the discourse-as-a-whole) becomes a necessary requirement to bridge the gap between the constitutive parts of discourse and discourse-as-a-whole.

The perlocutionary act manifests itself in the 'achievement of a perlocutionary object (convince, persuade) or the production of a perlocutionary sequel'. (Austin 1976, p. 181) This reference to some kind of continuation, connectedness, series or sequence can be interpreted as a requirement to connect a *situated speech act* (Mey 2011) with adjacent discursive parts composed of speech acts, and possibly with other more remote ones, bringing about the understanding of the meaning and force of the locution, thus construing discourse coherence, as is made explicit in the *coherence principle*, which goes beyond textual coherence, including coherence with respect to pragmatic presuppositions and illocutionary intention (Mey 2001). Against this background, Austin's inherently dynamic and dialogic conception of speech act and his differentiation between intended effects and unintended effects, and attempt and achievement (Fetzer 2002) provide the necessary requirements for a pragmatics-based analysis of discourse.

The extension of frame from sentences and speech acts to discourse and discourse purpose is a necessary step if discourse-as-a-whole is to be examined. In that scenario, the performance of discourse (as-a-whole) is functionally equivalent to the performance of a 'matrix of utterances' (Labov and Fanshel 1977, p. 30), or to a (macro) speech act. Complex sequences of speech acts, van Dijk (1980) argues, are mapped on more global macro acts in order to be able to plan them, execute them coherently, and in order to understand them, memorize them, and talk about them (cf. van Dijk 1980). Analogously to the performance of a (micro) speech act, which can be realized as a direct, indirect or conventionally indirect speech act, discourse (as-a-whole) can be realized as discourse with a direct, indirect or conventionally indirect force. In discourse with a direct force, the communicative intent and its linguistic realization as a sequence of one or more utterances are represented explicitly as regards force and content and thus are intended to be unambiguously clear, as is the case in legal discourse, e.g., pronouncement of judgement or cross-examination, and institutional discourse, such as application forms for citizenship or reminders. The linguistic realization of discourse with conventionally indirect force depends strongly on cultural conventions, as is the case with reviews, letters of recommendation or obituaries. Analogously to indirect speech acts, the communicative meaning of discourse with an indirect force depends strongly on the context, in which it is realized. Informal small talk or gossip may simply have a phatic function, but it may also serve as some kind of briefing, communicating relevant information about something or somebody.

The nature of the connectedness between (micro) speech acts and macro speech acts is complex. This is because there is no straightforward mapping from utterance to micro speech act and from micro speech acts to macro speech act. Rather, there are in-between-stages, or more and less global macro speech acts and thus discursive contributions with fuzzy boundaries, which also need to be considered in the corresponding mapping operations. Once utterances have been mapped onto micro speech acts and once they have been accommodated in the discourse common ground, they may be connected with their discourse-relation partners, thus forming larger discursive units. The less global macro speech acts are referred to as sequences in ethnomethodological conversation analysis (Schegloff 1995) and local communicative project in dialogue analysis (Linell 1998), and the more global, delimited sequences are referred to as global communicative project (Linell 1998), genre (Thibault 2003), or activity type (Levinson 1979), to name but the most prominent ones.

The structuring of discourse and its sequential organization make manifest the conventional effects of discursive contributions, which is examined in the following.

3.1   *Discursive Sequencing*

Discourse as a dynamic concept requires the explicit accommodation of co-operation, communicative action and felicity conditions as well as the embeddedness of discursive contributions in linguistic context, considering the contribution's doubly contextual status and thus both prior and succeeding contexts. This is because the sequencing of discourse makes manifest the contributions'(in Sbisà's terms moves') perlocutionary effects: 'When considering a sequence of moves, it is reasonable to view the output of one move as coinciding with the input for the next'. (2002a, p. 72) This means that the effects of the discursive contributions need to be considered explicitly with respect to cognitive effects, viz. the recipient's recognition of meaning and force, the construal of discourse common ground and the construal of intersubjective reality, and with respect to social effects, viz. discourse expectations, and rights and obligations from felicity conditions. However, it is not only discursive contributions that are situated in context, but also the context itself situates and conditions discursive contributions. This is particularly true for conversationally implicated meaning, which is what the context makes it to be. Conversely, a discursive contribution may create the context for which it is appropriate (cf. Mey 2011).

The linearization of discourse, or of conversation, has been examined in ethnomethodological conversation analysis and in interactional sociolinguistics. Both subscribe to the premise of indexicality of communicative action, and thus are appropriate frames of reference for examining the connectedness between discursive contributions and discourse-as-a-whole: 'Sequential organization refers to that property of interaction by virtue of which what is said at any time sets up expectations about what is to follow either immediately afterwards or later in the interaction'. (Gumperz 1992, p. 304).

The discursive constraint of *dovetailedness* as put forward in *Logic and Conversation* (Grice 1975) provides the necessary tool to account for the connectedness between discursive contributions and discourse-as-a-whole. Grice specifies the constraint by 'such as is required' (Grice 1975, p. 48) implying that conversational contributions are linked by one or more common goals manifest in prior and succeeding talk. Dovetailedness is intrinsically linked to the conversation-analytic conception of conditional relevance and to the sequence of adjacency pair, which, following Mey, 'is a case of coherent sequencing, but not all sequencing needs to be defined strictly in terms of adjacency'. (Mey 2001, p. 249) This is due to the fact that coherence and dovetailedness are related to felicity conditions, as well as to illocutionary force and illocutionary point, and to reasoning, as argued for by Levinson (1983, p. 293):'

> What makes some utterances after a question constitute an answer is not only the nature of the utterance itself but also the fact that it occurs after a question with a particular content –'answerhood' is a complex property composed of sequential location and topical coherence across two utterances, amongst other things; significantly there is no proposed illocutionary force of answering.

Discursive sequencing is both cognitive and social: it is reflected in the communicative status of a discursive contribution as a constitutive part of a pre-sequence, post-sequence or of the actual communicative action to be performed; and it is reflected in the administration of the cognitive construct of discourse common ground. A pragmatic theory of discourse needs this sort of dynamic accommodation, through which discursive input is administered. Discourse common ground is constantly negotiated and updated, i.e. modified and restructured, by storing new information and by updating already stored information, which may require the restructuring of the communicators' individual and collective discourse common ground (Fetzer 2007). Hence, discursive contribution and discourse are collective concepts, accommodating speaker and hearer, the set of speaker and hearer, as well as all other potential participants. The production and interpretation of discursive contributions and discourse are always goal- and participant-directed, and consequently, a collective endeavour.

It is at the interface between discursive contribution and discourse, where Austin's discussion of sequel becomes relevant. This holds in particular for the perlocutionary act and the speech act of expositive. Both are necessary for the construal of discourse coherence.

3.2 *Expositive*

In the research paradigm of speech act theory, speech acts have been classified as primary speech acts and secondary speech acts, accounting for the differentiation between direct and indirect speech act, and they have been classified as micro speech act and macro speech act, accounting for the larger unit of genre (van Dijk 1980; Fetzer 2002).

In *How to do things with words*, another class of speech acts with the illocutionary force of *expositive* is mentioned (Austin 1976). Expositives have the function of making plain how utterances fit into the course of an argument or conversation, of how speakers are using words, and of what they intend their words to count as. Possible realizations of expositives are 'I turn next to', 'I quote', 'I cite', 'I recapitulate', 'I repeat that', 'I illustrate', or 'I mention that'. To use Austin's (1976, p. 161) own words: 'Expositives are used in acts of exposition involving the expounding of views, the conducting of arguments, and the clarifying of usages and of references'. They are assigned a metacommunicative function as 'the expositive is the clarifying of reasons, arguments, and communications'. (Austin 1976, p. 163)

Expositives are different to classical speech acts, and that is why they count as more peripheral speech acts, this paper suggests. The conventional illocutionary effect brought about by an expositive is not a change in the world, which is described as a proposition, but rather a speaker comment on how she or he intends the speech act to be taken. For instance, the expositive 'turning to' communicates a change in the direction of the discursive sequence. That is, in saying an utterance as an expositive speech act, a speaker specifies the act in terms of a prior or succeeding illocutionary act, and, in doing so, builds a logical, or other kind of sequence of illocutionary acts. For this reason, the locution (or propositional act) of an expositive is not an independent locution (or propositional content) but rather the locution (or propositional content) of a prior or succeeding speech act. In that respect, expositives are different from ordinary speech acts, which are composed of illocutionary acts and locutionary (propositional) acts, but do not feed on contextualized propositional content.

Discourse connectives are indispensable to a theory of discourse in general and to a theory of discourse coherence in particular. Discourse connective is used as an umbrella term in this paper, including discourse marker, pragmatic marker or discourse particle, to name but the most prominent ones. Being processed bottom-up discourse connectives fulfill an important indexical function by connecting local domains of discourse with more global ones (Gernsbacher and Givón 1995; Schiffrin 1987). They may connect discursive contributions locally, they may connect local discursive contributions with the more global unit of a sequence, they may connect local discursive contributions with the global unit of genre, and they may specify the nature of the connectedness between discursive contribution and discourse topic. Because of their important metacommunicative function discourse connectives may signal the nature of connectedness between various coherence strands and between various planes of discourse.

In the Geneva model of discourse (Moeschler 2002; Roulet 1991), discourse connectives are referred to as text relation markers (Roulet 2006). They may indicate illocutionary relations between text segments (or text constituents) and information stored in the discourse memory, which has been referred to as the socio-cognitive construct of discourse common ground. Text relation markers are markers of illocutionary relations, and are functionally equivalent to illocutionary force indicating devices, providing instructions for the interlocutors to facilitate access to the relevant information. Roulet explicitly points out that text and text segments are not identical to speech acts because they do not need to have an illocutionary function. In this respect, they are different to expositives and to discursive contributions, which have illocutionary function.

Discourse connectives are not employed in an arbitrary fashion in discourse. Rather, they are used in a strategic manner. In spoken dyadic discourse, they may even occupy a full turn (Smith and Jucker 2002), thus counting as a move in the dialogic game. But would that minimal unit count as a speech act? Speech acts have been defined as composed of a locutionary (or propositional) act, an illocutionary act and, in Austin's framework, a perlocutionary act. Discourse connectives have illocutionary force, but they do not have propositional content. Rather, discourse connectives are discursive joints, expressing textual meaning about the status of a discursive contribution or larger discursive unit, thus instructing recipients how to interpret a contribution/unit at a particular stage in discourse. For this reason, they have illocutionary force. Thus, the difference between expositive and discourse connective does not lie in their function. But are discourse connectives speech acts?

Discourse connectives and expositives instruct the interlocutor how a particular discursive unit is to be connected with local linguistic context, and how the speaker intends it to be interpreted. For instance, the expositives 'I object' and 'I quote' may have the same function as the discourse connectives 'but' and 'like' in a sequence. In that respect, discourse connectives and expositives could be assigned the function of some kind of indirect directive, informing the interlocutor about local discourse expectations and requesting her/him to perform the corresponding inferencing processes, as for instance 'change your claim' for 'but' and 'I object', and 'I communicate second-hand knowledge' for 'I quote' and 'like'. This has also been pointed out by Thomason (1990, p. 355): 'Many implicatures are generated by such *discourse expectations*'. Thus, discourse connectives have illocutionary force, but they do not have proper locutions or propositional content. They are, per se, lexically marginal forms which have undergone a process of semantic bleaching (Traugott 1988; 1995). However, discourse connectives express procedural meaning (Brinton 1996) and because of that have illocutionary force and textual meaning. For this reason, they may count as a kind of discursive contribution.

4   Outlook: Speech Act Meets Discursive Contribution

The goal of this paper was to examine whether discourse constitutes some kind of macro communicative action and thus is compatible with speech act theory, or whether discourse was primarily descriptive and thus incompatible with speech act theory. The paper has shown that participants do things with discourse in context, that discourse is therefore intrinsically pragmatic, and that the basic premises of pragmatics, i.e. rationality, intentionality and cooperation obtain by default. Analogously to a (micro) speech act and its constitutive parts of illocutionary act, locutionary act (or: proposition) and perlocution, discourse can be conceptualized as some kind of macro speech act with illocutionary acts, locutionary acts (or: propositions) and perlocutions. Conceiving of discourse as a macro speech act composed of concatenated micro speech acts or a combination of micro and macro speech acts is too simplistic. This is because there is no direct mapping between a speech act and its linguistic realization as one utterance: a speech act can be realized by more than one utterance, and an utterance can count as more than one speech act. A string of concatenated utterances can thus not count as a string of concatenated speech acts.

Against this background, this paper proposes the concept of discursive contribution as unit of investigation with the term being adapted from the Gricean paradigm. Discursive contribution is a relational concept which is conceptualized as a cognitive prototype. To count as a discursive contribution *par excellence*, a discursive unit needs to have (1) illocutionary force, (2) propositional content, and (3) textual meaning. Classical discursive contributions have all three features, and less classical discursive contributions, such as discourse connectives, have illocutionary force and textual meaning but no propositional content. The inherent fuzziness of discursive contribution does not only allow for the differentiation into more and less fuzzy discursive contributions, but may also account for the dynamics of discourse and discourse processing. That is to say, discursive contributions may vary in seize, ranging from minimal contributions realized as discourse connectives, which only have illocutionary force and textual meaning, to larger contributions, for instance sequences with illocutionary force, propositional meaning and textual meaning.

Discourse constitutes communicative action by participants acting in accordance with generalized and particularized felicity conditions which hold by default. It is thus some kind of macro speech act. Analogously to the taxonomy of speech acts with respect to direction of fit, a taxonomy of discourse moving beyond discourse genre and communicative function seems plausible. Because of the inherent complexity of discourse, comprising various subdiscourses, the kind of macro speech act may fulfill a number of different communicative functions.

Bibliography

Asher, N. and A. Lascarides (2003). *Logics of Conversation.* Cambridge: Cambridge University Press.

Austin, J.L. (1976). *How to do Things with Words.* Cambridge: Cambridge University Press.

Bach, K. (1990). Communicative Intentions, Plan Recognition, and Pragmatics: Comments on Thomason and Littman and Allen. In: P. Cohen, J. Morgan and M. E. Pollack (eds.), *Intentions in Communication*, pp. 389–400. Cambridge: MIT Press.

Brinton, L. (1996). *Pragmatic Markers in English: Grammaticalization and Discourse Function.* Berlin: De Gruyter.

Bublitz, W., U. Lenk and E. Ventola, eds. (1999). *Coherence in Spoken and Written Discourse.* Amsterdam: John Benjamins.

Chafe, W. (1994). *Discourse, Consciousness and Time.* Chicago: Chicago University Press.

Clark, H. (1996). *Using Language.* Cambridge: Cambridge University Press.

Cohen, P., J. Morgan and M.E. Pollack, eds. (1990). *Intentions in Communication.* Cambridge: MIT Press.

De Beaugrande, R. and W. Dressler (1981). *Einführung in die Textlinguistik.* Tübingen: Niemeyer.

Fetzer, A. (2000). Negotiating Validity Claims in Political Interviews. *Text* 20(4), 1–46.

Fetzer, A. (2002). Communicative Intentions in Context. In: A. Fetzer and C. Meierkord (eds.), *Rethinking Sequentiality: Linguistics meets Conversational Interaction*, pp. 37–69. Amsterdam: John Benjamins.

Fetzer, A. (2004). *Recontextualizing Context: Grammaticality meets Appropriateness.* Amsterdam: John Benjamins.

Fetzer, A. (2007). Reformulation and Common Grounds. In: A. Fetzer and K. Fischer (eds.), *Lexical Markers of Common Grounds*, pp. 157–179. London: Elsevier.

Fetzer, A. (2010). Contexts in Context: Micro meets Macro. In: S. Tanskanen et al. (eds.), *Discourses in Interaction*, pp. 13–31. Amsterdam: John Benjamins.

Fetzer, A. (2013). The Pragmatics of Discourse. *Topics in Linguistics* 11, 5–12.

Fetzer, A. (2014). Conceptualizing discourse. In: K. Schneider and A. Barron (eds.), *Handbooks of Pragmatics. The Pragmatics of Discourse. Vol. 3*, pp. 35–61. Berlin: de Gruyter.

Fetzer, A. and A. Speyer (2012). Discourse Relations in Context. Local and Not-so-Local Constraints. *Intercultural Pragmatics* 9 (4), 413–452.

Gernsbacher, M. and T. Givón, eds. (1995). *Coherence in Spontaneous Text.* Amsterdam: John Benjamins.

Givón, T. (1993). *English Grammar: a Function-Based Introduction.* Amsterdam: John Benjamins.

Grice, H. P. (1975). Logic and Conversation. In: P. Cole and J.L. Morgan (eds.), *Syntax and Semantics. Vol. III*, pp. 41–58. New York: Academic Press.

Gumperz, J. J. (1992). Interviewing in Intercultural Situations. In: P. Drew and J. Heritage (eds.), *Talk at Work*, pp. 302–327. Cambridge: Cambridge University Press.

Halliday, M. A. K. (1994). *Introduction to Functional Grammar.* London: Arnold.

Halliday, M. A.K and R. Hasan (1987). *Cohesion in English.* London: Longman.

Heritage, J. (1984). *Garfinkel and Ethnomethodology.* Cambridge: Polity Press.

Jucker, A. and Y. Ziv, eds. (1998). *Discourse Markers. Descriptions and Theory.* Amsterdam: John Benjamins.

Kühnlein, P., Benz, A. and C. Sidner, eds. (2010). *Constraints in Discourse 2.* Amsterdam: John Benjamins.

Labov, W. and D. Fanshel (1977). *Therapeutic Discourse. Psychotherapy as Conversation.* New York: Academic Press.

Levinson, S.C. (1979). Activity types and Language. *Linguistics* 17, 365–399.

Levinson, S.C. (1983). *Pragmatics.* Cambridge: Cambridge University Press.

Levinson, S.C. (1995). Interactional Bias in Human Thinking. In: E. Goody (ed.), *Social Intelligence and Interaction*, pp. 221–260. Cambridge: Cambridge University Press.

Linell, P. (1998). *Approaching Dialogue.* Amsterdam: John Benjamins.

Maier, R., C. Hofmockel and A. Fetzer (2016). Spelling Out Discourse Relations: Co-Constructed Degrees of Overtness. *Intercultural Pragmatics* 13(1), 71–105.

Mey, J. (2001). *Pragmatics. An Introduction.* Oxford: Blackwell.

Mey, J, (2011). Speech Acts in Context. In: A. Fetzer and E. Oishi (eds.),3 *Context and Contexts: Parts meet Whole?*, pp. 171–180. Amsterdam: John Benjamins.

Moeschler, J. (2002). Speech Act Theory and the Analysis of Conversations. In: D. Vanderveken and S. Kubo (eds.), *Essays in Speech Act Theory*, pp. 239–261. Amsterdam: John Benjamins.

Reddy, M. (1979): The conduit metaphor. In: A. Ortony (ed.), *Metaphor and Thought,* pp. 284–324. Cambridge: Cambridge University Press.

Roulet, E. (1991). On the Structure of Conversation as Negotiation. In: J. R. Searle, H. Parret and J. Verschueren (eds.), *(On) Searle on Conversation*, pp. 91–100. Amsterdam: John Benjamins.

Roulet, E. (2006): The Description of Text Relation Markers in the Geneva Model of Discourse Organization. In: K. Fischer (ed.), *Approaches to Discourse Particles*, pp. 115- 132. Oxford: Elsevier.

Sbisà, M. (1991). Speech Acts, Effects and Responses. In: J. R. Searle, H. Parret and J. Verschueren (eds.), *(On) Searle on Conversation*, pp. 101–111. Amsterdam: John Benjamins.

Sbisà, M. (2002a). Cognition and Narrativity in Speech Act Sequences. In: A. Fetzer and C. Meierkord (eds.), *Rethinking Sequentiality: Linguistics meets Conversational Interaction*, pp. 71–97. Amsterdam: John Benjamins.

Sbisà, M. (2002b). Speech Acts in Context. *Language and Communication* 22(4), 421–436.

Schegloff, E. A. (1995). Discourse as an Interactional Achievement III: The Omnirelevance of Action. *Research on Language and Social Interaction* 28(3), 185–211.

Schiffrin, D. (1987). *Discourse Markers*. Cambridge: Cambridge University Press.

Searle, J. R. (1969). *Speech Acts*. Cambridge: Cambridge University Press.

Searle, J. R. (1983). *Intentionality*. Cambridge: Cambridge University Press.

Smith, S. and A. Jucker (2002). Discourse Markers as Turns. In: A. Fetzer and C. Meierkord (eds.), *Rethinking Sequentiality: Linguistics meets Conversational Interaction*, pp. 151–178. Amsterdam: John Benjamins.

Speyer, A and A. Fetzer (2014). The Coding of Discourse Relations in English and German Argumentative Discourse. In: H. Gruber and G. Redeker (eds.), *The Pragmatics of Discourse Coherence. Theories and Applications*, pp. 87–119. Amsterdam: John Benjamins.

Thibault, P. J. (2003). Contextualization and Social Meaning-Making Practices. In: S.L. Eerdmans et al. (eds.), *Language and Interaction. Discussions with John J. Gumperz,* pp. 41–62. Amsterdam: John Benjamins.

Thomason, R. H. (1990). Accommodation, Meaning, and Implicature: Interdisciplinary Foundations for Pragmatics. In: P. R. Cohen, J. Morgan and M. E. Pollack (eds.), *Intentions in Communication*, pp. 325–363. Cambridge: MIT Press.

Traugott, E. C. (1988). *Approaches to Grammaticalization*. Amsterdam: John Benjamins.

Traugott, E. C. (1995). Subjectification in Grammaticalization. In: D. Stein and S. Wright (eds.), *Subjectivity and Subjectivisation*, pp. 31–54. Amsterdam: John Benjamins.

Van Dijk, T. (1980). *Macrostructures*. Hillsdale, NJ: Earlbaum.

Van Dijk, T. (2008). *Discourse and Context. A Sociocognitive Approach*. Cambridge: Cambridge University Press.

Werlich, E. (1975). *Typologie der Texte. Entwurf eines textlinguistischen Modells zur Grundlegung einer Textgrammatik*. Heidelberg: Quelle und Meyer.

Widdowson, H. (2004). *Text, Context, and Pretext. Critical Issues in Discourse Analysis*. Oxford: Blackwell.

Witczak-Plisiecka, I. (2013). 2013. *From Speech Acts to Speech Actions*. Łódź: Łódź University Press.

Witek, M. (2015a), An Interactional Account of Illocutionary Practice. *Language Sciences* 47, 43–55.

Witek, M. (2015b). Linguistic Underdeterminacy: A View from Speech Act Theory. *Journal of Pragmatics* 76, 15–29.

Witek, M. (this volume). Coordination and Norms in Illocutionary Interaction. In. M. Witek and I. Witczak-Plisiecka (eds.), *Normativity and Variety of Speech Actions*, pp. 66–97. Leiden: Brill (*Poznań Studies in the Philosophy of the Sciences and the Humanities* 112).

CHAPTER 5

Silence as Speech Action, Silence as Non-speech Action

A *Study of Some Silences in Maeterlinck's* Pelléas et Mélisande

Dennis Kurzon

Abstract

This paper takes a look at the phenomenon of silence, both as speech action and as non-speech action, in Maurice Maeterlinck's symbolist drama, Pelléas et Mélisande (1892). Of the four types of silence set out by the author in his typology (Kurzon 2007), two are focussed upon here in relation to the drama. Firstly, "situational silence" in which the women servants of the castle, where the action of the play takes place, silently enter the chamber in which Mélisande, the heroine, is dying. This silence seems to follow conventions well known among the women. The second type of silence is "thematic silence." This is not silence in the strict sense that no one is speaking, but "silence about," where the speaker does not mention a particular topic while talking. In Maeterlinck's play, Mélisande avoids answering questions that delve into her past. There is also a connection between silence and telling or not telling the truth. Mélisande not only violates the maxim of quality by not answering questions; she violates the cooperative principle by telling different versions of the same event, and by keeping silent. If a person maintains silence, suggests a servant in the final act of the play, this means one does not tell the truth.

1   Introduction

The interpretation of silence in social interaction is totally dependent on the context, unlike spoken utterances or written texts which may, to a great extent, be interpreted semantically. Since silence has no verbal form, though in many instances it may be replaced by a verbal form, its interpretation derives not from its semantics -- it has none, but solely from its pragmatics. Silence should be considered an action – either a speech action if it can be *replaced* by words, i.e. what the silent person would have said if s/he had spoken, or a non-speech action when the silence cannot be replaced by words even in social interaction. The meaning or function of silence as non-speech action may, of course, be given by an observer.

Silence which may be replaced by words is often intentional in that the silent person decides not to say something even when s/he is participating in an interaction, as, for example, in everyday conversation. The silence of a person who deliberately remains silent when asked a question or who is expected to respond to something that has been said but does not may be glossed "I will not speak," if s/he decided on his/her own not to participate, or "I may not speak," if there is some external pressure on him or her not to participate (following Kurzon 1998). Suspects under police investigation may refuse to answer questions, viz. maintain their right of silence, because they have decided not to speak. These are well-rehearsed suspects, but there are suspects who decide not to speak out of fear that their circle of acquaintances/colleagues would harm them if they do speak. Moreover, it is possible that at a certain point in a conversation, a participant, though s/he has been talking, feels that s/he has nothing to say, and so decides that instead of muttering "Uhh" or "hmm," which may still invite another participant to ask him/her to contribute to the ongoing conversation, s/he doesn't open his/her mouth.

Just as intentional silence may be modally glossed (with *will not* or *may not*), so can unintentional silence, though in this case with *cannot*. This silence tends to be psychological in origin. The person who does not respond verbally may feel embarrassed or even shy to participate actively in the interaction. This silence may be glossed "I cannot speak," which is of course the gloss attributed by the observer to the silence of the silent person and not by the silent person him/herself, since s/he cannot verbally communicate in the given situation.

In this paper, silence as speech action and as non-speech action is analyzed in a play, *Pelléas et Mélisande*, written by the Belgian symbolist writer Maurice Maeterlinck (1862–1949), who was awarded the Nobel Prize for Literature in 1911. For Maeterlinck silence was highly important. In an essay he wrote in 1896, "Le silence" (Maeterlinck 1902), he compares silence with speech, arguing that while speech is ephemeral, what is meaningful in human relations is silence:

> L'instinct des vérités surhumaines que nous possédons tous nous avertit qu'il est dangereux de se taire avec quelqu'un que l'on désire ne pas connaître ou que l'on n'aime point; car les paroles passent entre les hommes, mais le silence, s'il a eu un moment l'occasion d'être actif, de s'efface jamais, et la vie véritable, et la seule qui laisse quelque trace, n'est faite que de silence. (Maeterlinck 1902, p. 10)

> The instinct of superhuman truths that we all possess warns us that it is dangerous to remain silent with someone you do not want to know or whom you do not like at all, for words pass between men, but silence, if it has had

for a moment the occasion to be active, of never being erased, and true life, and the only one that leaves some trace, is made up only of silence.[1]

He also talks of the silence of love, death and destiny, focusing on the silence of love, since this silence is controlled by the persons in love. Death and destiny are out of people's hands. He refers to these three states as "des choses les plus graves" ("the gravest things of all"; Maeterlinck 1902, p. 21). The silence associated with these three states is the truth: "il restera toujours entre nous une vérité qui n'est pas dite, qu'on n'a même pas l'idée de dire" ("there will always remain between us a truth that is not said, that we have not even thought of saying"; Maeterlinck 1902, p. 22). In this brief essay, he describes the role of silence in love:

> Si je dis à quelqu'un que je l'aime, il ne comprendra pas ce que j'ai dit à mille autres peut-être; mais le silence qui suivra, si je l'aime en effet, montrera jusqu'où plongèrent aujourd'hui les racines de ce mot, et fera naître une certitude silencieuse à son tour, et ce silence et cette certitude ne seront peut-être pas deux fois les mêmes dans une vie ...
>
> If I tell someone that I love him – as I may have told a hundred others – my words will convey nothing to him; but the silence which will ensue, if I do indeed love him, will make clear in what depths lie the roots of my love, and will in its turn give birth to a conviction, that shall itself be silent; and in the course of a lifetime, this silence and this conviction will never again be the same ... (Maeterlinck 1902, p. 23)

In her study of Maeterlinck, Spies (citing Daniels (1953)) says that "Maeterlinck embraces the idea that 'one mysterious spirit flows through the universe and through the beings that people it.'" (Spies 2009, p. 52) Silence, Daniels goes on to argue, is

> the element in which this mystic communion takes place. As the universal spirit is hidden deep, it can be perceived only when superficialities of everyday life are laid aside. Human speech is regarded as one of these superficialities. (Daniels 1953, p. 46–47)

According to Spies, then, words "fail to represent the real nature of things and consequently do not succeed in revealing the essence of the truth." (Spies

---

1   This translation, by Alfred Sutro, was published by George Allen, London, originally in 1897, and reprinted four times until 1905. https://archive.org/stream/treasureofhumbleoomaetu-oft/ treasureofhumbleoomaetuoft_djvu.txt, accessed October 20, 2015.

2009, p. 53) In Maeterlinck's play, silence is indicated not only by stage directions such as

> *Golaud la poursuit à travers le bois, en silence.* (4.4)
> *Golaud follows her through the woods in silence.*

but also by characters' comments, e.g.

> PELLÉAS: La nuit tombe très vite ...
>   *Un silence.*
> GENEVIÈVE: Personne ne parle plus? ... Vous n'avez plus rien à vous
>   dire? ... (1.4)

> PELLÉAS: The night falls very quickly ...
>   *A silence*
> GENEVIÈVE: No one speaks anymore? ... You have nothing more to say
>   to each other? ...

or by a series of three periods, as may be seen in this last example. There are almost one thousand instances of these silences or pauses in what is a fairly short play.

Maeterlinck was probably the first of a long series of playwrights who used silence extensively. The most prominent of them are Anton Chekhov, Samuel Beckett, Harold Pinter and Edward Albee (Kane 1984), though the motivation behind the use of silence changes over time. The silence of post-Second World War drama, for example, affecting Pinter, Albee and others, perhaps reflects Theodor Adorno's well-known dictum "Nach Auschwitz ein Gedicht zu schreiben ist barbarisch" ("the writing of poetry after Auschwitz is barbaric"; Adorno [1977] 1983).[2]

Shortly after Maeternick's play was put on stage the French composer Claude Debussy (1862–1918) became interested in it as the libretto for an opera. He asked the author's permission, not only to use the play as a libretto but to make cuts in it and make some minor changes, to which Maeterlinck agreed. Debussy's opera is far better known than the play, and is performed far more often than Maeternick's play. The present article, however, deals with the original play with some of its silences, and not Debussy's silences or representations of silence in the opera.

Moreover, further analysis of the complexity of Maeterlinck's views on silence, especially as a symbol in his writings, would divert this discussion from

---

2   But see Martin (2006), who argues that Adorno (1983 [1977]) has been misunderstood as far as silence is concerned.

one on pragmatics to one on symbolic literature; I would leave the latter to literary scholars. Our interest here is the analysis of some of the silences in the play from a pragmatic perspective. Instances of silence will be examined to see what types of silence do occur in the play (Section 2.), and how the distinction between silence as speech action and silence as non-speech action can be shown (Sections 4–6). Section 3 presents a synopsis of Maeterlinck's play, and the article closes with a brief conclusion (Section 7).

2 Types of Silence

For this analysis, I have selected three cases of silence in the play, illustrating several of the types of silence I have previously posited (Kurzon 2007): conversational silence, textual silence, situational silence and thematic silence. Conversational silence is the most frequent type of silence, and is the one usually discussed in the literature on pragmatics, as illustrated in the situations discussed above, in which a participant in a social interaction does not participate at a certain point – s/he either does not answer a question or does not respond to what is being said by the other participants.

As for textual silence and situational silence, these occur in fairly specific circumstances. The first, textual silence, refers to the silence in a situation in which one or more persons are silent while reading or looking at a specific text, or even reciting a text by heart. This may occur in a library where silence tends to be the rule (perhaps more broken nowadays than obeyed). Library users may be looking at a book or an article or a microfiche that interests them, or may simply be looking at the online catalogue on a computer screen. Textual silence may occur in the classroom when the teacher asks the class to read silently to themselves a passage or a page of a book. Reciting a prayer in silence is a further instance of textual silence. It may also occur at home when members of the family are all sitting in the living room, but each of them is reading something else – in silence without disturbing anyone else. These examples may be somewhat ideal. Comments such as "Did you see this in the newspaper?" may be uttered when members of the family are all reading their individual reading material. Children at the back of the classroom may be talking quietly among themselves without the teacher noticing. But all of these instances of textual silence can and do occur, perhaps with less frequency than formerly.

Situational silence is similar to textual silence in that a person or a group of people are silent in a specific situation, but in this case no particular text is being read or recited by heart. Situational silence occurs mostly at institutionalized events, for example war remembrance ceremonies with its one- or two-minute silence, though words may be said quietly by individuals who say a prayer to themselves, but these words are not laid down. Another example of an institutionalized silence is the somewhat controversial "moment of silence" at the start of the school day in many of the states of the USA (see, e.g., Kurzon 2011). Less institutionalized situations – and that is what we are looking at in the play under discussion – include police or army ambushes, where the men (usually, but not necessarily) in the ambush are waiting for the quarry or quarries who should not be made aware of the presence of those waiting in ambush. Silence is necessary, even if the people to be ambushed are in a vehicle and cannot hear what is going on in the vicinity. Radio silence is also necessary in case the other side has broken the code and is listening in.

An informal example of situational silence is a surprise party. The guest of honour should not be made aware that people are waiting for him/her to come and surprise him/her. This is often, but not necessarily, accompanied by a blackout, or at least the major lights of the house and/or garden are turned off.

Another instance of informal situational silence was suggested by Alfred Schutz (1966), inspired as it were by G.H. Mead's (1937) description of two wrestlers who communicate with each other by a "conversation of gestures" which enables either of the participants to anticipate the other's behavior and to orient his own behavior by means of such anticipation (Schutz 1966, p. 160). Schutz refers, among other situations, to the silence of a couple "making love together." (*ibid.*, p. 162) Jaworski (1993, p. 83) also uses a similar example, but in Polish:

> "Kochali się w milczeniu" ("They made love in silence"), to illustrate how silence may be conceptualized metaphorically as a container (cf. Lakoff and Johnson 1980).

Some cases of situational silence may be action, as in making love, while others may be considered non-action, e.g. the one-minute silence, or waiting for the guest of honour at a surprise party. Nothing happens until the guest arrives, and then the action begins! Furthermore, situational silence tends to be intentional. People deliberately keep silent when standing for a one-minute silence at a remembrance ceremony. Likewise, soldiers in an ambush deliberately do not speak so as to be effective when the enemy passes.

What these three types of silence have in common is that they may all be timed. In conversational silence, even a pause of half a second or so may be perceived as silence, given the circumstances. If there is a silent but physically present participant in the conversation, his or her silence could last for quite some time. Reading a page in silence can be timed, and teachers asking their students to do that would judge how much time is needed. In institutionalized instances of situational silence, the length of silence is laid down by law or by convention as in the one-minute silence.

The fourth type of silence in my typology (Kurzon 2007) – thematic silence – is in effect not silence, though it is referred to by this word in many languages, including English.[3] This type of silence may be glossed as "to be silent *about*" as opposed to "to be silent," as in the other three types. Typical instances of this type of silence are in the speech of politicians, who may avoid mentioning something to their detriment, or in the speech of diplomats, who avoid disclosing, among other things, secret negotiations. Omitting something – deliberately or not – may also, of course, occur in everyday conversation.

In this paper, I have limited the analysis of silence to several instances in Maeterlinck's drama. These instances may be discussed within the typology I have presented. The silences to be analyzed as speech actions and non-speech actions are those that are labeled as silence in the text, and those silences that are discussed by the characters. But first, to set up the context, a necessary prerequisite to discussions on silence, I present a synopsis of the play in the next section.

3   Synopsis

Here follows a synopsis of the play, based on Goehr (2001), to which I have also added Act and Scene number so as to help contextualize the instances of silence to be analyzed. Some of the wording has also been changed:

1.1.   *The gate of the castle.* Servants working in front of the castle.

1.2.   *A forest.* Golaud, grandson of King Arkel of Allemonde, has lost his way hunting in a forest. He sees Mélisande crying beside a pool of water. Afraid and avoiding questions, she tells him she comes from a place to which she does not wish to return. He offers to retrieve her crown, which he sees lying in the water; she forbids him.

1.3.   *A hall in the castle.* Geneviève, Golaud's mother, and Arkel learn of Golaud's marriage to Mélisande.

1.4.   *An apartment in the castle.* Married, they return to his family castle. Mélisande meets Golaud's half-brother, Pelléas, who is about to visit a dying friend but is delayed because of his father's illness.[4]

---

3   But not in, for example, in languages such as French, Persian, Chinese or Korean in which one would have to say something like "S/he did not speak about X."

4   Golaud and Pelléas have the same mother, Geneviève, but a different father. Pelléas's father is reported to be ill until Act 4, when he is said to have recovered. He does not, however, appear on stage.

2.1. *A fountain in the park.* Pelléas and Mélisande meet at the Fountain of the Blind. At midday she lets her wedding ring drop into the water. At the same time Golaud falls from his horse while hunting. Pelléas tells Mélisande to tell her husband the truth about the ring.

2.2. *An apartment in the castle.* Injured, Golaud returns to the castle. He is upset by the loss of Mélisande's ring. Ignoring Pelléas's advice to tell the truth, she says she lost it in the sea vaults.

2.3. *Before a grotto.* Golaud sends her and Pelléas to look for it.

2.4. *An apartment in the castle.* Arkel tells Pelléas to stay in the castle until his father is better.

3.1. *An apartment in the castle.* Pelléas and Mélisande talk about Golaud. His son, Yniold, from his previous marriage (his wife had died), comes in, and waits for his father's return from a hunt.

3.2. *One of the towers of the castle.* Mélisande sits by a window in the castle tower. Pelléas arrives and entangles himself in her hair, which cascades down the wall. Golaud arrives and warns them against these "childish games."

3.3. *The vaults of the castle.* Golaud takes Pelléas down underneath the castle with its "smell of death."

3.4. *Exit to vaults.* He repeats his warning to Pelléas concerning Mélisande, telling him to stay away from her, and suggests she might be pregnant.

3.5. *Before the castle.* He uses Yniold to spy on the lovers, but Yniold does not answer his questions the way Golaud wants him to. He says Pelléas and Mélisande are standing silently, staring into the light.

4.1. *A corridor in the castle.* Pelléas tells Mélisande that his father has recovered his health, which allows Pelléas to leave now.

4.2. *An apartment in the castle.* Arkel tells Mélisande he hopes she will bring happiness to the castle. Golaud enters the room and shows his fury toward Mélisande.

4.3. *A terrace of the castle.* Yniold is trying to lift a boulder, and watches a herd of sheep go pass.

4.4. *A fountain in the park.* Pelléas and Mélisande meet to say farewell. They openly declare their love. Golaud arrives, kills Pelléas, and slightly wounds Mélisande.

5.1. *A lower hall in the castle.* The women servants are discussing the situation – with Pelléas dead and Mélisande dying (not from the wound).

5.2. *An apartment in the castle.* Shortly after Mélisande has given birth to a daughter, she dies. The women servants come in to be present when she dies. Calm, forgiving, but still stubborn, she does not appease Golaud's jealous torment. Arkel comments at the end that the baby will continue the life cycle: "C'est au tour de la pauvre petite ..." – "It is the poor little one's turn ...."

4   Situational Silence

The prominent example of situational silence in *Pelléas et Mélisande* is in the last act when Mélisande lies dying. The women servants in 5.1. relate how they are trying to silence the children in the castle quiet:

> DEUXIÈME SERVANTE: Il faudrait faire taire les enfants ... Ils crient de
> toutes leurs forces devant le soupirail ...
> TROISIÈME SERVANTE: On n'entend plus ce qu'on dit ...
> QUATRIÈME SERVANTE: Il n'y a rien à faire; j'ai déjà essayé, ils ne veu-
> lent pas se taire ...

> 2nd SERVANT: We should make the children keep quiet ... They are
> screaming with all their might in front of the basement window ...
> 3rd SERVANT: You can't hear yourself speak ...
> 4th SERVANT: There's nothing you can do; I've already tried, they won't
> keep quiet ...

Silence is for Maeterlinck the sign of death (see Section 1 above), but only when there is complete silence, among the servants, does the climax of the final scene of the play occur – Mélisande's death. At the opening of this scene, we see her lying in bed dying either as a result of giving birth or from a broken heart; this is deliberately kept vague.[5] In the room we find Golaud, who feels guilty that he is the cause of her death, and a doctor who cannot help Mélisande. The servants enter the bedroom. As described in the stage directions:

> *La chambre est envahie, peu à peu, par les servantes du château, qui se*
> *rangent en silence le long des murs et attendent.*

---

5   In the world of opera, Mélisande's death seems as mysterious as Dido's in Purcell's *Dido and Aeneas*, and Isolde's in Wagner's *Tristan und Isolde*. One of the many comparisons and contrasts between Debussy's opera and the earlier Wagner opera (Abbate 1981) is that both more or less end with a *Liebestod* ("love in death").

The room has been gradually invaded by the women servants of the castle, who range themselves in silence along the walls and wait.

Golaud does not understand what is happening. He asks them why they have come, who has asked for them, and demands an answer, but "Les servantes ne répondent pas" ("the servants do not reply"). No one has called them in, no one has told them to be silent, but the presence of the silent women seems to be a natural phenomenon. Their presence in their silence anticipates death – that is what they are waiting for. This is a ritual, conducted in silence. It is a vigil carried out until the person dies, but whether the women deliberately enter the death chamber or whether this is carried out instinctively is left vague, as many things are in Maeterlinck's work. We see the same phenomenon a short time later, when Mélisande dies:

> *En ce moment, toutes les servantes tombent subitement à genoux au fond de la chambre.*[6]
> ARKEL, se tournant: Qu'y a-t-il?
> LE MÉDECIN, s'approchant du lit tâtant le corps: Elles ont raison ...
> *Un long silence.*
> ARKEL: Je n'ai rien vu. – Êtes-vous sûr? ...
> LE MÉDECIN: Oui, oui.

> *At this moment, all the servants fall suddenly on their knees at the back of the room.*
> ARKEL, turning: What's the matter?
> DOCTOR, approaching the bed and feeling the body: They are right ...
> *A long silence.*
> ARKEL: I didn't see anything – Are you sure? ...
> DOCTOR: Yes, yes.

The women servants acted instinctively at the moment Mélisande dies. No one tells them to do anything, and they do not say anything, only act – a non-speech action – in silence.

---

6 In the French version of the play I am using, the subject of the sentence is printed "*toutes les servants.*" This is obviously a typographical error: the predeterminer *toutes* is feminine in form as is the pronoun *elles*, in the doctor's declaration that follows ("Elles ont raison" – "They are right"), that relates to the noun phrase.

5   Thematic Silence

The instances of thematic silence that I would like to discuss are answers to questions which Mélisande is asked. In thematic silence, the speaker is not silent, but is speaking. The silence is in essence "silence about." In other words, the speaker does not mention a topic or does not refer to a topic which may be salient in the context. We find among politicians that when they give speeches they may deliberately leave out something, since it may embarrass them or simply they have nothing to say on the specific topic (see for example Kurzon 2017). In Mélisande's case, we already see her avoiding answering a question in the second scene of Act 1, when we meet her for the first time. After asking Golaud why he is at the spring, he says:

> GOLAUD: Je n'en sais rien moi-même. Je chassais dans la forêt. Je pour-
> suivais un sanglier.
> Je me suis trompé de chemin. – Vous avez l'air très jeune. Quel âge
> avez-vous?
> MÉLISANDE: Je commence à avoir froid ... (1.2.)

> GOLAUD: I do not know myself. I was hunting in the forest, I was chas-
> ing a boar. I got lost.
> You look very young. How old are you?
> MÉLISANDE: I am beginning to feel cold ...

To Golaud's question about her age, she does not answer – she is silent about her age, changing the topic to her feeling cold (a topic that occurs several times in the course of the drama).

In the first scene of Act 2, Mélisande is with Pelléas next to a fountain in the castle park. Pelléas wants to know what happened when Mélisande met his half-brother by the spring for the first time (in 1.2). After Mélisande speaks of her long hair, there is a silence, then Pelléas asks:

> PELLÉAS: Que vous a-t-il dit?
> MÉLISANDE: Rien; – je ne me rappelle plus ...
> PELLÉAS: Était-il tout près de vous?
> MÉLISANDE: Oui; il voulait m'embrasser ...
> PELLÉAS: Et vous ne vouliez pas?
> MÉLISANDE: Non.
> PELLÉAS: Pourquoi ne vouliez-vous pas?
> MÉLISANDE: Oh! oh! j'ai vu passer quelque chose au fond de l'eau ... (2.1.)

> PELLÉAS: What did he say to you?
> MÉLISANDE: Nothing. I can no longer remember ...
> PELLÉAS: Was he close to you?
> MÉLISANDE: Yes. He wanted to kiss me ...
> PELLÉAS: And did you want to?
> MÉLISANDE: No.
> PELLÉAS: Why wouldn't you have wanted?
> MÉLISANDE: Oh, oh. I saw something at the bottom of the water ...

Mélisande again doesn't answer the question, though this time it is Pelléas who asks it. In the first act she does not want to give her age, and in this scene she does not want to give information concerning her personal feelings. She is again silent about a topic she does not want to talk about. It is quite clear that these instances of thematic silence are deliberate. Mélisande intentionally changes topic.

6   Not Telling the Truth

Furthermore, in her response in the previous extract, we may also see that Mélisande is not telling the truth, and this is the third case of silence in the play. There is no indication in the text of the second scene of Act 1 that Golaud does try to kiss her. He persuades her to come with him, but she will not even take his hand so he can guide her out of the place. Golaud himself does not know where they are: "Je suis perdu aussi ..." (1.2.; "I am also lost ...").
A further example of telling the truth or non-truth concerns the wedding ring that Golaud had given her and which Mélisande drops into the fountain in the park (2.1). She asks Pelléas what she should say to Golaud:

> MÉLISANDE: Qu'allons-nous dire à Golaud s'il demande où il est?
> PELLÉAS: La vérité, la vérité, la vérité ...
>
> MÉLISANDE: What are we going to tell Golaud if he asks where it is?
> PELLÉAS: The truth, the truth, the truth ...

But when Golaud does confront her about the ring in the following scene, we find Mélisande telling a story different to what had actually happened:

> MÉLISANDE: Non, non; elle est tombée ... elle doit être tombée ...
>   mais je sais où elle est; ...

GOLAUD: Où est-elle?

MÉLISANDE: Vous savez ... vous savez bien ... la grotte au bord de la mer? ...

GOLAUD: Oui.

MÉLISANDE: Eh bien, c'est là ... Il faut que ce soit là ... (2.2.)

MÉLISANDE: No, no. It fell ... It must have fallen ... but I know where it is; ...

GOLAUD: Where is it?

MÉLISANDE: You know ... you know well ... the grotto by the sea-shore? ...

GOLAUD: Yes.

MÉLISANDE: Well, it's there ... it has to be there ...

There is a connection in the play between telling and not telling the truth, on the one hand, and silence, on the other. Lying is a topic that has been widely discussed. Mahon (2015), for example, has surveyed a number of definitions of "lying," analyzing each one to show their strengths and weaknesses. One of his own definitions, which he cites from a previously published article, is

> To lie = $_{df}$ to make a believed-false statement (to another person), either with the intention that that statement be believed to be true (by the other person), or with the intention that it be believed (by the other person) that that statement is believed to be true (by the person making the statement), or with both intentions. (Mahon 2008, pp. 227–228)

Not telling the truth is of course a speech action, and may be analyzed in terms of speech act theory. A person who is telling a lie is uttering an assertive speech act, and one of the felicity conditions of a speech act is sincerity. When uttering an assertive speech act, a speaker is said to commit him-/herself in varying degrees to the truth of the proposition expressed in the utterance – from simply saying that p, to asserting that p through to insisting that p. The propositional content of the assertive has, then, truth value: it may be true or false. Unless the hearer knows otherwise, the speaker is assumed to be saying something s/he believes to be true. But what happens when the speaker says p, and s/he actually means $\sim p$? For example, the speaker says:

> John got the book he wanted. = p

when the truth is

> John didn't get the book he wanted. = $\sim p$

The hearer believes that the speaker believes that p, without knowing that the speaker is, in Austin's (1962) terms, abusing the sincerity condition. The speaker should have the appropriate attitude towards what s/he is saying – that it is true. If not, then s/he is insincere, and the assertive is a lie.

Another factor that may have to be taken into account is the question of deception. It has been argued that lying may take place without deceiving the hearer as in business negotiations when two experienced negotiators tell each other "That is the highest I can go," when both know that it is an untruthful statement, but is part of the technique of negotiating (Mahon 2015). But in many other cases of lying, the aim is partly at least to deceive the hearer to believe that p is true.

Lying may also be seen, for example, as violating the maxim of quality in Grice's (1975) scheme of the cooperative principle (see Sbisà this volume, p. 29 on the weakness, as it were, of the sincerity condition vis-à-vis the strength of the maxim of quality). In general, Mélisande's verbal behavior may be considered a violation of the principle, not only of the maxim of quality. She does not want to tell anyone where she comes from, who she is (e.g. her age), her personal feelings (e.g. whether she wanted to kiss Golaud or not).

Let us look at the situation in which the speaker who is expected to utter an assertive is silent. On the one hand, we may argue that speech act theory plays no part, but, on the other, we have seen that many instances of silence may be replaced by verbal utterances. Sometimes, the contents of these utterances are known. But more often, it is only the illocutionary force that may be worked out through the context. If a speaker asks someone a *wh*-question, we expect an assertive utterance as response, e.g.

A. What time is it?
B. (It is) four o'clock

A. Where is the dog?
B. (The dog is) in the kennel.

This is even the case with answers to polar interrogatives. The short response "yes" or "no," which may be called polar pro-sentences, may be said to replace a declarative sentence functioning as an assertive, e.g.

A. Did John manage to get the book he wanted?
B. Yes

or, either retaining or omitting the polar pro-sentence,

B.   (Yes,) he did manage

or

B.   (No,) he didn't manage.

To continue with this exercise, let us take away B's response in all these cases. We are left with silence, but a silence that may be replaced by an utterance some of whose content may be guessed at. Admittedly, I am using rather simple examples. Nevertheless, if such is the case, we may say that B would have said the truth if s/he had spoken or that B would not have said the truth, i.e. s/he would have told a lie, if s/he had spoken.

A further example of silence and the issue of truth and falsity occurs in the first scene of Act 5 when the women servants are talking about the gradual silence that is permeating the castle. After the old servant describes how she found Mélisande and Golaud by the gate of the castle after the events of 4.4., when Golaud kills Pelléas, the conversation turns to Pelléas' fate:

TROISIÈME SERVANTE: C'est comme le bon seigneur Pelléas ... où est-il? – Personne ne le sait ...
LA VIEILLE SERVANTE: Si, si; tout le monde le sait ... Mais personne n'ose en parler ... On ne parle pas de ceci ... on ne parle pas de cela ... on ne parle plus de rien ... on ne dit plus la vérité ... (5.1.)

3rd SERVANT: It is like the good lord Pelléas ... where is he? – No one knows ...
THE OLD SERVANT: Yes, yes; everyone knows ... But no one dares to speak of it ... You don't speak of this ... you don't speak of that ... you don't speak any more about anything ... you don't speak the truth any more.

What the old servant seems to be saying here is that if you are silent, you cannot speak the truth. But even if you do speak, there is no guarantee that you will speak the truth. In the lie concerning the ring discussed above, Pelléas tells Mélisande to tell the truth. Mélisande fabricates a story about dropping it in the grotto. In speaking, she is lying.

But in keeping silent, does she tell the truth? First of all, in those instances of thematic silence, when she does not want to answer a question, we may say that she is silent about a personal matter, her age for example, so she changes the topic of conversation. It is possible to maintain that in order not to lie, she is silent about the specific topic salient in the conversation, for example an answer to a question. When she does respond to a question or comment, she may lie, but not only to Golaud as in the example above concerning the ring. She also lies to Pelléas concerning the first meeting with Golaud – that he wanted to kiss her, which according to the second scene of Act 1, he did not.

In 5.2., Golaud asks Mélisande, when she is on her death-bed, to tell him the truth about Pelléas, whether she loved him "d'un amour défendu" ("with a forbidden love"). Mélisande denies it and asks why he wants to know:

> GOLAUD: ... dis-moi la vérité pour l'amour de Dieu!
>
> MÉLISANDE: Pourquoi n'ai-je pas dit la vérité?
>
> GOLAUD: Ne mens plus ainsi, au moment de mourir!
>
> MÉLISANDE: Qui est-ce qui va mourir? – Est-ce moi?
>
> GOLAUD: Toi, toi! et moi, moi aussi, après toi! ... Et il nous faut la vérité ... Il nous faut enfin la vérité, entends-tu! ... Dis-moi tout! Dis-moi tout! Je te pardonne tout! ...
>
> MÉLISANDE: Pourquoi vais-je mourir? – Je ne le savais pas ...
>
> GOLAUD: Tu le sais maintenant! ... Il est temps! Il est temps! ... Vite! vite! ... La vérité! la vérité! ...
>
> MÉLISANDE: La vérité ... la vérité ...
>
>
> GOLAUD: ... tell me the truth, for God's sake!
>
> MÉLISANDE: Why have I not told the truth?
>
> GOLAUD: Don't lie any more, at the moment of death!
>
> MÉLISANDE: Who is going to die? – Is it me?
>
> GOLAUD: You, you! and me, me also, after you! ... And we must have the truth ... We must have the truth at last, do you hear me? ... Tell me everything! Tell me everything! I forgive you all! ...
>
> MÉLISANDE: Why am I going to die? – I didn't know that ...
>
> GOLAUD: You know it now! ... It's time! It's time! ... Quickly! Quickly! ... The truth! The truth! ...
>
> MÉLISANDE: The truth! The truth! ...

In his bumbling way, Golaud tells her that she is dying and the truth should be told in one's last moments. Mélisande denies committing adultery with Pelléas, but Golaud is aware that she does not always tell the truth. She changes the topic when Arkel and the doctor enter the room by asking whether winter is coming because it is cold. When Arkel asks her whether she does not like the winter, she answers "J'ai peur du froid – Ah! J'ai peur des grands froids ..." ("I am afraid of the cold – Oh, I am afraid of the great cold"), which may be interpreted as death. Maeterlinck associates what he has termed passive silence with three elements: death, sleep and non-existence. It is passive because people have no control over it.

The truth about Mélisande is found in her silence. Whoever she is or was is now concealed in the silence of death. As Arkel says:

> C'était un petit être si tranquille, si timide et si silencieux ... C'était un pauvre petit être mystérieux, comme tout le monde ... ... Je n'y comprendrai rien non plus ... (5.2.)

> She was a little being so quiet, timid, so silent ... She was a poor little mysterious being, like everybody ... I shall never understand it all ...

7   Conclusion

We have looked at instances of silence in Maeterlinck's symbolist drama *Pelléas et Mélisande*, distinguishing silence as speech action from silence as non-speech action. It has been suggested that where silence may be replaced by words such as unuttered responses to questions or where a topic is silenced, while the person is speaking, viz. thematic silence, these types of silence are speech actions in that they are still meaningful in the sense that there is an utterance which may replace the silence – whether it is conversational silence or thematic silence in Kurzon's (2007) typology. Silence as non-speech action occurs in the play as situational silence. People are silent and no apparent text is being read or recited. Moreover, their silence, here I am referring specifically to the women servants, is instinctive. They do not act intentionally, so their unintentional silence in entering the chamber and in kneeling is non-speech action.

As for the play, not only are there instances of silence as speech action and as non-speech action in the play, the action itself – whether speech or non-speech – is ineffectual, as Pataky-Kosove concludes, and we leave her to say the final words: "if one defines the tragic outlook as embracing a belief that our actions can control events, we have, in *Pelléas et Mélisande*, a play in which action is seen as futile." (Pataky-Kosove 1967, p. 783)

Bibliography

Abbate, C. (1981). Tristan in the Composition of Pelléas. *19th-Century Music* 5 (2), 117–141.
Adorno, T.W. ([1977] 1983). Cultural Criticism and Society. In R. Tiedeman (ed.), *Prisms*, *pp.* 17–34. Cambridge, Mass.: MIT Press.

Daniels, M. (1953). *The French Drama of the Unspoken.* Westport, Conn.: Greenwood Press.

Goehr, L. (2001). Radical modernism and the failure of style: Philosophical reflections on Maeterlinck-Debussy's *Pelléas et Mélisande. Representations* 74 (1), 55–82.

Grice, H.P. (1975). Logic and Conversation. In P. Cole and J.L. Morgan (eds.), *Syntax and Semantics III: Speech Acts*, pp. 41–58. New York: Academic Press.

Jaworski, A. (1993). *The Power of Silence.* Newbury Park: Sage.

Kane, L. 1984. *The Language of Silence: On the Unspoken and the Unspeakable in Modern Drama.* Madison, NJ: Fairleigh Dickinson University Press.

Kurzon, D. (1998). *Discourse of Silence.* Amsterdam: John Benjamins.

Kurzon, D. (2007). A typology of silence. *Journal of Pragmatics* 39, 1673–1688.

Kurzon, D. (2011). Moment of Silence: Constitutional transparency and judicial control. *International Journal for the Semiotics of Law* 29 (2), 195–209.

Kurzon, D. (2017). Thematic silence as a speech act. In P. Cap and M. Dynel (eds.), *Implicitness: From Lexis to Discourse*, pp. 217–232. Amsterdam: John Benjamins.

Lakoff, G. and M. Johnson. (1980). *Metaphors We Live By.* Chicago Il.: Chicago University Press.

Maeterlinck, M. ([1892] 2006). Pelléas et Mélisande. Ebooks libres et gratuits. http://fr.groups.yahoo.com/group/ebooksgratuits (last accessed: 12 October 2015).

Maeterlinck, M. ([1896] 1902). Le silence. In *Le Tresor des Humbles*, pp. 2–25. Paris: Mercure de France.

Mahon, J.E. (2008). Two Definitions of Lying. *International Journal of Applied Philosophy* 22, 211–230.

Mahon, J.E. (2015). The definition of lying and deception. *The Stanford Encyclopedia of Philosophy* (Winter 2016 Edition), Edward N. Zalta (ed.), URL = <https://plato.stanford.edu/archives/win2016/entries/lying-definition/> (last accessed: 12 October 2015)

Martin, E. (2006). Re-reading Adorno: The "after-Auschwitz" Aporia. *FORUM: University of Edinburgh Postgraduate Journal of Culture and the Arts* 2, 1–13.

Mead, G.H. (1937). *Mind, Self, and Society.* Chicago, Il.: University of Chicago Press.

Pataky-Kosove, J. (1967). Maeterlinck's *Pelléas et Mélisande. The French Review* 40 (6), 781–784.

Sbisà, M. (this volume). Varieties of speech act norms. In. M. Witek and I. Witczak-Plisiecka (eds.), Normativity and Variety of Speech Actions, pp. 23–50. Leiden: Brill (Poznań Studies in the Philosophy of the Sciences and the Humanities 112).

Schutz, A. (1966). Making music together. In: *Collected Papers*, Vol II, *Studies in Social Theory*, pp. 159–178. The Hague: Martinus Nijhoff.

Spies, M.M. (2009). *Pelleas et Melisande* as Symbolist Opera. MA thesis, University of Cape Town.

CHAPTER 6

The Dynamics of Conversation: Fixing the Force in Irony. A Case Study

Cristina Corredor

Abstract

The aim of this paper is to analyse, from an interactionalist and normative point of view, an actual case of re-assignment of force to a public statement, in which the original intentions of the speaker were correctly identified but not accepted as determinative of the illocutionary force of his statement. The case under study, one of parodic irony in a personal blog, brought about a longer sequence of interaction and ended up with the initiator being held accountable for the straight, "literal" meaning of his words. Yet the uptake and normative stance on the part of the addressee have to be completed with a third turn-taking on the part of the initiator himself, who acknowledged the addressee's interpretation and thus agreed with the re-assignment of force to his own statement. I will contend that there is a need in the interactionalist account to be complemented with an account of the initiation-response-evaluation sequence that jointly contribute to fix the meaning and force in communicative interaction.

1 Introduction

The interactionalist view of communication contends that the force of a speech act (in the sense of Austin 1962) does not merely depend on the communicative intentions of a speaker, as the Gricean tradition holds.[1] Instead, the recognition of the addressee is co-determinative of the illocution. According to the proponents of this interactionalist view (Sbisà 2006; 2009; 2013; this volume; Carassa and Colombetti 2009; Witek 2015; this volume; see also Ball this volume), the

---

1 I am deeply grateful to the journal editor, Dr. Maciej Witek, and to two anonymous reviewers. Their comments greatly helped to improve an earlier version of this manuscript. Any errors that remain are my sole responsibility. I should also acknowledge the financial support of the Spanish Ministry of Economy, Industry and Competitiveness through research projects FFI2012-33881 and FFI2014-54681. An earlier version of this paper was accepted for presentation at the International Symposium of Epistemology, Logic and Language (Lisbon, 2012).

characteristic conventional effect of illocutionary acts is to create, cancel or change deontic states of affairs in the domain of commitments, obligations, rights, entitlements, and the like that articulate the intersubjective relations of the interactants in the ongoing interaction. This view is thus internally related to a normative conception of communication. Conversations are considered to be forms of joint action, in which the interactants negotiate meaning to eventually agree upon the fact that a particular speech act has been performed, thus bringing about its conventional effect in virtue of this very agreement.

Moreover, within the framework of discourse analysis it has been contended that the minimal sequence in a conversation can be analyzed as a three-step one, with a first initiative move from the speaker, followed by the response of the addressee (recognition, rejection, or a new proposal), and finally a turn of validation or repair from the first interactant (Schegloff 2006). This dynamics is determinative of the fact that what is done with words "is held to emerge from the contextualization of utterances in conversational sequences or sequences of interactional moves" (Sbisà and Turner 2013, p. 5). In my view, this three-step sequential unit is not only complementary to the interactionalist view, but it represents a necessary theoretical recourse in order to satisfactorily account for many cases of communicative exchanges where meaning is jointly co-determined by the interactants in a dynamic process of meaning negotiation and fixation.[2]

This viewpoint is commonly illustrated in the literature by means of simplified examples in which the addressee fails to recognize the communicative intentions of the speaker, bringing about a sequence through which the interlocutors repair the broken understanding by negotiating and (possibly) reaching an agreement on the meaning and force of the initiator's utterance. My aim is to analyze, from an interactionalist and normative point of view, an actual case of re-assignation of force to a public statement, in which the original intentions of the speaker where correctly identified but not accepted as determinative of the illocutionary force of his statement. This analysis can thus help test the main contention of the interactionalist view. At the same time, it may allow us to identify some limits and constraints of this view. Although obviously a single case study cannot give support to general conclusions, it can contribute to elucidating some aspects of the phenomenon in play and help identify key issues for a satisfactory theoretical account.

In what follows, I will be endorsing the interactionalist view on communication.[3] Nevertheless, my analysis will not focus on the respective normative

---

2 For a reference to the process of meaning negotiation, see also Fetzer this volume, section 2.1.

3 In relation to the terminological distinctions introduced in Witek this volume, my account attempts to combine an *Austinian* and an *interactional* approach to speech acts. I am

stances of the interactants, but on the dynamics of the interaction and the way in which this interaction leads the participants to the co-determination of meaning. In this respect, I will resort to a three-step sequential analysis aiming to show how meaning can become jointly co-determined by the interactants, with the addressee playing an active role in this fixation and even if the agreed-upon meaning and force of the initiator's utterance were not the ones originally intended by him. We will begin by a brief exposition of the above-referred example. It is a case of parodic irony in a personal blog that brought about a longer sequence of interaction, which ended up with the initiator being held accountable for the straight, "literal" meaning of his words. In order to analyze it, we will take into account some relevant theoretical approaches to irony, trying to apply their alternative explanations to the case under study. Finally, some suggestions will be put forward concerning the theoretical conceptualization of communicative interaction as such.

2   A Case Study: "No jokes with the Holocaust"

On the 6th of February of 2011, the Spanish journal *El País* published an editorial note signed by its ombudsperson in which, under the title "No jokes with the Holocaust," she gave a detailed account of an event in which the journal had been involved. A few days before, on the 29th of January, Nacho Vigalondo, a film director that had been hired by the journal to conduct and star a TV advertising campaign and that authored a blog on cinema in the digital edition, reached 50.000 followers in his personal Twitter account. Commenting on that, he wrote, "Now that I have more than 50.000 followers and I have drunk four glasses of wine, I'll be able to state my message: the Holocaust was a hoax!," and he added, "I have something more to tell you: the magic bullet that killed Kennedy has not yet landed!" (Pérez

particularly interested in the way in which speakers negotiate the meaning and force of their speech acts in the course of their interactions and, in this perspective, I am convinced that, in many communicative dialogues in non-institutional settings, the normative positions that they assign and recognize each other depend on their jointly agreeing on the fact that these normative positions have taken effect. To that extent, the addressee's response can be seen as partly determining the illocution (in closeness to the *interactional* approach in the sense of Witek 2015 and this volume). But, at the same time, I think that negotiation of meaning can only take place against a background of necessary conditions for the force of speech acts; moreover, these necessary conditions, in their turn, can be accounted for in terms of the interlocutors' normative positions associated with each illocutionary type (in line with the *Austinian* account; see Sbisà 2006; this volume).

Oliva 2011, my translation)[4] According to the editorial note, the blog post immediately led to replies from the author's followers. Many of them considered that the joke had exceeded reasonable limits that should be respected. Vigalondo's answer consisted of a series of Jewish jokes and jokes about the Holocaust, thus provoking new reactions, particularly among descendants of victims. Finally, the journal released a formal statement informing of its decision to put an end to its collaborative relation with the film director. The journal's statement asserted that the above-mentioned comments were "unacceptable and incompatible with its editorial line" and apologized for the unhappy sequel of events. The same day, the film director wrote a last post and a letter to the journal where he announced his decision to close the blog and said, "I apologize for the suffering that my *tweet* is causing. I want to clarify that I am neither anti-Semitic nor negationist," and declared that the questioned *tweet* was not the statement of a revisionist but "the parody of such an attitude." (*ibid.*)[5]

A first, informal approach to the full sequence of interaction shows great complexity and the intervention of several interactants. There is a first, initial communicative move from a speaker/writer, followed by a sequel of replies from his addressees (the readers of his blog) that motivated the initiator's second intervention (a series of new jokes on the same subject), who could then be seen as reaffirming himself in his first move. After the second sequel of critical reactions, addressed not only to the speaker but also to the journal in the form of letters to the editor, the journal (its board of directors or responsible persons) decided to issue a statement of condemnation, besides taking more direct action in what concerned the journal's professional relation to the first speaker. Finally, the speaker himself made a last move that can be interpreted as an attempt to repair the damaged understanding with his interlocutors, by means of explicitly stating his very ideological stance (in fact, by negating a presumed erroneous attribution of the opposite, censured position) and "literally" saying how he intended his initial move to be taken.

---

4 Given that this second fragment in the statement did not play an explicit part in the interactional sequence that followed, I won't deal with it here, although it was intended by the speaker to make his communicative intentions clear.

5 Once the journal's editors intervened, the original blog post was soon cancelled. This is why I have had to resort to the ombudsperson's account as the sole source to be accessed. Nevertheless, and for the sake of checking versions, it seems relevant to take into account that in a later blog post the film director Vigalondo offered a version of the incident that was entirely in line with the journal's ombudsperson. This latter reply can be accessed on the URL: http://blogs.elpais.com/nachovigalondo/2011/02/holocausto-vigalondo.html (last accessed: 31 August 2018).

From a theoretical point of view, it does not seem unjustified to focus on the main turns in the interaction and consider the other interventions as contextually influencing and contributing to explain the former. Hence, we will center our attention on the sequence that consists of three moves: the first move by the speaker/initiator, the second move as accomplished by the journal's reply, and the third, final move of repair by the first speaker. Furthermore, there are some conceptual distinctions that should be taken into account. In his last intervention, the initiator describes his first move as a parody. The editorial note, in its turn, uses the word "joke." As I will argue, the first utterance is to be typified as parodic irony.

3   Theoretical Approaches to Irony

Although in its ordinary-language sense the word "irony" covers a wide range of loosely related phenomena, these are theoretically different The traditional, pre-theoretical concept of irony is defined as "the use of words to express something other than and specially the opposite of the literal meaning." (Merriam-Webster Dictionary) More generally, irony can be defined as saying something while meaning something else. This operational concept is nevertheless in need of theoretical accuracy. Following Attardo, there are two principal types of theories or approaches. The first one considers irony as a trope or figure of speech, whereas the second one is based on the language/metalanguage distinction and is known as the theory of irony as mention/pretense (Attardo 2000, p. 794). The last two concepts are related to Grice's seminal work and have led to two influential but differentiated accounts.

Before we briefly review those accounts, it is worth making a methodological point. The case under study is to be typified as parodic irony, a special subclass of irony understood as a figure of speech. The approaches to be considered here deal with irony as a general phenomenon, and to that extent they are applicable to parodic irony as well. This concerns the two-stage-processing approaches to be considered below, but not the echoic approach due to the proponents of Relevance Theory, where parodic irony is acknowledged to involve pretense. In due course, these specifications will be taken into account.

3.1   Grice's Views on Irony
Grice began by assuming that irony is closely related to the expression of a (usually negative) attitude, feeling, or evaluation. He writes, "I cannot say something ironically unless what I say is intended to reflect a hostile or derogatory judgment or a feeling such as indignation or contempt." (Grice 1978,

pp. 53–54) Moreover, "[t]o be ironical is, among other things, to pretend (as the etymology suggests), and while one wants the pretense to be recognized as such, to announce it as a pretense would spoil the effect." (*ibid.*) Grice's theory of irony explains it then as a case of implicature, particularly as a case of flouting the cooperative principle by violating the maxim of quality: "Do not say what you believe to be false." Grice 1975, p. 46; *ibid.*, p. 53)

3.2   *The Echoic Account in Relevance Theory*

Notwithstanding its seemingly explanatory character, Grice's theory has been criticized in several respects. One main shortcoming is the fact that the violation of other maxims can be shown to trigger irony (cf. Attardo 2000, p. 798). This has led to formulating alternative accounts within the neo-Gricean tradition. One of the most influential is the echoic (or mention) theory of irony, firstly presented and later revised by Sperber and Wilson (1981; 1995; 2012). The central claim of the echoic theory is that "the point of an ironical utterance is to express the speaker's own dissociative (e.g. mocking, scornful, or contemptuous) attitude to a thought similar in content to the one expressed in her utterance, which she attributes to some source other than herself at the current time." (Wilson 2013, p. 7) Moreover, the thought being echoed need not have been overtly expressed in an utterance. When this is the case, and the pretend speech act exploits resemblance to the form of the targeted utterance, it is a parody of an actual speech act, "there is indeed a target for irony." (*ibid.*, p. 12)

Wilson criticizes other approaches for being inaccurate in that they conflate irony and parody. On her view, the object of an ironical attitude does not have to have a real-life counterpart, and is unlikely to have one. Therefore, most ironical utterances are not parodies, but have as its target a thought or the person to whom a thought is attributed. In parody, the (mocking, scornful or contemptuous) attitude conveyed is not to an echoed thought but to a real speech act or, more in general, to a piece of observable behaviour. When this happens, it seems legitimate to typify such cases as parodic irony, as we did above. Therefore, in Relevance Theory the phenomenon of parodic irony is to be seen as a case of pretence (in the sense to be further developed below).

The echoic (or mention) theory has in its turn been criticized for a number of reasons. Attardo (2000) argues that mentioning is neither a necessary nor a sufficient condition for irony. For one thing, there are non-ironical mentions, as well as cases of irony that can be satisfactorily explained without introducing the concept of mention (cf. *ibid.*, pp. 805–807). Moreover, Giora (2003) contends that literal meanings should still be available after non-literal meanings have been activated (an output that contradicts the one-stage processing, where the non-literal meaning should be directly accessed). Furthermore, she claims that ironical interpretations are less salient than literal readings and hence they should take longer to process (a prediction consistent with available evidence; cf. Giora 2003, pp. 63–65).

In what concerns the latter criticism, however, the following should be noticed. According to the echoic view, the literal meaning of the utterance must be decoded from the logical form and inferentially processed, inasmuch as this element is needed to arrive at the ironic meaning.[6] In the case under study, however, my contention will be that the interactant needs more than just to arrive at the ironic meaning by way of decoding the logical form of the utterance. The literal meaning of the assertion "I'll be able to state my message ..." must be available as an ingredient part of a turn of initiation, effectively performed, for the interactant to take it at its face value and appropriately respond to it. I will contend that it was not only the instrumentation of the subject matter in the irony but also the fact that, in order to convey the irony, the prohibited statement had to be literally expressed in a communicative act of self-allowance ("I'll be able to state my message. ...") that together prompted the response

In this very respect, the echoic account has been considered a one-stage-processing account, in contrast with other approaches that appeal to a two-stage process.

3.3   Two-Stage-Processing Accounts. Giora and Attardo

The echoic theory is mainly intended as an alternative to the traditional Gricean view. Coming back to this account, the recognition of an utterance as ironical involves a two-stage process, in which the interpreter has to recognize the utterance as communicating something non-literally on the basis of its incongruity with the context or with the set of beliefs, etc. that she can ascribe to the speaker. Only then is the speaker's non-literal intended meaning inferentially looked for, by using the cooperative principle and its maxims. Taking a point of departure in Grice's original work, some authors have developed alternative proposals within the framework of a two-stage theory that are intended not to be prone to the same difficulties. Giora (1995; 2003) proposes an account of irony that is based in the two concepts of indirect negation and graded salience. She notices that indirect negation does not make use of an explicit negation marker, but a usually affirmative expression "is used to implicate that a specific state of affairs is different or far from the taken-far-granted, expected (or more desirable) state of affairs explicitly indicated by the same

---

6   The echoic view should not be taken as indicating that the literal meaning is not accesible to the hearer for further processing. I am grateful to an anonymous referee for highlighting this point to me.

affirmative expression." (Giora 1995, pp. 240–241) As a result, irony as indirect negation does not cancel the indirectly negated message, nor does it necessarily implicate the opposite. Its import is rather that "it entertains both the explicit and implicated messages so that the dissimilarity between both can be computed." (*ibid.*)

The graded salience hypothesis states that for information to be salient (i.e., for it to be foregrounded in one's mind), it needs to be stored or coded in one's mental lexicon, a process that is termed consolidation. Salience admits degrees, with the effect that more salient meanings have priority in interpretation (an hypothesis formulated for figurative language). Salience is dependent on conventionality, frequency, familiarity, or prototypicality (cf. Giora 2003, p. 10, 15 ff., 69). Both notions, graded salience and indirect negation, allow for an account of irony in the following terms. The salient literal meaning of irony functions as a "reference point relative to which the ironicized situation is to be assessed and criticized," thus conveying frustration or dissociation from what is referred to (Giora 2003, p. 94)

Attardo, in his turn, proposes to define as ironical "an utterance that, while maintaining relevance, explicitly or implicitly violates the conditions for contextual appropriateness." (Attardo 2000, p. 817) This author advances the following operational definition for the notion of appropriateness: "an utterance u is contextually appropriate iff all presuppositions of u are identical to or compatible with all the presuppositions of the context C in which u is uttered." (*ibid.*, p. 818 and ff.) He then contends that purposeful inappropriateness (which is still seen as a violation of the cooperative principle) is a necessary and sufficient cause of irony in an utterance. Violation of contextual appropriateness includes violation of both sincerity and cultural norms or expectations and other forms as well (e.g., deictic inappropriateness). To that he adds a principle of least disruption, to the effect that the speaker is to limit his or her violation of the cooperative principle to the smallest possible conversational unit (one utterance, one conversational turn, one speech exchange) and to try to link the entire unit violating the cooperative principle to the rest of the interaction (for example, by finding a certain appropriateness to this very unit) (*ibid.*, pp. 814–815). A final point worth mentioning is his claim that the concepts of mention and pretence are very close to each other, but that mention is a more restricted concept that pretence. This is relevant in our context, since it is pretense, and not mention, what is exploited in parodic irony.

As already mentioned, Giora's and Attardo's accounts can be seen as revisions and extensions of Grice's original theory. Both share the view that the priority of literal meaning must be rejected and instead postulate other principles –the priority of salient meanings in Giora and the necessity and sufficiency of the search for contextual appropriateness in Attardo. Both consider that the processing of irony is two-stage in that it requires backtracking and reinterpretation. Explanatory as they are, we can see that these accounts explain irony as a question of the speaker's intentions, and only that. The interpreter's role is to correctly infer the speaker's communicative intentions.

The theoretical accounts so far considered describe the conditions that allow the interpreter to carry out her interpretation. Interestingly, Attardo conceptualizes irony as a violation of contextual appropriateness, where this last concept involves norms and expectations that are both cultural and related to the knowledge by the participants of the opinions and belief systems of the speakers. Hence, his view allows for a consideration of the role that the social context may play in ironical interaction.

3.4   *The Pretence Theory*

This aspect is explicitly part of the last account that is worth considering here, the pretense theory of irony due to Clark and Gerrig (1984). According to its proponents, this theory may be expressed as follows. In speaking ironically to the hearer A, the speaker S pretends that he or she is a different speaker S' speaking to the hearer A' (a pretend hearer, who can be present or absent, real or imaginary). Moreover, the attitude of the ironist S is critical towards what S' is saying, something that is, in one way or another, "patently uninformed or injudicious, worthy of a 'hostile or derogatory judgment or a feeling such as indignation or contempt.'" (Clark and Gerrig 1984, p. 122, quoting Grice) A' is intended to miss this pretense and take S as speaking seriously, but A is assumed to be able to see all the above. The authors point to one merit of their account, namely, that the victims of the irony can be of two kinds. The first is the pretend speaker S', seen as an injudicious or uninformed person; the second one is the pretend hearer A', who takes S' words at its face value.

This shows the need to take into account not only the speaker's intentions, but some other conditions having to do with the social context as shared by speaker and hearer. Clark and Gerrig consider this aspect when they observe that "A listener's understanding of an ironic utterance depends crucially on the common ground he or she believes is shared by the ironist and the audience— their mutual beliefs, mutual knowledge, and mutual suppositions." (*ibid.*, p. 124) Thus, the pretense theory makes clear how common ground, a common social context, is needed in irony.[7]

---

7 It is worth mentioning that there have been hybrid echoic-pretence accounts contending that irony is necessarily attributive but that it also necessarily involves pretence (e.g. see Kumon-Nakamura et al. 1995).

3.5   *Balance*

Although taking the common ground into account undoubtedly helps to explain ironical interactions like the one under study (more on that below), there is still a point that should be noticed. It would seem that a real audience A that, in the course of the interaction, behaves like A' deserves a negative assessment for its incomprehension. Nevertheless, it seems fair to say that there are situations, like the one under study, where a real audience can understand all the above and at the same time take the speaker's words at its face value. This situation strongly suggests that the addressee (the real audience A in Clark and Gerrig's terms) is also contributing to the co-determination of the (ironical or other) force of the utterance, as far as the interactional sequence is concerned. In what follows, we will focus on the case under study, in order to closer analyze it and try to determine whether the above-mentioned theories allow for a satisfactory explanation of the interaction. In order to do that, some contributions will be taken into account concerning the reception of irony from the part of the addressees.

4   Responding to Irony: the Dynamics of Interaction

Before that and for the sake of clarity, we state here again the interactional sequence under study. As said before, I take this sequence to be constituted by three steps.

Initiator's first turn [T1]:

> Now that I have more than 50.000 followers and I have drunk four glasses of wine, I'll be able to state my message: the Holocaust was a hoax!

Interactant's turn [T2]:

> The journal considers the given commentaries to be unacceptable and incompatible with its editorial line.

Initiator's second turn [T3]:

> I apologize for the suffering that my *tweet* is causing. I want to clarify that I am neither anti-Semitic nor negationist." [The questioned *tweet* was] "the parody of such an attitude

Both the first and second turns by the initiator can be seen as complex utterances, intended as complex communicative acts. In [T1], the initiator may be

seen as intentionally pretending to be the type of negationist, anti-Semitic person that would utter the words he wrote, with the reflexive intention that this
first intention of pretense be recognized, and with the further intention that
this recognition trigger on the part of the addressees an inferential process that
would eventually allow them to recover the speaker's intended meaning. In the
case under study, one may conjecture that this intended meaning had to do with
pointing at the extraordinary power of the Internet to spread and make believe
almost anything, however absurd it may seem. Yet in order for this communicative intention to succeed, the addressees would have to carry out the required inference, and for that they would need to have at their disposal the contextual and
background information that would allow them to detect the speaker's flouting
of the maxim of quality. Interestingly, in his last intervention the speaker seems
to have felt the need to make this information explicit, when he adds, "... Anyone that knows my career can test that I have never approached such positions
[negationism and anti-Semitism], which I strongly condemn." (Pérez Oliva 2011)

   This later self-clarification seems to give empirical support to Grice's explanation of irony as a case of flouting the maxim of quality (i.e., of saying
something patently insincere), thus prompting in the hearer the search for another meaning that may be congruent with the maxim. Furthermore, it seems
to support the view that both the literal and the non-literal meanings must be
available in the course of the interaction, to allow for the required process of
backtracking and reinterpretation. In contrast, the one-stage account seems
to find more difficulties to give an explanation that is congruent with the full
sequence, since the ironical meaning should have been directly accessed (provided that the communicative act was successful, as we may assume it was).
Given that according to the one-stage account other possible meanings are
discarded and are no longer available for processing, it remains unexplained
why the interaction might retain both senses, as it in fact did.

   Additionally, the communicated content seems in the context slightly irrelevant (given that the blog was personal, why an increase in followers should lead
the speaker to general considerations about the Web power to induce false beliefs?) and even self-defeating (is the speaker suggesting to his readers that he is
really to do so?), unless one attributes to the speaker the ironic intention of indirectly negating what he was saying, namely, that he was really in a situation to induce false beliefs of any kind. But the way he proceeded strongly suggests that he
was motivated by a further secondary intention. This would be a non-declared
intention to show off, to impress and evoke admiration in view of the speaker's
powerful capacity to influence opinions. Yet this type of intention is not a communicative one, because "recognition of the intention might militate against securing the effect and promote an opposite effect." (Strawson 1964, p. 452) This

secondary intention, that cannot be manifested if the speech act is to attain its intended perlocutionary effect, was not taken into consideration in the sequence of turns that followed the first one and played no role in the interaction. It helps to explain, however, the speaker's attitude in the course of events.

The fact that this secondary intention played no role in the interaction could be explained by recourse to some of the above-considered theoretical notions. The inappropriateness of the utterance (Attardo) and the consequently in-ferred ironical intention were to be assessed independently of the psycholog-ical motives that the author had to adopt such an ironical attitude. Moreover, salience of meaning (Giora) seems also to have constrained the relevant inter-pretation for the non-literal meaning of the utterance, notwithstanding other secondary, non-communicative intentions of the speaker.

Until now, then, it seems that a two-stage account in line with Grice's theory may provide a satisfactory theoretical framework to account for the case under examination. The difficulty arises when we remember that, in the course of the complete interactional sequence and particularly in [T2], the relevant address-ees (the journal's responsible persons) seem to have correctly understood the speaker's ironical intent, but have consciously refused to cooperate with him and have rather taken his words at its face value, so to say. From an interaction-alist point of view, this would explain the speaker's second turn [T3], which implicitly acknowledges the interlocutor's interpretation and tries to repair the broken understanding. It is nevertheless implausible that the interlocutors had not grasped the speaker's ironical intention.

In order to account for this seemingly incongruent second turn, it is worth considering a further theoretical approach that takes into consideration the reception of irony. Kotthoff (2003) provides empirical data to convincingly support the view that in irony both the implicated and the literal meanings are processed, and that "if there are responses to the literal meaning, this does not necessarily indicate that the listener was not able to bridge the ironic gap." (Kotthoff 2003, p. 1387) According to her findings, the way an addressee reacts to irony is influenced by the way he or she is affected by it. This helps to explain the fact that addressees can and do often react to both levels of meaning: to what is said and to what is implicated (the non-literal, ironical meaning). Moreover, in this way they "shape the meaning of the emergent conversation-al sequence." (*ibid.*) Finally, and crucially to our case study, Kotthoff (quoting other authors) contends that the specific opposition between what is said and what is implicated, between the literal and the non-literal is located not sim-ply on the level of the proposition (semantic level) or illocution (pragmatic level of speech acts), but rather "on the level of evaluation." (*ibid.*, p. 1389) The concept of evaluation is explained as follows. It is an activity in which a person assigns a value (within a continuous scale) to the object of evaluation; it is done from a perspective that takes specific attributes as relevant and assigns them a normative value; finally, the relationships among the object of evaluation, the evaluation aspect, and the standard of evaluation are conventional and come from the practical activities in which the object is integrated.

In the case under study, ultimately, the second interactant (the journal's editors) may be seen as reacting to the instrumental use that the first speaker was making of negationist and anti-Semitic opinions. The intended ironical message, having to do with an ironical negation of the speaker's ability to induce false beliefs in the situation, was not in itself the object of the evaluation. But in order to convey this intended meaning, the speaker instrumentally resorted to some (for him, and he assumed that also for his readers) extremely absurd views. It was his instrumentation of the subject matter together with the need, for the irony to work, to express literally such views which made his utterance not only inappropriate but also unacceptable for the second interactant. Thus the evaluation took those particular aspects as the ones that ought to be assessed. As the formal statement of reply made explicit, the standards of evaluation were both moral (the sequel of events, together with the uttered words were considered "unacceptable") and related to the journal's ideological background (since the words were "incompatible with its editorial line"). Of course, there are good reasons to suspect that other motives (like trying to avoid a negative impact on the journal's reputation and on its sales) were playing their part in the sequence of events. But, as before in the case of the speaker's motives, these aspects did not become explicit in the interaction and are therefore put aside.

The editorial note from which the case under study is taken suggests that it was not only the first (ironic) utterance, but also the initiator's response to the criticisms by means of a series of jokes with the Holocaust which prompted the journal's formal statement. Yet it should be noticed that, for some of the readers (especially for those that were descendants of victims), it was the instrumentation of such negationist and anti-Semitic views together with the explicit repetition of them which was censurable in the strongest terms. It does not seem unfair to consider that this fact played a central role in the issue of the journal's response. This is even highlighted by the very title of the editorial note, "No jokes with the Holocaust."

5   Joint Meaning and Accountability

If this analysis is correct, it seems then that the journal's reply was simultaneously reacting to both literal and implicated meanings. The negative evaluation

undoubtedly concerned the instrumentation of the subject matter, which presupposes a meta-pragmatic perspective on the part of the evaluator. At the
same time, this negative assessment seems to also apply to the very utterance
of the words, thus considering its literal meaning at its face value (as we have
argued before, this interpretation is supported by the initiator's last response).
From a theoretical perspective, the second interactant's reply seems to introduce two different interpretations and attribute two different illocutions to
the speaker. One may wonder whether this is possible and, in such case, what
makes it so.

The fact that the same utterance may be taken as performing different illocutions is a well-known phenomenon, firstly observed by Austin (1962) and
since then almost universally accepted among scholars. It should be noticed
that when we categorize irony as an (indirect) illocution we are departing
from Austin, who dismissed the special circumstances in which language was
"used not seriously, but in ways *parasitic* upon its normal use." (Austin 1962,
p. 22) Searle in his turn mentions irony as a an indirect speech act in which
sentence's meaning and speaker's meaning are different, arguing that it is the
inappropriateness of the utterance that prompts the reinterpretation (Searle
1975, pp. 112–113). Afterwards, there have been several attempts to analyze irony
as an indirect speech act, mainly as an insincere one that is in need of reinterpretation. To this extent, Attardo's assessment that "these could be considered
as Gricean theories as well" (Attardo 2000, p. 801) seems well founded. Here
we have been assuming that irony is an (indirect) illocutionary act, susceptible
of being analyzed in its own terms. For that, we have taken into consideration
some relevant approaches that help to illuminate the phenomenon.

Yet the question about the conditions that contribute to determining the
illocution in context seems less straightforward. For one thing, Gricean theories and usual theories of irony as an indirect speech act rely on the speaker's
intention as determining the illocutionary meaning of his or her utterance.
The discussions have evolved around the conditions (e.g. salience or inappropriateness) that constrain and make possible for the addressee the inferential process that leads him or her to correctly grasp those intentions. However,
Kotthoff's approach to the reception of irony has highlighted an aspect of the
phenomenon so far unnoticed. Namely, the possibility that the addressee interprets the utterance in a way that was not intended by the speaker, notwithstanding the fact that he or she has correctly grasped the speaker's intentions.
This fact points to an active role of the addressee in determining the illocutionary force of the utterance, and to a more complex and interactive process
in the course of the communicative sequence. With this in mind, we may try
to reassume our case study.

As said before, under one interpretation, the speaker utterance reached in the course of the interaction an illocutionary force that was different from the one intended by him. It was the literal meaning, and not the non-literal, which constituted the joint meaning of the utterance. The last turn on the part of the initiator, explicitly negating that these views were really his own, paradoxically confirms the second interactant's interpretation as one that is available in the sequence. The notion of joint meaning, stemming from Clark (1996), is defined as follows: "Joint meaning is formed every time a speaker and a hearer jointly commit to the fact that a specific communicative act has been performed." (Carassa and Colombetti 2009, p. 1849) This type of meaning involves a commitment on the part of the interactants that a specific speech act has been performed. Therefore, joint meaning is not just common belief of what has been said, but carries deontic implications in what concerns the commitments, as well as the corresponding legitimate expectations that the interactants recognize and ascribe to each other.

This view on communicative interaction has been developed by a number of authors (Clark 1996; 2006; Carassa and Colombetti 2009; Sbisà 2006; 2009; Haugh 2013). The common tenet in all of them is the claim that communicative interaction is normative, in that it creates deontic relationships between the interactants that may be accounted for in terms of the specific responsibilities and obligations, as well as entitlements and rights, etc., instituted through the interaction. Furthermore, it is contended that these relationships are constituted by the (possibly tacit) acceptance of the participants. It is in this sense that Austin's (1962) notion of "uptake" is reinterpreted in what concerns the attribution of an illocutionary force to an utterance: the illocution can be described by saying how the interpersonal relationship of the interactants has been affected by it, and its conventional effects on the interactant's relationship come into being by being agreed upon by the relevant people involved (Sbisà 2009, p. 49).

Coming back to the case under study, we may see that the first meaning intention of the initiator was not accepted by the second interactant. Thus the intended ironical force of the utterance was not to constitute the joint meaning as an agreed upon fact. Instead, it was the second interactant's interpretation which was joined in by the initiator. He tacitly recognized his words to have the literal meaning they had, but tried to dissociate his own system of beliefs from it.

Turning now to the second available interpretation, it is apparent that the addressee, the second interactant, correctly grasped the speaker's ironic intention. Nevertheless, far from joining in the ironic meaning with a cooperative attitude (see Clark 1996, pp. 369–374 for a notion of irony as joint pretense), the addressee moved to a meta-pragmatic, evaluative stance in order to critically assess the initiator's utterance as an unacceptable instrumentation of the subject matter. Under this interpretation, the aspect for the evaluation was not the one intended by the speaker but a different one. Moreover, the second interactant held the speaker accountable for his move, taking into account the real-world consequentiality of his words.

This social dimension of accountability has recently been studied by Haugh (2013), who revises the notion of speaker meaning to contend that whether a linguistic act constitutes speaker meaning "depends on whether or not the speaker is held accountable for it"; moreover, to be held accountable here "refers to participants treating the speaker as socially committed to and/ or responsible for the meaning representation(s) in question." (Haugh 2013, pp. 47–48) This responsibility refers not only to the truth or sincerity of the uttered contents, but to "the real-world social or interpersonal consequences of it." (*ibid.*) As Haugh notices, there are also cases in which the participants dispute the speaker meanings because of their real-world consequentiality. This kind of disagreement is notably present in our case study, in that the ironic intention is correctly grasped but not joined in as a humorous interchange.

Nevertheless, and unlike Haugh's account, I do not take the interlocutors' evaluative stance to be merely explainable in terms of the "moral order" (*ibid.*) that frames the dialogue. It seems to me that this view is not fair to the intuition that certain speech acts should be and in fact are critically assessed both according to their compliance with their corresponding necessary conditions and on the basis of their *objective* correctness (Sbisà this volume, section 4), notwithstanding other social criteria. In this sense, evaluation should be understood within the Austinian framework of regulated procedures and objective requirements.[8]

6   Conclusion

The case study under consideration, as described in Section 2, has allowed us to see how meaning is jointly established in the course of the interaction, with the addressee playing an active role in the determination of the illocutionary force of the utterance. The first speaker's intention is confronted with a counter-perspective on the part of the second interactant, who adopts an

---

8   Still, I take it that some evaluative stances can be grounded on the preceding interactional history and posterior patter-recognition on the part of the interactants, in line with the view put forward by Witek (2015; this volume). I am nevertheless reluctant to join in a naturalistic foundationalism as the one he seems to suggest. I am aware that this suggestion is in need of development and support, something out of the scope of this paper.

evaluative stance to hold the speaker accountable in a double concern. Firstly, the literal meaning of the utterance ("... the Holocaust was a hoax!") is taken at its face value and evaluated with respect to the real-world consequences of expressing such an opinion. Secondly, the speaker's ironic intention is grasped but not joined in by the addressee, who adopts an evaluative stance with respect to the instrumentation of the subject matter (the Holocaust) with a humorous attitude.

Under both interpretations, the last turn on the part of the initiator shows his attempt to repair the broken relationship (by apologizing), in congruency with the second interpretation (meta-pragmatic level). At the same time, he attempts to repair the broken understanding on the level of the illocution, by making explicit a content ("I am neither anti-Semitic nor negationist") that was a crucial ingredient of the background information needed to recover the indirect, non-literal illocution.

It still makes sense to question whether it is rational that the same addressee assigns two different interpretations to the same initial move. We should notice here that both correspond to different evaluative aspects and are, in this sense, two different criteria to hold the speaker accountable for the consequentiality of his words.

Finally, in my view the interactionist account of irony is able to answer to aspects of the phenomenon that other accounts overlook. In particular, the addressee's active intervention in interpreting (and evaluating) the initiator's utterance, to the effect that it assigns to it a meaning and a force beyond the initiator's first intentions. This uptake and normative stance on the part of the addressee are only completed with a third turn-taking on the part of the initiator, accepting the interpretation and thus agreeing with the assignment. According to the interactionist view, this process of negotiation of meaning and final agreement (on the meaning and force of the utterance) is what determines the illocutionary effect. But notice that it has been indispensable in our analysis to take into account a three-step sequence. I contend that there is a need in the interactionist account to be complemented with an account of the initiation-response-[evaluation] sequence that jointly fixes the meaning and force in communicative interaction.

Bibliography

Attardo, S. (2000). Irony as relevant inappropriateness. *Journal of Pragmatics* 32, 793–826.
Atardo, S. et al. (2006). Reactions to irony in discourse: evidence for the least disruption principle. *Journal of Pragmatics* 38, 1239–1256.

Austin, J.L. (1962). *How to do things with words*. Oxford: Oxford University Press.

Ball. B. (this volume). Commitment and Obligation in Speech Act Theory. In: M. Witek and I. Witczak-Plisiecka (eds.), *Normativity and Variety of Speech Actions*, pp. 51–65. Leiden: Brill (*Poznań Studies in the Philosophy of the Sciences and the Humanities* 112).

Carassa, A. and M. Colombetti (2009). Joint meaning. *Journal of Pragmatics* 41, 1837–1854.

Clark, H.H. (1996). *Using language*. Cambridge: Cambridge University Press.

Clark, H.H. (2006). Social actions, social commitments. In: S. C. Levinson and N. J. Enfield (eds.), *Roots of human sociality: Culture, cognition, and human interaction*, pp. 126–150. Oxford: Berg Press.

Clark, H.H. and R.J. Gerrig (1984). On the pretense theory of irony. *Journal of Experimental Psychology: General* 113 (1), 121–126.

Fetzer, A. (this volume). Speech acts in discourse. In: M. Witek and I. Witczak-Plisiecka (eds.), *Normativity and Variety of Speech Actions*, pp. 101–121. Leiden: Brill (*Poznań Studies in the Philosophy of the Sciences and the Humanities* 112).

Giora, R. (1995). On irony and negation. *Discourse Processes* 19, 239–264.

Giora, R. (2003). *On our mind: salience, context and figurative language*. Oxford: Oxford University Press.

Grice, H.P. (1975). Logic and Conversation. In: P. Cole and J.L. Morgan (eds.), *Speech acts*, vol. 3, pp. 41–58. New York: Academic Press.

Grice, H.P. (1978). Further considerations on logic and conversation. In: P. Cole (ed.), *Pragmatics*, vol. 9, pp. 113–127. New York: Academic Press.

Irony. In *Merriam-Webster Dictionary*, accessible in http://www.merriam-webster.com/dictionary/irony (last accessed: 2 May 2017).

Haugh, M. (2013). Speaker meaning and accountability in interaction. *Journal of Pragmatics* 48, 41–56.

Kotthoff, H. (2003). Responding to irony in different contexts: on cognition in conversation. *Journal of Pragmatics* 35, 1387–1411.

Kumon-Nakamura, S. et al. (1995). How about another piece of pie: the allusional pretense theory of discourse irony. *Journal of Experimental Psychology: General* 124, 3–21.

Pérez Oliva, M. (2011). Ninguna broma con el holocausto. *El País*, 6 February 2011 (printed edition). Also accessible in http://elpais.com/diario/2011/02/06/opinion/1296946805_850215.html (last accessed: 2 May 2017).

Sbisà, M. (2006). Communicating citizenship in verbal interaction: principles of a speech act oriented discourse analysis. In: H. Hausendorf and A. Bora (eds.), *Analysing citizenship talk*, pp. 151–180. Amsterdam: John Benjamins Publishing Company.

Sbisà, M. (2009). Uptake and conventionality in illocution. *Lodz Papers in Pragmatics* 5 (1), 33–52.

Sbisà, M. (2013). Locution, illocution, perlocution. In: M. Sbisà and K. Turner (eds.), *Pragmatics of speech actions*, pp. 25–75. Berlin and Boston: De Gruyter Mouton.

Sbisà, M. (this volume). Varieties of speech act norms. In: M. Witek and I. Witczak-Plisiecka (eds.), *Normativity and Variety of Speech Actions*, pp. 23–50. Leiden: Brill (*Poznań Studies in the Philosophy of the Sciences and the Humanities* 112).

Sbisà, M. and K. Turner (2013). Introduction. In: *id.* (eds.), *Pragmatics of speech actions*, pp. 1–21. Berlin and Boston: De Gruyter Mouton.

Schegloff, E. A. (2006). *Sequence Organization in Interaction*. Cambridge: Cambridge University Press.

Searle, J.R. (1975). *Expression and meaning*. Cambridge: Cambridge University Press.

Sperber, D. and D. Wilson (1981). Irony and the use-mention distinction. In: P. Cole (ed.), *Radical Pragmatics*, pp. 295–318. New York: Academic Press.

Sperber, D. and D. Wilson 1995. *Relevance: Communication and Cognition*, 2nd ed. Oxford: Blackwell.

Strawson, P.F. (1964). Intention and convention in speech acts. *The Philosophical Review* 73 (4), 439–460.

Wilson, D. (2013). Irony comprehension: A developmental perspective. *Journal of Pragmatics* 59 (A), 40–56.

Wilson, D. and D. Sperber (2012). Explaining irony. In: D. Wilson and D. Sperber (eds.), *Meaning and Relevance,* pp. 123–145. Cambridge: Cambridge University Press.

Witek, M. (2015). An interactional account of illocutionary practice. *Language Sciences* 47, 43–55.

Witek, M. (this volume). Coordination and norms in illocutionary interaction. In: M. Witek and I. Witczak-Plisiecka (eds.), *Normativity and Variety of Speech Actions*, pp. 66–97. Leiden: Brill (*Poznań Studies in the Philosophy of the Sciences and the Humanities* 112).

CHAPTER 7

Forms of Aggressive Speech Actions in Public Communication

Milada Hirschová

Abstract

The paper focuses on the phenomenon of aggression in speech actions performed in public communication events. The relation among the notions of speech act and speech action, as well as among un/im/politeness, rudeness, verbal aggression (the last two mostly described as intentional use of vulgarities), and aggressive communication are all discussed in speech act-theoretic perspective. Analyses of relevant dialogues, being extracts from TV shows and a recording of an interview, demonstrate that aggressive, openly offensive communication can be seen not just as a borderline case in the periphery of impoliteness, but, more accurately, as a parallel phenomenon, a communicative strategy in which vulgarities can be present or not. It is evident that within this strategy, speech actions such as accusations (statements concerning the past or current oponents' activities), defamations and rhetorical questions are among the most frequent types of such verbal actions.

1   Speech Acts and Speech Actions

A speech act has been, in the times of the origin of the theory, conceptualized as a discrete unit (cf. Austin 1962).[1] Its main distinctive feature, its illocutionary force, ensued from speaker's intention, i.e. the relevant illocutionary point, and, in a prototypical case, materialized in an utterance with specific properties given mainly by the presence of an illocutionary verb used performatively, or from speaker's use of some other illocutionary force indicating device as elaborated later by Searle (cf. 1969). While an utterance as a speech item can be seen as a discrete, limited unit without major uncertainities (unmarkedly, its boundaries are delimited by intonation), the discrete nature of an act (already

---

1   I express my thanks to the editors of this volume, especially to Prof. Iwona Witczak-Plisiecka, for their useful comments and suggestions.

when performed by the speaker) is far from being unambiguous. For instance, if we consider 'acts' related to speech act verbs such as *confide* (*something in somebody*), *gossip* (*about somebody*), it is clear that they do convey an item of information, i.e. they could be listed as assertives, but, at the same time, in every day ('real') communication they most probably would not be executed as a single utterance. Communicative events of *confiding* or *gossiping* have both in common that they transmit a piece of information (whose propositional content is) of a specific kind: either it is something personally relevant for the speaker (and not publicly known at the moment of *confiding*), or it is something relevant for the speaker and (presumably) for the addressee. Most importantly, a content of a *gossip* concerns a third party, a non-present person, in an unfavourable way. Such information can hardly be conveyed instantly, directly, without at least minimal preparatory steps, i.e. preliminary announcement or notification. There are common opening phrases of the kind: *If you do not mind, there is something I need to tell you; You know, I think that you should be aware of ...,* etc. Moreover, *confiding* would probably be followed by a request that the addressee should keep the information for him/herself (e.g. *don't tell anyone, ok?*) and a *gossip* by an assertion cancelling or weakening the speaker's commitment towards the truthfulness of the content (e.g. *well, that's what I have heard*), or transferring the burden of evidence to some other person (e.g. *that's what A.B. told me!*). In their common most expected forms both *confiding* and *gossiping* are represented by sequences of utterances (each of which can have its own subsidiary function) creating a complex unit covered by one major, macro illocutionary function (cf. van Dijk 1980).

Another example of common speech act-clusters are requests or pleas which quite regularly are preceded by apologies for bothering the addressee (e.g. *sorry, but ...; Sorry to bother you but ...*) and followed by explanations why the speaker wants the addressee to do *p* – *Open the window, please / Would you mind opening the window, please? It is hot in here; I think we need some oxygen,* etc.). Performing illocutionary acts of *confiding, gossiping, requesting* (including, with the exception of some ritualized declarations, most of the others, no matter which classification we use) in the form of a plain, isolated utterance is in most cases unusual, unconventional, and can be viewed as less felicitious. Illocutionary acts are more commonly performed as sequences consisting of smaller steps towards one major point, so we dare to conclude that it is more appropriate to describe doing things with words as continuous succession of minor actions aimed at a major goal than singular, discrete acts (cf. also the German concept of *sprachliche Handlung*). This view has already been acknowledged in pragmatics literature, e.g. as a concept of subsidiary illocution (Rosengren 1983 and from other angles by e.g. Hirschová 2004; Mey 2001;

Witczak-Plisiecka 2013a; 2013b). Nevertheless, the idea of speech acts as unitary utterances is still rather well established in general linguistics handbooks and in general educational contexts.

Following the above-mentioned complexity, it seems that the most cogent concept of particular classes of illocutionary acts might be to picture them as blocks of actions unified by speaker's goal; an illocutionary point of a speech event can be seen as a flagpole or the main pillar supported by particular actions serving as foundations for its erected structure. The main purpose in such speech actions is recognized and secured step by step. The borderlines between such blocks are far from being clear-cut – indirectness is the most common way of fulfillment of speakers' goals in conversation and, as G. Leech (1983, p. 175) suggests '... illocutions are in many respects (...) distinguished by continuous rather than by discrete characteristics.' In addition, illocutionary acts can often be 'negotiated' (*ibid.*, p. 23). It has also been suggested (Leech 2014, pp. 56–58) that the *pragmatic meaning* of what was said resides in the speaker's communicative intention, but its interpretation depends on the recognition of that intention (cf. Corredor this volume), which can also be seen as a goal, by the addressee (or by some third party). In this perspective what is fundamental for pragmatic interpretation is therefore the complex inferential process that is always present, which can also be related to the notion of an *interactional effect* (cf. Witek this volume).

2   Aggressive Speech Actions

In order to successfully deal with aggressive speech actions, it is necessary to take a standpoint and elucidate the relation between aggressive communication and the notions and concepts of impoliteness, rudeness and verbal aggression. In a classificatory perspective on communicative conduct, impoliteness seems to be particularly difficult to grasp in a systematic way. A thorough discussion of politeness-oriented literature is not something to be attempted within the scope of this paper, but it is worth noting that our discussion does not follow too closely the line of thinking as present in politeness theory in the tradition of Brown and Levinson (1987) as our focus is not on persuasive strategies, but rather on the very phenomenon of aggression and related 'impolite' speech actions. At this point, let us stress two elements which we find important and which are asserted in literature in the most often quoted mantras: a) there are hardly any means of language which would be inherently polite or impolite; their polite or impolite nature is mostly a matter of speaker's use in a particular discourse (Watts 2003); b) the assessment of a piece of communication as impolite is a matter of addressee's (or a third party's) interpretation – impolite is that communicative behaviour that is interpreted as impolite, as imposing, offensive, etc. (cf. Culpeper 1996; 2011; Haugh 2015). It means that impoliteness does not need to be intentional, a superficially, formally identical utterance can be assessed differently by different listeners and a piece of communication assessed as impolite need not include impoliteness-marked means of expression. (Rudeness, on the other hand, can always be identified because of speaker's use of marked vocabulary, i.e. vulgarism. It is also accompanied by the speaker's communicative goal which is obvious and linked to the concept of rudeness in the relevant context. Rudeness can certainly do harm and be offensive, which for instance can be seen in a context when a person is being called names). However, rudeness can also merely appear to vent one's emotions, which is a common reason for cursing. It can also be directed towards a particular addressee, and sometimes can be meant as quite neutral, almost normative means of communication; for instance within some social groups or in certain communicative situations, such as the army training (cf. Bousfield 2008). Rudeness can neighbour jokes, i.e. it can sometimes be used jestingly, performed in order to cheer up or encourage the addressee, or as a contrastive means in the language comic.

Verbal aggression can be partly identified with the offensive use of marked vocabulary, but among its important constituents, often the most relevant ones, there are the suprasegmental elements of speech, i.e. the volume and tone of voice, mimics, etc. Compared to rudeness or cursing (which can be related to expressives), aggressive communication seems apt to be understood as an independent communicative strategy related to a struggle for power. It is based on speaker's effort to harm the addressee (or the discussed object) and to dominate the conversation. It can include (even though not necessarily) impoliteness, rudeness, as well as a marked tone of voice, i. e., as a strategy it is a more complex phenomenon than the aforementioned ones. Aggressive communication can be paralleled to an effort to defend or extend one's territory, and it can be defined as an effort to assert, forward, and pursue one's own agenda. Typically, its core is materialized as linguistic attacks at the addressee's face, i.e. his or her positive social value, an image of the self (cf. Goffman 1971, pp. 5–45). It is quite common that in later works on im/politeness (e.g. Spencer-Oatey 2005; 2007; Culpeper 2011, pp. 26–31) the concept of face includes the notions of integrity and identity, whether professional, qualitative, social, relational, or other.

Verbal attacks need not be explicitly vulgar. The triggering mechanism of aggressive communication emerges in a aprticular communicative situation – an individual starts or joins a particular communicative event with the agenda to achieve his or her goal/s showing minimal or zero considerations for the interlocutor/s. It may also be the case that he or she finds him/herself under pressure because of being put into a position perceived subjectively as disadvantaged. A person communicating aggressively either feels him/herself in the position of power or wants to prevail over the opponent. Seen in a broader perspective of social interactions, aggressive communication occurs in two basic forms: a) as hostile aggression which is impulsive, driven by anger and primarily aiming at offending and harming the target; and b) as instrumental aggression which is premeditated as a means of retaliation or obtaining some goal, mostly to boost up speaker's position.

3   Aggressive Communication on TV

The very topic of this study, aggressive speech actions in public communication, emerged while conducting an analysis of a popular media genre, TV talk shows, in which various issues were targeted (Hirschová & Svobodová 2014). Among the analysed problems there were issues that due to their gravity and frequency had grown to be considered influential and the shows proved to be part of an important genre, operative in showing contemporary (not only Czech) language use and patterned ways of communication. For instance, in Czech public space, the influence of talk shows can be seen in the increasing tolerance towards colloquial language and forms which circa two decades ago were deemed unacceptable in mass media, in casual or trivial forms of discussing a variety of (sometimes rather serious) issues, and, more importantly, in public presentation of not-quite conventional, or even entirely anti-conventional communicative strategies. This is true not only of talk shows concerning life style, gossip, etc., but specifically about talk shows (and interviews) discussing economic or political topics, with well-known active politicians as participants. Even though media discourse is primarily a domain of first-level politeness, non imposing communication conventionally expected in the public, in certain subgenres of TV talk shows the participants' identity (i.e. their opinions, attitudes, professional competence, even personality traits) is openly attacked with criticism, mockery, irony, which can sometimes be accompanied by the use of open vulgarities. Such offensive speech actions executed in the form of accusations of the opponents or even calling them names are nevertheless tolerated by the show interlocutors, and received without reservation on the part of the audience. The reason is that the performers usually are speakers in a position demanding (at least in their own eyes and in the eyes of their supporters) to show off, to project the air of decisiveness and to show their ability to boost up their social position at the expense of their opponent as the issue of power becomes dominant.

The above-mentioned kinds of controversial patterns of communicative behaviour are tolerated by the media authorities since they are seen as instrumental in building the show's attractiveness and also seen as instrumental in increasing its rating. Expectedly, perception of such communicative behaviour on the part of the public is ambiguous – it is accepted or approved by the speaker's partisans or supporters and rejected by others. In the extracts presented below, there are examples of both hostile aggression and instrumental aggression, as well as patterns being combinations of the two types. The cited examples have been selected from the recordings of the Czech public TV stations CT1, namely the weekly talk show *Máte slovo* (Eng. 'The floor is yours') and CT24 – daily news and commentaries (*Studio 24*).

3.1 The *Máte Slovo* Talk Show

In *Máte slovo*, there is always a topic which would currently provoke public discussion and controversy. The main specific feature of the show is that there is not only the host and her guests (regularly, there are two guests presented as 'supporters' of certain opinion or solution and two opponents), but also the audience is present in the studio. First, the host presents pre-recorded questions asked by the viewers on the phone, later she moderates the discussion with direct questions from the audience on site. The show aims to expose controversy and to allow for resolving disagreement (with any kind of establishment). Thus, the show's major purpose and the role of the host is to provoke an outcry, rather than simply to lead the discussion. The atmosphere is competitive from the very beginning, the typical feature of the situation being the struggle for self-presentation on the part of the guests (as there are usally politicians exercising some marketing strategy) and the pre-established uncompromising antagonistic attitude of the host, enhanced by the incessant efforts on the part of the audience to impose and disturb the guests' self-image and possibly to contradict his or her opinions taking the role of a kind of 'vox populi.'

3.2 *Hostile Communications*

Open hostile communication often occurs in (anonymous) viewers phone calls always released as an introduction to each part of *Máte slovo*. It is common practice that at the end of every episode, the following week's topic and the names of the invited guests are announced together with the phone numbers which can be used by those who want to ask them questions or make comments related to the prospective discussion. It is obvious, though, that individual entries are purposefully selected, and even edited, by the TV production team, predictably in view of their aggressivness, thus in other words with the intention to increase the show's attractivity. The samples below illustrate some of the typical communications:

(1)

The introduction of the part discussing restitutions of the church property (February 28, 2013):
Call no. 1: no vrátit majetek církvím v době kdy je většina národa pod hranicí bídy a lidi
well to return the property to the church at the time when the majority of the nation live under the border of poverty and people

spávaj pod mostem máme tady spoustu bezdomovců, to je úplně absurdita ale
sleep under bridges, we have lots of the homeless here, it is entirely absurd but

naše vláda to dělá proto aby měla potom mít kde azyl až je vodsaď poženeme a co
our government does it in order to have an asylum after we will have chased them out of here and what

z toho bude mít církev? akorát budou mít větší zlatý řetězy kolem krku
will the church have? just thicker golden chains on their necks

Call no. 2: samozřejmě že to je krádež století církev si nahromadila majetek tím že
of course it is the theft of the century; the church had piled their possessions by
vykořisťovala ty nejchudší lidi pokud věřící potřebujou ty kněžoury tak ať si je platí
exploiting the poorest ones; if worshippers need those pulpiteers then let them pay for them

Call no. 4: prosím vás, dyť církvi nebylo nikdy ... ani nedokázala vona kde ten majetek který
excuse me it has never been ... the church has never proven where the property being

se jí teďka vrací vona získala? dyť vona ho taky ukradla a nikdy to nebylo nikomu
*returned to it was obtained? it had stolen it anyway and nothing was ever
returned to anybody*

vrácený tak jaká je to? dyť je to zlodějna prosím vás normální
then what is it? it is a regular rip-off

(II)

The introduction of the part discussing the prices of electricity in Czech
Republic (March 7, 2013):
Call no.3: elektrika bude tak drahá, jak jim to dovolíme, až kam můžou
zdražovat takže
  *electricity will be as expensive as we let them make it, as much as we let
  them raise the prices so*

Bulharsko, Albánie nám ukázaly cestu[2]
Bulgaria, Albania have shown us the way to go

Call no. 4: poďte do nich, dokud do nich nepudem a nevymlátíme je tam tak
to prostě bude
  *let's go after them as long as we don't knock them out of their heads it
  will be more*

dražší a dražší budeme sedět jednou při svíčkách akorát kecaj ty na-
hoře voni si to
*and more expensive and we will sit at candlelight they just babble those
up there they*

domluvili a my to platíme a to je úplně se vším
*have made a deal and we pay for it and it is all the same with every-
thing*

Let us comment on the extracts (I) and (II). Anonymous callers express radical
opinions which might be interpreted as majority attitudes of the society; what
is typical in this context is the deictic positioning of the exclusive 'we' (i.e. the

2 What is meant here are incidents in Bulgaria and Albania where the clients of CEZ (the biggest Czech elctricity company, operating also in the mentioned countries) stopped their pay-
   ments as a form of protest against the high prices.

people) against 'them' (the establishment), and general negativity. The speech actions they perform are a mixture of complaints, unsubstantiated statements (*majority of the nation lives under the poverty line; people sleep under bridges,* I/1; (the church) *had stolen it* (the property) *anyway, it is a regular rip-off,* I/4), and threats (*let's go after them,* II/4). There are also open calls for aggressive behaviour (II/4). The targets to be offended (objects of dehonestation) are the members of the 'establishment' (in I: the clergy, in II: energy companies and government). Due to the fact that in *Máte slovo* half of the discussants would always represent either the 'parties,' i.e. the 'adversary,' such offense is aimed more directly at them. The callers do not use any rational arguments, they predominantly vent their disapproval (with almost anything concerning the establishment) and frustration. Since the host of this talk show predominantly mediates the opinions expressed by 'simple people' and the audience in the studio mostly joins the callers, the position of the guests, including the 'opponents,' can be difficult. Having accepted the invitation to the show, they are obliged to respond to attacs of that kind but, for obvious reasons, they cannot react with the same strength, with the same level of aggression as, *inter alia*, they are publicly known; they cannot even show that the other persons' utterances have been perceived as offensive, and as a result hardly any serious discussion will ever take place. It can be concluded that aggressiveness, hostile communication patterns, are not only tolerated but also invited in the show, and that the show's main attractivity consists in showing the public persons being scandalized.

3.3   *The Combination of a Hostile and an Instrumental Aggressive Communication*

There is a frequently occurring communicative phenomenon which is a combination of a hostile and of an instrumental kind of aggression. This type can be illustrated in the following extracts culled from *Máte slovo* and dealing with the quality of imported groceries (February 14, 2013).

(iii)

(1) FJ (importer of Polish groceries): vy tady mluvíte, že jako to Polsko, ale já to budu
You say here like, it is Poland but I will make it

zkracovat, proč mám jít kolem omáčky, a co když to je úplně jinak? protože víte
short why to beat around the bush what if everything is different? because you know

Česká republika jo, to je, jak se říká, stát podvodníků jo? prostě lhářů
(…) a proč si
The Czech Republic it is as people say nation of crooks ok? of simply liars
(…) and why not to

neudělat tenhleten systém, já si nechám udělat výrobky (…) Polsko mi
to přebalí
make such a system, I have some groceries produced (…) in Poland I have
it re-packed

vrátím to zpátky do České republiky, (…) a najednou bác jo, je to Polsko
jdete stíhat
and import it back to the Cz. Rep. (…) and all of a sudden bang, yes it is it
is Poland you go chase

Poláky, uděláme plošný zákaz dovozu z Polske, a já vám něco řeknu
(…) já sem něco
Poles, let's ban the overall import from Poland, and I tell you something
(…) I have

prožil, jasně to je záměr (…) a polské potraviny, jestli chcete ochutne-
jte, jo?
seen a lot, clearly this is intentional (…) and Polish food if you want try, ok?

(2) MJ (talk show host): a pane, pane J., vy tedy (říkáte) že to je záměr (…)
a vy tady
And, Mr., Mr. J., so you (say) that it is intentional (…) and here

máte polské potraviny, ano no počkejte a jako můžem to ochutnat jo?
you have Polish food, yes well, wait and so we can try it, ok?

(3) FJ: ano, můžete to ochutnat, můžete to ochutnat co se zlíbí
yes you can try it, you can try whatever you like

(4) AB (owner of the biggest Czech agricultural and food company): já
bych po panu J.
I would after Mr. J.

aby to vyzkoušel nejdřív pan J. sám jako? (laughter and applause of the
audience)
rather let Mr. J. try it first, like?

(5) FJ: nebojte neotrávíte se
don't worry you will not get poisoned

(6) AB: a vy ste Čech nebo Polák, když říkáte že Česko je krajina podvodníků?
*and are you Czech or Polish since you say that Czechia is a nation of
crooks?*

(7) FJ: já su, já su Moravák, a my na Moravě mluvíme česky[3]
I am, I am Moravian, and we in Moravia speak Czech

(8) AB: tak proč říkáte, že Česko je krajina podvodníků?
then why do you say that Czechia is a nation of crooks?

(9) FJ: já vám nabízím klobásku z Polska, pěkně z vepřového, vy to potřebu-
jete
I am offering you a Polish sausage, a nice pork one, that's what you need

(10) AB: ale ne, jděte s tím. já to nejím ty vaše sračky
oh no, go away with it, I don't eat that crap of yours

Let us discuss the extract III in more details. In (1) the speaker FJ reacts to
the context of the previous conversation in which specifically imported Polish foods were specifically criticized; he opens the core of his contribution
with a rhetorical question (*a co když to je úplně jinak? / what if everything is
different?*) signalling that he is going to express an opposite opinion. Then
he attacks his opponents with an offensive remark based on their nationality (the Czechs cannot rightfully criticize anyone because they are a *nation
of crooks, simply liars*), supports his accusations by an allegedly generally
accepted opinion (*as people say*), describes a possible system of cheating
and adds an accusation concerning efforts to harm Polish producers (puts
the criticism as a part of the business rivalry); at the end of his turn he
wants to prove that the quality of Polish food is good. It is also significant
that the way FJ speaks Czech shows that he obviously is a native speaker of
Polish – *zákaz dovozu z Polske,* etc. In (4), the attempt of FJ is used by AB to
strike back. The attack is first indirect – AB suggests the interlocutors and
the audience as well as the viewers that FJ cannot be trusted (FJ should try

---

3   There is a large Polish minority (Czech citizens of Polish ethnicity) living in the Northern part
of Moravia, a region of the Czech Republic.

the offered sausage himself first), while later, in (6) and (8) he suggests that FJ's allegations amount to an instance of slander (the speaker is Polish himself, therefore he defends Polish foods by all means). In (10), AB openly dehonestates both FJ's professional competence and his nationality (*that crap of yours* means Polish food). AB's turn can be grasped as a kind of retaliation for (1). As the response of the present audience (applause, laughter) shows, AB intentionally and succesfully aims at winning the favour of the public, i.e. he uses the open hostile aggression (with the use of vulgar vocabulary) instrumentally.

4 Instrumental Aggressiveness

Offensive and aggressive speech actions need not always use offensive language. An instrumental aggressive communication, a mostly deliberate effort to dominate, can take more refined forms and dispense with profanities or vulgarities. An instructive instance of instrumental aggression in communication can be seen in the interview conducted by a TV anchor DT with Czech president's aide LJ broadcasted by CT24.[4]

Let us begin by sketching the background. In his last New Year's presidential speech on January 1st 2013, Vaclav Klaus declared an extensive amnesty which would put an end to prosecution of many persons and litigation against them in connection with problematic cases of privatization or other economic affairs in the Czech Republic; the cases had started in 1990s. The amnesty was met with vast public protests and many politicians demanded that the Office of the President would make public the names of the lawyers – authors of the amnesty. The immediate context, released before the very interview, is a recording of an indignant speech made by a prominent member of the Czech Social Democratic Party, LZ, who, with strong criticism, enumerates the names of the presumed lawyers.

(IV)

(1) DT: introduces Mr. LJ who joins the live broadcasting on the phone and continues:
Odpovíte panu Z, pane J?
Will you give an answer to Mr. Z, Mr. J?

---

4 *Studio 24,* January 18, 2013, full recording available at https://www.youtube.com/watch?v=QoueR4AD2ag.

(2) LJ: já bych chtěl pozdravit diváky ČT z polské Wisly kde teď momentál-
ně jsme
I would like to greet the viewers of the CT from Wisla in Poland where we
currently are

s panem prezidentem (...)
together with Mr. President

(3) DT: i z Polska nám pane J můžete odpovědět, jestli odpovíte panu Z
nebo ne (...
even from Poland, Mr. J, you can tell us if you are going to respond
to Mr. Z

(4) LJ: ... a věřte tomu, že pan prezident tady má na programu jinou agen-
du a jiné věci
and believe it, Mr. President's agenda here is different

než vyřizování pošty
from dealing with mail

(5) DT: přesto bych si s dovolením trval na té odpovědi. víte nebo nevíte ...
despite that I must insist that you answer do you know or not ...

(6) LJ: já vím že musíte vypadat v tom rozhovoru aktivně a já vám to klidně
řeknu ale
I know that you must make an active appearance during this interview,
and I will tell you that without a problem

(7) DT: no tak prosím, na to čekáme
then go ahead, please, we are waiting for it

(8) LJ: ano
yes

(9) DT: a nemusím vypadat nijak (dotčený výraz obličeje). jenom prosím
trvám na
and I need not make any appearance (he looks irritated) *I just insist*

konkrétní odpovědi
that you provide a concrete answer

(10) LJ: já vás poslouchám jak pořád mluvíte spíš než se ptáte … ano dobře
*I am listenning to you you keep talking all the time, more than you ask
questions … well ok*

(11) DT: už jsem se ptal třikrát
I have asked you the question three times

(12) LJ: ano, i k nám se do Polska došplouchla ta informace o (nesrozumitel-
né)
yes, even to us to Poland has slopped the information about (indistinguished)

hrubém a neslušném projevu pana Z … já nevím já teď neumím říct
jestli pan
*the rude and indecent speech of Mr. Z … I don't know I cannot say wheth-
er Mr.*

prezident na to bude odpovídat podle mého hlubokého přesvědčení
ze zákona
*President will respond to it, I strongly believe that there is no legal obli-
gation*

na to odpovídat jednak nemusí a jednak ten dotaz ani nemá náležito-
sti podle
for him to respond, and the query has no legal relevancy anyway

onoho zákona ale všichni dobře víme proč pan Z. takováto takováto
gesta dělá
but we all know why Mr. Z performs gestures like that

dělají je lidé kteří ze sebe potřebují dělat ty největší statečné bojo-
vníky proti
*these things are done by people who need to present themselves as the
boldest*

lumpárnám v sociální demokracii největším takovým řečníkem byl DR
dokud u
*evil combatants, in the Social Democratic Party the major one was Mr.
DR until*

něj nenašli miliony v krabici od vína
he was caught with the wine-box stuffed with millions

já si myslím že bude velmi zábavné si číst věty pana Z
I think it will be very funny to read Mr. Z's sentences

až na něj prasknou jeho jeho věci ...
when his issues come into the open

(13) DT: počkejte jaké věci? co praskne na pana Z?
wait a minute what issues? what is to come out about Mr. Z?

(14) LJ: pan Z kolem sebe kope křičí ve stylu zloděj křičí chyťte zloděje a snaží se
Mr. Z is kicking around and yelling in the style stop thief! and he has tried

ze sebe udělat toho nejčestnějšího, přesně tento typ lidí má nejvíc másla na hlavě
to present himself as Mr. Most Honest, exactly these people are the most blemished

(15) DT: s dovolením pane J nebudeme řešit pana Z budeme řešit odpověď
excuse me, Mr. J, we will not deal with Mr. Z, we will deal with

prezidenta republiky panu Z ...
Mr. President's response to Mr. Z

(16) LJ: takový zákon se vztahuje na správní orgány (...)
the legal obligation to respond is relevant for public administration

prezident republiky není správní orgán, amnestie byla vyhlášena prezidentem, on ji podepsal
President of the Czech Republic is not a body of public administration, the amnesty was declared by Mr. President, he has signed it

The dialogue cited above is asymmertical in such a way that in its original media form one of the interlocutors is visible, while the other one is present only through his voice and a small picture in the corner of the screen, even though it is obvious that he is watching the programme (see his comment in (6)). Such partial anonymity of the interviewee can be considered an advantage here since his body language and face expression remain hidden. The anchor opens the interview in a standard way and so does LJ in

(2). Most probably, LJ had been informed about the topic to be discussed in advance but he avoids a relevant reaction – his information in (4) is irrelevant and his description of the required response is inadequate (*vyřizování pošty* – dealing with the mail). When the anchor insists on getting an answer, LJ's reaction (6) evidently intentionally misinterprets his utterance as an inappropriate eagerness. In fact, LJ attacks the anchor's professional competence by judging it as a mere effort to build his image, i.e. he mocks him. In (7), the anchor's response is already impatient; he uses the exclusive 1st person plural form *čekáme* meaning 'I and the viewers,' diváci). Another openly uncooperative turn of LJ (8) provokes the anchor to an unprofessional reaction (he slips off his role, which is obvious in the first part of (9), explicitly rejecting (6)). In (10), LJ again, in place of a required answer, comments on anchor's utterances and only in (12), after a strong reminder that the question had been asked three times, he starts to answer, nevertheless, not directly the question asked in (3). The first part of (12) dehonestates the introductory information, the actual impulse towards the interview (the information about the LZ's speech *slopped* to the presidential team), later on he subjects LZ's speech to severe criticism (it was *rude and indecent*). The only relevant part of his reaction (in his opinion, the President has no legal obligation to inform the public who were the law experts involved in designing the amnesty) is evasive and does not include the required information. Furthermore, the next turn (12) can be described as another sidestep: instead of complementing the primary general answer, LJ attacks LZ and presents several unsubstantiated accusations aimed at him. He even compares him to a defendant in a fraud case of another SD allegedly corrupt politician, i.e. he brings in a piece of information being totally irrelevant at the moment, apparently with an intention to create a defamating parallelism. This approch of his is marked by the use of the inclusive first person plural (*všichni dobře víme* meaning 'we all know well'), which recognizably is meant as a piece of evidence of general consensus embracing the viewers and also the anchor DT. It implies that the pressupposed information included in the extract 'not even you can be naïve to the point that you would believe Mr. Z to be Mr. Honest.' In other words, it is one more step aside serving the purpose of diverting the main line of the discussion. In (13) the anchor tries to bring LJ back to the topic showing the irrelevance of his utterance, but, in turn (14) LJ continues LZ's dehonestation. The rumor (LJ's belief) that Mr. Z may be involved in doings similar to those of the indicted politician, is presented as a generally shared knowledge, i.e. a fact not needing any proof. This way, LJ uses the time space of the interview for dehonestation of third parties and at the same time he tries to justify his own effort to avoid the direct answer. In (15), the anchor states rather firmly that it is necessary to get to the point (here, the inclusive 1st person plural concerns the anchor and Mr. LJ). In (16) which has been abridged here (at the recording, it is almost two minutes long) LJ finally provides the relevant information why the President will not make public the names of councellors and legal experts who participated at the declared version of the amnesty. Thus, the first and only relevant piece of information in the interview could be heard at the point of 5.50 minute (the whole duration of the recording is 10.21). For the rest of the interview, LJ pursues the chosen strategy. He keeps repeating his statement made in (16) in an almost identical form and rejects all the anchor's objections together with his effort to ask some additional questions. During the whole interview LJ, thanks to a presumably pre-planned strategy, wins and holds a dominating, even domineering position for which his inconsiderate, sometimes even unscrupulous communicative behaviour was the main tool. The speech actions he utilizes (usubstantiated statements, defamations) together with his deliberate uncooperativeness (he avoids to answer anchor's questions for five minutes) makes him the winner – he presents the presidential point of view and does not admit any doubt. He does not hesitate to attack both the anchor and other persons (in the interview, the anchor was treated as a part of the 'enemy line') knowing that the anchor, due to his professional ethics, is not in a position to get even with him. His openly aggressive communication is instrumental, purpose-oriented, and, at certain points, is also endowned with traits of hostility – towards his (and the president's) political opponents, or even towards the anchor (turns (4) and (6) are patronizing, almost mocking). On the part of LJ, there is no visible strife for popularity, on the contrary, he seems to enjoy the 'villain' position.

5   Closing Remarks on Verbal Aggressiveness as Speech Action

Although conflicts and controversies in public communication do not take place only in political discusions broadcast by nationwide TV stations, and can certainly be encountered at other shows or other programmes, it seems significant that in the Czech TV shows dealing with political topics, aggressive communicative patterns of behaviour have become almost standard, and the most important instrument how to forward one's atittudes and position. Interlocutors holding different opinions often do not hesitate to call each other liars, accuse each other of criminal activities (most popular allegation being bribery), or even use vulgar language. This kind of verbal aggressiveness appears to be predominantly instrumental because similar dialogues are primarily targeted at the supporters of a particular politician. Performers of such offensive speech actions are persons in a position demanding (at least in their own eyes and in the eyes of their supporters) to show that they are decisive and able to boost up one's position at the expense of their opponent. Evidently, the issue of power becomes dominant in such contexts.

Our brief survey has shown, though, that aggressive communicative behaviour need not use marked vocabulary. What seems to be a stronger weapon in the struggle for dominance is strong-mindedness, a resolution to pursue one's agenda and daring to be persistently uncooperative and indecent and the last one does not necessarily need to be synonymous with being rude or vulgar. In this perspective, aggressivity in speech does not simply mark excessive impoliteness; it is an independent kind of communicative behaviour aiming at winning a prevailing position in a particular constellation of communicative roles.

In the original concept of 'speech acts,' general semantic-pragmatic actions ruled and constituted by general principles, there was hardly any space for a detailed description of inferential processes underlying everyday communication. In the analyses of real communicative interactions the experience has shown that without extensive context and without data defining the communicative situation an adequate interpretation is not possible. In G. Leech's *politeness principle* there is a strong correlation between politeness and indirect speech actions. Similar connection has been proposed in the traditional theory of politeness (Brown & Levinson 1987) – indirectness (off-record strategies) is the most common way of fulfillment of speakers' goals in conversation even though there are types or classes of speech actions that are inherently polite (e.g. offers) and inherently impolite (direct requests or orders). Later studies specifically aimed at impoliteness have shown that a) it can be addressee's interpretation (perlocutionary effect) that assesses an utterance (or an action) as polite or impolite (in certain situation, direct or even rude orders need not be perceived as impolite), and b) it is a constellation of social roles (relational work) among interlocutors that enables some of them to act and communicate in a direct way. In many situations a person in a conventionally superior position feels entitled to pursue one's communicative (interactional) goal directly, which often means that his or her speech can be perceived as impolite or inconsiderate. In this perspective, impolite, rude or even aggressive communicative behaviour is not necessarily linked to any particular class of speech acts or actions; it is rather a type of interaction which allows for communicative behaviour aiming at offending (harming) an interlocutor (cf. aggressive facework as discussed in e.g. Watts 2003, pp. 259–260). In psychology and in sociology the origins of aggression are often sought in the instinctive self-defence (Lorenz 1969, Anderson & Bushman 2002). It means that the triggering mechanism of aggressive communicative behaviour originates in the communicative situation itself. A person communicating aggressively either feels himself or herself in the position of power or wants to prevail over the opponent. Seen in a broader framework of social interaction, aggressive communication occurs in two basic forms: a) as hostile aggression which is impulsive, driven by anger and primarily aiming at offending and harming the target; b) as an instrumental aggression which is premeditated as a means of retaliation or obtaining some goal, mostly to boost up speaker's position. In this view, speech acting hostile aggression is mostly direct; it is openly rude (it aims at harming addressee's self-esteem) and often uses vulgar language as well as marked volume and tone of voice. Instrumental aggression, on the other hand, can involve rudeness (as an instrument to fulfil speaker's goal), too, but more often it is indirect. It makes use of statements or rhetorical questions the real (intended) meaning of which can be interpreted only in a broader context of the communicative event. Especially instrumental aggressive communication can be considered an independent communicative strategy related to the struggle for power. It is based not only on speaker's effort to harm the addressee (or the discussed object) but primarily on the effort to project and boost speaker's position and to secure dominance in the conversation. As a type of speech action, aggressive communicative behaviour can be seen as a blend, an amalgam of direct and indirect communication and, at the same time, as a superstructure built on simultaneous speech acting on several levels.

Bibliography

Anderson, C.A. and B. Bushman (2002). Human Aggression. *Annual Review of Psychology* 53 (1), 27–51.

Austin, J.L. (1962). *How to Do Things with Words*. Oxford: Oxford University Press.

Bousfield, D. (2008). *Impolitenes in Interaction*. Amsterdam/Philadelphia: John Benjamins Publishing.

Brown, P. and S.C. Levinson (1987). *Politeness*. Cambridge: Cambridge University Press.

Corredor, C. (this volume). The dynamics of conversation: fixing the force in irony. A case study. In M. Witek and I. Witczak-Plisiecka (eds.), *Normativity and Variety of Speech Actions*, pp. 140–158. Leiden: Brill (*Poznań Studies in the Philosophy of the Sciences and the Humanities* 112).

Culpeper, J. (1996). Towards an Anatomy of Impoliteness. *Journal of Pragmatics* 25, 349–367.

Culpeper, J. (2011). *Impoliteness*, Cambridge: Cambridge University Press.

Goffman, E. ([1956] 1971). *The Presentation of Self in Everyday Life*. Harmondsworth: Penguin.

Hirschová, M. (2004) Řečový akt, řečové jednání a komunikační funkce výpovědi (Speech act, speech action and communicative function of an utterance). *Slovo a slovesnost* 65 (3), 163–173.

Hirschová, M. (2009). Speech Acts in Slavic Languages. In S. Kemgen, P. Kosta, T. Berger, K. Gutschmidt (eds.), *Die slavischen Sprachen – The Slavic Lnguages 1*, pp. 1055-1-90. Berlin/New York: Walter de Gruyter.

Hirschová, M. (2013) *Pragmatika v češtině*. Praha: Karolinum.

Hirschová, M. and J. Svobodová (2014). *Komunikační strategie v jednom typu mediálního diskursu*. Olomouc: Vydavatelství UP.

Haugh, M. (2015). *Im/Politeness Implicatures*. Berlin/Munich/Boston: DeGruyter Mouton.

Leech, G. (1983). *Principles of Pragmatics*. London: Longman.

Leech, G. (2014). *The Pragmatics of Politeness*. Oxford/New York: Oxford University Press.

Lorenz, K. (1969). *On Aggression*. New York: Harcourt, Brave & World.

Mey, J. (2001). *Pragmatics: An Introduction*. (2nd ed.) Oxford: Blackwell.

Searle, J.R. (1969). *Speech Acts: An Essay in the Philosophy of Language*. Cambridge: Cambridge University Press.

Rosengren, I. (1983). Die Textstruktur als Ergebnis strategischer Überlegungen des Senders. In I. Rosengren (ed.), *Sprache und Pragmatik. Lunder Symposium 1982*, pp. 157–191. Stockholm: Almquist & Wiksel International.

Spencer-Oatey, H. (2005). (Im)Politeness, Face and Perceptions of Rapport. Unpackaging Their Bases and Interrelationships. *Journal of Politeness Research: Language, Behaviour, Culture* 1, 95–119.

Spencer-Oatey, H. (2007). Theories of Identity and the Analysis of Face. *Journal of Pragmatics* 39, 639–665.

Van Dijk, T.A. (1980). *Text and Context*. London: Longman.

Watts, R.J. (2003). *Politeness*. Cambridge: Cambridge University Press.

Witczak-Plisiecka, I. (2013a). Speech action in legal contexts. In M. Sbisà & K. Turner (eds.), *Pragmatics of Speech Actions* [Handbook of pragmatics; Part 2], pp. 613–658. Berlin/Boston: Mouton de Gruyter.

Witczak-Plisiecka, I. (2013b). *From Speech Acts to Speech Actions*. Łódź: Łódź University Press.

Witek, M. (this volume). Coordination and Norms in Illocutionary Interaction. In M. Witek and I. Witczak-Plisiecka (eds.), *Normativity and Variety of Speech Actions*, pp. 66–97. Leiden: Brill (*Poznań Studies in the Philosophy of the Sciences and the Humanities* 112).

CHAPTER 8

A Theory That Beats the Theory?
Lineages, the Growth of Signs, and
Dynamic Legal Interpretation

Marcin Matczak

Abstract

Legal philosophers distinguish between a static and a dynamic interpretation of law. The former assumes that the meaning of the words used in a legal text is set at the moment of its enactment and does not change with time. The latter allows the interpreters to update the meaning and apply a contemporary understanding to the text. The philosophy of language seems to provide greater support to the static approach to legal interpretation. Within this approach, represented by the theory of legal interpretation called 'originalism', interpretation is a quest for the speaker/lawmaker's intention or the public meaning that prevailed at the time of enactment. Neither the intention nor the public meaning are considered to have changed over time. In this paper I argue that the philosophy of language provides the dynamic approach with an equally robust support as it does the static one. This support comes from an externalist perspective in semantics, rooted in philosophical pragmatism and supported by Ruth Millikan's concept of meaning as proper function and a Peircean idea of semeiosis. Grounding the dynamic approach in a well-founded linguistic philosophy rises to the challenge presented by the originalists' declaration that 'it takes a theory to beat a theory'.

1   Introduction

Who decides on the meaning of legal text?[1,2] The traditional approach in jurisprudence endows the lawmaker with this privilege. The theoretical basis for this approach is intentionalism: the intention of the speaker gives the meaning

---

1   The author would like to thank all who kindly provided their comments to the earlier drafts of this paper, in particular all the commentators taking part in the discussion session organized at academia.edu, the participants to the legal philosophy seminar at the Warsaw University, two anonymous reviewers and Maciej Witek.
2   The kind of meaning this paper is dedicated to is *linguistic* meaning (communicative content), not *legal* meaning. The significance of this distinction is rightly underlined by Solum

to their words; without intention there is no meaning (Fish 2008). Even those who criticize the intentionalist approach locate the source of a text's meaning at the moment when it was created. For instance, the versions of originalism based on the original public meaning claim the meaning of a legal text is defined by the linguistic conventions prevailing at the time of its enactment.[3]

Any proposals to treat subsequent linguistic practice as having any decisive influence on the meaning of the legal text are considered suspect for at least two reasons. First, such proposals seem to lack support from the philosophy of language and as such are theoretically weak. An expression of these suspicions is the originalists' bon-mot 'it takes a theory to beat a theory'.[4] Second, admitting that the meaning of the legal text changes over time is felt to undermine the stability of the law, increase the interpreters' discretionary powers or even lead to judicial lawmaking. The corollary is a perceived threat to the rule of law by the rule of men.

In this paper I provide a counter-argument to these reservations and a theoretical basis for the claim that linguistic practice subsequent to a legal text's enactment can and should influence its meaning. First, I prove that there exists a convincing linguistic theory which explains how the meaning of the language evolves over time. Secondly, I argue that the evolution of meaning is entirely independent from any individual language user. This evolution is a traceable, relatively transparent and verifiable process: the individual interpreter's discretionary authority over meaning is thus strictly curtailed.

In the first part of this paper I briefly present the current debate on optimal approach to interpreting legal texts, focusing on the dispute between static and dynamic theories of interpretation. Originalism and living constitutionalism respectively represent each theory. I go on to examine theoretical and philosophical backgrounds for static and dynamic theories, showing how opposite semantic frameworks justify opposing approaches: internalism for static theories and externalism for dynamic ones. I conclude that the philosophical justification for semantic externalism, supported by the framework build around a Peircean idea of semeiosis, is robust enough to provide a theory that can beat the theory.

(2015, p. 2). Therefore, the paper does not deal with the accounts of legal meaning, e.g. as those proposed by the argumentative theories of legal interpretation. The author is grateful to an anonymous reviewer for indicating this distinction.

3   See Solum 2008.

4   As Scalia (1989) puts it, '[a]part from the frailty of its theoretical underpinning, nonoriginalism confronts a practical difficulty reminiscent of the truism of elective politics that 'You can't beat somebody with nobody'. It is not enough to demonstrate that the other fellow's candidate (originalism) is no good; one must also agree upon another candidate to replace him'. (Scalia 1989, p. 855)

2   Static and Dynamic Legal Interpretation –
         Two Approaches in Legal Philosophy

Lay people may perceive legal interpretation as an automatic, algorithmic process that is carried out in a similar way by all judges and lawyers, no matter
where or when it takes place. In fact, lawyers disagree profoundly as to the
optimal way legal texts should be interpreted and propose entirely different
interpretive strategies. A key dispute is whether legal text can change its meaning over time, and two competing theories propose opposing answers. Static
theories hold that the meaning of a legal text is set at the moment of the text's
enactment and does not change subsequently. Accordingly, the only way to
change the meaning of the text is to amend the text itself. By contrast, dynamic
theories hold that the meaning of the legal text can evolve over time. Consequently, lawyers are entitled to update the meaning of the legal text according
to the linguistic conventions prevailing at the moment of its interpretation.

    The resolution of the dispute between the static and the dynamic theories
has significant practical ramifications. Legal texts provide patterns of behavior for individuals and corporations, and refusal to follow those patterns may
result in serious sanctions. The patterns are encoded in the text and decoded
through legal interpretation. Consequently, the way the interpretation is carried out has a crucial impact on the final shape of the encoded patterns. The
8th amendment to the US Constitution provides a clear exemplification of this
relationship.[5] The linguistic content of the crucial phrase 'cruel and unusual
punishment ...' depends on the interpretative approach one takes. A static approach will result in endowing the term with the meaning prevailing at the end
of the 18th Century. A dynamic approach will lead to interpreting the phrase
in accordance with the most contemporary understanding of what is cruel.[6]

    A prominent example of a static theory of legal interpretation is originalism,
a theory of constitutional interpretation especially popular in the US. This theory comes in two versions: the originalism of original intentions and the originalism of original public meaning (Calabresi 2007, p. 154). The first presents
'the view that the original intentions of the Framers should guide constitutional interpretation'. (Solum 2011, p. 8). The second argues that 'constitutional

---

5   'Excessive bail shall not be required, nor excessive fines imposed, nor cruel and unusual pun-
    ishments inflicted'.
6   Again, we are talking here about the linguistic meaning of 'cruel', not the legal one (Solum
    2015, p. 2). The originalist theory is capable of justifying a change in the legal meaning of cru-
    elty, while at the same time maintaining that the linguistic meaning of that phrase as used in
    the US Constitution has not changed.

law includes rules with content that are fixed by the original public meaning of the text – the conventional semantic meaning of the words and phrases in context'. (Solum 2008, p. 2)

A crucial semantic thesis defended by originalists of all stripes is the so-called fixation thesis. As Solum claims 'almost all originalists agree, explicitly or implicitly, that the meaning (or 'semantic content') of a given Constitutional provision was fixed at the time the provision was framed and ratified. We can call this idea the fixation thesis'. (Solum 2008, p. 2)

Dynamic theories of legal interpretation can be exemplified by the theory presented by Eskridge (1987) and a group of theories collectively known as 'living constitutionalism' (Strauss 2010). Contrary to originalists, dynamic theories assumed that interpreters should update the meaning of the legal text, adjusting it to the linguistic conventions prevailing at the moment of interpretation, rather than to those that were in force at the moment of the text's enactment. Eskridge distinguishes between three perspectives in legal interpretation. The first, a *textual perspective*, is taken by an interpreter who focuses on the text as a formal factor limiting the number of available interpretive options. The second, a *historical perspective*, primarily takes into consideration the expectations of the historical lawgiver. The third, *an evolutive perspective*, allows the interpreter to account for the change in the context in which legal text operates, in particular change in the social and legal environment since its enactment. The main thesis of Eskridge's work is that the evolutive perspective should prevail over the textual and historical ones (Eskridge 1987, p. 1484).

The proposal to substitute the textual perspective with the evolutive one is a weakness of Eskridge's theory in particular, and traditional dynamic theories in general, because it is based on a false dichotomy. In this paper I demonstrate that the textual perspective in fact encompasses the evolutive one. A different theory of language than that assumed by the static theories of interpretation is required to show how the meaning of legal texts evolve. To this end, in the next section I first outline the theory of language assumed under the static approach and then compare it with one that can support the dynamic approach.

3   Static Theories of Interpretation and the Philosophy of Language

Originalism, the paragon of static theory, comes in two forms: the originalism of original intentions[7] and the originalism of original public meaning. Let us

---

7   The originalists do not define the nature of the 'original intentions' in precise terms. In particular, it is not clear whether those intentions are locutionary or illocutionary in nature,

evaluate the respective philosophical justifications of these two forms, extract their essence, and present an alternative theoretical framework – one within which the dynamic theory of interpretation appears equally viable.

3.1   *Originalism of Original Intentions – a Theoretical Background*
The intention-based static theories of legal interpretation can be justified by a group of linguistic and philosophical theories called 'semantic internalism'. These theories hold that internal mental processes, in particular a speaker's intention, are the crucial factors influencing meaning. According to Barwise and Perry, those theories

> stress the power of language to classify minds, the mental significance of language, and treat the classification of events as derivative. Thus John Locke held that words, in their primary signification, stand for ideas. They stand for objects in the world derivatively, since the ideas stand for those objects. (Barwise and Perry 1983, pp. 3–4)

According to this approach, the meaning of an utterance is constituted by the state of mind of a speaker (writer). As such, meaning happens inside the speakers' heads, and words and sentences reflect the ideas in their minds, not the external world.

Below I take issue with the main assumption of the intention-based originalism, namely that historical intention is a primary factor constituting the meaning of a legal text. To this end I apply the theory of meaning called 'semantic externalism', in particular Ruth. G. Millikan's concept of lineages and her theory of meaning as proper function (Millikan 1984; 2005). My aim is to prove that the meaning of a legal text is the product of an evolution that starts before the moment of the enactment of the legal text and does not end at that point. Individual intentions of speakers do not play a crucial role in this process.

3.2   *Originalism of Original Intentions – an Alternative Framework*
Semantic internalism does not enjoy a monopoly over the philosophy of language. One can describe an alternative approach thus:

> A second approach is to focus on the external significance of language, on its connection with the described world rather than the describing

---

nor if they are prospective, communicative Gricean intentions or rather basic, retrospective intention which indicate the convention a speaker wants to deploy in his or her communication. The lack of clarity brings about several misunderstandings in the theoretical discussion on the originalists' theses.

mind. Sentences are classified not by the ideas they express, but how they describe things to be. (Barwise and Perry 1983, p. 4)

A useful umbrella term for a group of theories that oppose semantic internalism is semantic externalism. Those theories can be generally described by Putnam's famous phrase 'Meaning just ain't in the head' (Putnam 1975). The idea that meaning resides outside the mind, in the relations in the external world has been also proposed by Barwise and Perry:

> Meaning's natural home is the world, for meaning arises out of the regular relations that hold among situations – bits of reality. (Barwise and Perry 1983, p. 16)

and D. Brink:

> Language users interact with their natural and social environment in certain ways; in particular they introduce terms (e.g. names and general terms) to pick out interesting features of their environment. (Brink 1989, p. 182)

Semantic externalism advocates the idea of meaning autonomous of individual users of a language, be they speaker or recipient. Meaning evolves in the process of repeatable co-occurrence of words (sentences) and states of affairs. A name co-occurs with a person, a noun co-occurs with a thing, a predicate co-occurs with a given attribute. The co-occurrence can be physical (words and things or qualities are present at the same time and place), or of a historical-causal nature (as in Kripke-Putnam semantics, in which our current reference extends back to the first use of the word). As a result of this co-occurrence, historical chains of usages come into existence – Millikan calls them 'lineages'.[8] In this conception, linguistic signs behave similarly to natural signs – they co-occur with states of affairs in the world, like smoke co-occurs with fire and dark clouds with rain. Unlike natural signs, linguistic signs are produced by individuals, not by the laws of nature; however, they operate in a way similar to natural signs.

---

8 'The phenomenon of public language emerges, I believe, not as a set of abstract objects, but as a real sort of stuff in the real world, neither abstract nor arbitrarily constructed by the theorist. It consists of actual utterances and scripts, forming crisscrossing lineages'. (Millikan 2005, p. 38)

A lineage starts the moment a word is used in a particular way for the first time. This moment is called 'the original baptism' or 'the naming ceremony'. (Kripke 1980) At this moment, the speaker for the first time points out to a particular element of reality (a state of affairs, a quality) and uses the word to refer to this element of reality. Subsequent usages of this word are anchored in this first moment. The users of language borrow the reference from the previous uses of the language. By doing so, the users take part in the chain of usages and thereby in the tradition of this word's use.[9]

At the naming ceremony and at each subsequent instance of a word's use, a co-occurrence takes place between an utterance of the word and the state of affairs in which a designate of this word is instantiated. The chain of co-occurrences (a lineage) leads a so- called 'stabilizing function' of signs to emerge (Millikan 1984). The stabilizing function means that irrespective of a particular user's intention, a word refers to a state of affairs to which it referred in the past.[10] What defines the reference is the link between the word and the state of affairs typical to it; the link has been constituted by a critical mass of cases in which users referred by this word to that state of affairs. In this way a public language emerges, consisting of the history of usages and a relatively stable semantic link between the words and reality that constitutes meaning. Individual intentions are far from central to this process.

The vision of language proposed by Millikan is based on the assumption that linguistic signs sufficiently often refer to states of affairs, understood as certain configurations of elements of reality. This systematic link between a sign and a reality has been recognized by the members of a linguistic community because they benefited from doing so.[11]

---

9   The concept of lineages is a more widely applicable version of M. Devitt's concept of multiple groundings. As Rauti points out: 'Since at least Gareth Evans' work, proponents of anti-descriptivism have been aware of the need to account for the phenomenon of reference change. Some attempts to do so have emphasised the fact that the link between singular terms and their referents is not fixed once and for all. The link is rather established and re-established, reinforced in certain ways and weakened in other ways. Michael Devitt has introduced the apt expression 'multiple grounding' and claimed that proper names and natural kind terms are multiply grounded. Hilary Putnam has endorsed the idea: '(As Devitt rightly observes, [natural kind terms] are typically 'multiply grounded')'. (Rauti 2012, p. 1)

10   See Witek this volume who elaborates on the co-ordinative function of language conventions in Millikan.

11   Millikan indicates that within her theory at least two interlinked aspects of meaning can be identified: meaning as a semantic mapping function (a relation between a sign and a state of affairs it refers to) and meaning as a stabilizing function (an impact the sign has on the audience). The emergence of the semantic mapping function is a pre-requisite for the emergence of the stabilizing function: the sign must sufficiently often map on reality

Millikan (1984) provides a good illustration of that benefit in the communication between beavers. In case of danger, those creatures splash water with their tails as a sign of warning. Millikan explains that in the evolutionary history of beavers the signal of splashing sufficiently often correlated with a state of affairs that involved danger (e.g. the approach of a predator) to produce a habitual reaction to that signal. Beavers learned to recognize the signal of splashing because they benefited from such recognition. This kind of benefit is referred to as 'survival value' by Millikan (1984): recognizing the sign makes one better-off than failing to recognize the sign. The beavers who failed to recognize the sign for approaching danger probably also failed to survive, and whatever individual meaning they assigned to tail-splashing disappeared with them.

Human language is a complex system of signs that as a whole helped *homo sapiens* to survive and to dominate the globe. However, a particular sign – a word or a phrase – does not need to increase our survival chance directly, but simply to be useful for some purpose: very often as an element of a bigger structure of signs. In this sense both the word 'danger' and the connector 'and' have a survival value. 'Danger' has a survival value for humans, similar to that of the beavers' splashing, but 'and' is almost equally useful as a sign that indicates an important relation of conjunction between two things. In a similar vein, cardinal numbers, punctuation marks and intonations have survival value. They all are copied by the members of a linguistic community because they work: they help their users in achieving their vital purposes and so are reproduced, creating a historical chain of usages.[12] Those chains are sets of tokens of a particular sign, used many times for a similar purpose. This purpose or the reason why a sign is useful and is reproduced is this sign's 'proper function':[13] the function

---

for its use to have an impact on the audience. On those two aspects of meaning see Millikan 2005, pp. 53–76.

12 See Sbisà this volume, p. 44 and her remarks on the precedential nature of conventions in Millikan.

13 This is how Millikan defines the proper function: 'Where m is a member of a reproductively established family R and R has the reproductively established or Normal character C, m has the function F as a direct proper function iff: (1) Certain ancestors of m performed F. (2) In part because there existed a direct causal connection between having the character C and performance of the function F in the case of these ancestors of m, C correlated positively with F over a certain set of items S which included these ancestors and other things not having C. (3) One among the legitimate explanations that can be given of the fact that m exists makes reference to the fact that C correlated positively with F over S, either directly causing reproduction of m or explaining why R was proliferated and hence why m exists'. (Millikan 1984, p. 28)

the sign performs in a particular linguistic community. In the pragmatic framework, the proper function equates with the meaning of the sign.

To take a more abstract example of the survival value and proper function,
one which is closer related to the real world of constitutional interpretation,
let us analyse Richard Bernstein's (2010, p. 159) exemplification of the predicate 'is cruel'. One cannot properly apply this phrase, for example, to a state
of affairs in which a woman helps a blind man to cross the road. This results
from the lineage of the predicate 'is cruel' containing states of affairs whose
characteristics are very different from those in which one person helps another: 'is cruel' refers to states of affairs where the suffering of one person
is caused by another person. Since that feature is not present in the case of
woman helping the blind man, it is not possible to use the predicate 'is cruel' with reference to that case. To put it another way, if applied to a helpful
gesture, the predicate 'is cruel' will not perform its proper function in relation to the state of affairs at hand, and will thereby threaten the stability of
the use of that predicate. The lesson from this and similar examples is that
meaning is a product of relations in the world, not the relations within someone's mind: through a process of use, recognition and re-use, some relations
become semantic relations, and others not. Those semantic relations in turn
cause the stabilizing function to emerge: because a sign sufficiently often
refers to a particular state of affairs, the use of that sign is recognized as signaling that a particular state of affairs occurs, and a proper reaction to that
state of affairs is performed by the hearers.

In terms of an interpreter's work, to determine the meaning of a sign is not
to determine the intention of an individual user, but rather to determine the
sign's proper function. The meaning does not depend on an individual user's
intention or their states of mind, but is created by a long-lasting practice of a
community that keeps reproducing the signs in order to influence their environment. As a consequence, the meaning becomes not only autonomous from
individual intention, but sometimes even conflicts with it. Getting back to
the example of beavers, an individual beaver could on some occasions splash
water with its tail with an intention to express joy. Nevertheless, the sign the
joyful creature would produce by doing so would cause other beavers to flee.
The reason for the discrepancy between the beaver's intention and its fellow
beavers' interpretation would be the historically shaped proper function of the
sign which is to warn against an imminent danger.[14]

---

14   Naturally, if a sign is sufficiently enough used not in line with its proper function, this
        function can be changed or the sign can lose it completely. Millikan indicates that for
        a proper function to emerge and last, a critical mass of cases in which this particular

The proper function of linguistic instruments (words, sentences, punctuation marks, voice intonations etc.) constitutes what we call public language. To be stable enough to allow co-ordination of behaviors among members of a community, this language must be to some extent independent from the intention of an individual user. If the meaning of public language depended on an *ad hoc* intention of a particular user, it would differ significantly from instance to instance. Were this the case, we would find ourselves in the position of Humpty-Dumpty,[15] and not only we but also the stability of our linguistic practice would risk a great fall.

To conclude, we have seen why the lawmaker's intention is not crucial for setting the meaning: because no individual user's intention can define the meaning of public language. As Millikan shows, a chain of using the linguistic instruments in a public language has to be in place before the lawmaker's first use. Otherwise, the lawmaker's words and sentences cannot have a proper function, as no such function could have developed. Without a proper function there is no public language, and consequently no public meaning. If the sounds or marks used by the lawmaker are produced for the first time in history, they would come across as gibberish. On the other hand, if there is a history of using the words and sentences before they become elements of a legal text, the meaning of those words and sentences is defined by this history, not by the intention of the lawmaker.

3.3 Originalism of Original Public Meaning – a Theoretical Background

A linguistic justification for the second form of originalism, that of original public meaning, is based more on conventions than intentions. This newer version of originalism is a response to the argument that the intention-based approach is non-viable, not least because of the impossibility of identifying and aggregating the legislators' intentions (Ekins 2013). To meet this challenge, the focus of originalists has shifted from original intentions to original public meaning. The essence of this type of originalism is nicely presented by Solum:

> [I]magine that you are reading a text written quite some time ago – a letter written in the thirteenth century, for example. If you want to know what the letter means (or more precisely, what it communicates), you will need to know what the words and phrases used in the letter meant at the

---

function is performed must take place. If signalling joy is a function of tail-splashing in a sufficient number of cases, it can become the sign's new proper function.

15 'When I use a word (…) it means what I choose it to mean – neither more nor less'. (Carroll 1872)

time the letter was written. Some words may be archaic – no longer used
in contemporary English. Other words may have changed their meaning
over time – and you would want to know what their meaning was in the
thirteenth century. (...) All of this seems uncontroversial when the text
we are interpreting is a letter. It is hard to imagine someone saying that
we should use twenty-first century linguistic practices to understand a
thirteenth-century text. And it would be very odd indeed for someone to
suggest that we could better understand the letter if we were to disregard
the thirteenth-century context in which it was written and instead imagine that the letter had been written today under different circumstances.
Ignoring the time and place at which the letter was written would seem
like a strategy for misunderstanding! (Solum 2015, p. 2)

Such a simple and powerful approach to communication *via* legal texts poses
a difficulty for a critic, as it seems to require them to take a less straightforward
one. The 13th century letter argument is so obvious it seems irrefutable, except
by some convoluted approach. But let us take that road less travelled and see if
there is a viable and non-circuitous alternative to Solum's argument.

3.4   *Originalism of Original Public Meaning – an Alternative Framework*
When evaluating the intention-based originalism, I argued against its main
thesis and showed that it is not the historical intention that constitutes meaning. Similarly, in the case of convention-based originalism I will argue that the
historical convention does not set the meaning of the legal text. The father
of semantic externalism, Charles S. Peirce, has provided the tool to prove this
thesis, namely his theory of 'the growth of signs'. Let me first outline the theory
and then indicate how it justifies my thesis.
     According to Peirce, signs operate not as two-element entities (consisting of
sign and object), but as three-element entities, the third element of which he
calls an 'interpretant:'

I define a sign as anything which is so determined by something else,
called its Object, and so determines an effect upon a person, which effect
I call its interpretant, that the latter is thereby mediately determined by
the former. (Peirce 1998, p. 478).

In the broadest terms, the interpretant is the way the relationship between the
sign and the object is recognized by the interpreter. There are at least a two
types of interpretants – a dynamical interpretant and the final interpretant.
The dynamical interpretant is the way the relationship between the sign and

the object is perceived at a particular moment in time.[16] The 'final interpretant' according to Peirce, is the way a sign-object relationship is understood 'at the end of the inquiry'.[17]

The inquiry Peirce refers to is a process of 'semeiosis': a long-lasting effort of the linguistic community to define and understand the true meaning of the signs this community uses. This process encompasses defining the signs by using other signs to make them clearer and better understood (when we explain the meaning of lesser known words by providing definitions), as well as translating signs into action, e.g. when we use signs as instructions. The process of semeiosis is possible thanks to the ongoing and unceasing nature of linguistic practice. Both the translation of signs into signs, and the translation of signs into actions are performed by using the signs in real life situations.

The process of translating signs into signs must be closed at some point. This point is called the 'final interpretant', and can be simultaneously understood in two ways. One way is as the final translation of the sign into the action we undertake with regard to reality (a result of interpreting the sign). For example, when one is given an order, one can translate the words used in the order into simpler terms to understand the order in an optimal way, but finally the order must be translated into a particular action – that which was ordered.

The other way of understanding the final interpretant consists of the way the community interprets the sign at the end of the process of semeiosis, understood here as a social process of gathering knowledge on the object of the sign and the relation of that object to the sign:

> the Final Interpretant is the one Interpretative result to which every Interpreter is destined to come if the Sign is sufficiently considered ... The Final Interpretant is that toward which the actual tends. (Short 2007, p. 190)

In other words, translating signs into other signs and translating signs into action increase the social knowledge about the signs' real meaning. Thanks to

---

16 Short (2007, p. 188), quoting Peirce from his letter to Lady Welby: 'The Dynamical Interpretant is a single actual event. (...) My Dynamical Interpretant is that which is experienced in each act of Interpretation and is different in each from that of any other'.

17 Short (2007, p. 190): 'The picture evoked is that of scientific inquiry, conceived by Peirce as an indefinitely prolonged 'fixation of belief' carried out by an indefinitely extended community of inquirers, all of whom have the same ultimate purpose. (...) interpretants, including final interpretants, may be actions, feelings, or habits, as well as representations'.

this, as Peirce puts it, the signs 'grow' (see Nöth 2014); this growth is a form of evolution that changes the meaning of those signs:

> I believe in mooring our words by certain applications and letting them change their meaning as our conceptions of the things to which we have applied them progress.[18]

and

> Every symbol is a living thing, in a very strict sense that is no mere figure of speech. The body of the symbol changes slowly, but its meaning inevitably grows, incorporates new elements and throws off old ones. (CP 2.222, 1903)

In Nöth's interpretation of Peirce:
a)   Signs grow with the increase of knowledge or amount of information that they have accumulated in the course of time. This knowledge grows in parallel with the growth of science: 'The woof and warp of all thought and all research is symbols, and the life of thought and science is the life inherent in symbols' (Nöth 2014, p. 178, references in the original omitted).
b)   Knowledge grows through interpretation, or as Peirce puts it: 'in their interpretants, signs grow in information'. Knowledge is produced in a process in which a sign is interpreted in the form of a new and more informative sign, the latter being the interpretant of the former (Nöth 2010, p. 179, references in the original omitted).
c)   Signs grow through both the addition and the subtraction of characteristics attributed; by doing so, signs made progress in their fitness to represent the object of the sign (Nöth 2014, p. 179).

A revealing example of sign growth provided by Nöth is the history of the word 'electricity'. It started its life as a vague notion which covered some processes

---

18   Short (2007, p. 287), quoting Peirce's statement dated 1861. As Short comments in another place: 'This presupposes that a term's reference can be fixed independently, or to some degree independently, of its meaning, which is assumed in this passage to be conceptual. That overturns the familiar view that a term's reference is determined by its meaning, that is, that it refers to that of which a concept is true. The same passage entails that the meaning of a term will change or can be changed with the growth of our knowledge of the world. And that undercuts definitions of philosophy as 'conceptual analysis', that is, as usefully employed in explicating received meanings. The point is not to understand our meanings but to change them'. (Short 2007, p. 264)

not fully understood by scientists. With time, the knowledge on what electricity is has grown. An important factor in this process was the scientific practice which consists in applying the word 'electricity' to natural world phenomena and finding out what the real nature of those phenomena is.

Peirce bases the concept of the growth of signs on two ideas: 'indexical signification' and 'hypostatic abstraction'.[19] The former is derived from the difference between 'index' and 'icon' as aspects of a sign. In general terms, an index is an aspect of sign that points to a feature or a phenomenon, and an icon is an aspect of a sign that represents that feature or phenomenon. The index is deprived of any content, it only indicates. The icon reflects the nature of the thing indicated. People frequently use indexes when not sure about the real nature of the thing they indicate. Indexes are particularly useful in a process Peirce calls 'hypostatic abstraction' (Short 2007, pp. 267–268). Having experienced a series of similar states of affairs, we abstract a feature that is common to those states of affairs and give it a name. This name is a sign and it is mainly an index, as our knowledge of the feature is limited. This hypostatic abstraction is a working hypothesis that gets tested in subsequently experienced states of affairs. If the ability to indicate the feature in subsequent states of affairs proves useful for practical reasons, the sign is reused and copied by others. If not, the sign is abandoned. The only way to understand the real value of a sign is to put it into practice and observe how it works. The crucial element of the Peircean theory of signs is practice: signs are constantly being used in permanent semeiosis, in order to confirm the usefulness of the hypostatic abstraction that had been made.

Let us move now from the linguistic background to the legal context. In what follows I assume that legal terms are subject to permanent semeiosis both at the individual and social level and that they very often work as indexes, not icons in the process of hypostatic abstraction. That legal terms are subject to semeiosis means that they are permanently being translated into each other in the legal practice that encompasses both legal academia and judicial review. Moreover, in the work of courts the signs are translated into actions, i.e. the signs are applied to reality, to the facts of the case and ultimately this

19   Short (2007, pp. 264–265), describing two elements of Peirce's doctrine of signs' growth: 'One was the idea of indexical signification, as depending on causal or other existential relations rather than on thought or general precepts or habits of interpretation. Only so could the reference of a term be fixed independently, to a degree, of what it means. Another was the idea of hypostatic abstraction. By hypostatic abstraction, an entity can be introduced into discourse independently of direct characterization of it. Only so could we have some idea of what we are referring to, independently of knowing what it is'.

application influences people's behavior: they pay fines, go to prison or simply stop doing illegal things. That legal terms work as indexes can be seen in their indicating a feature or phenomenon without defining it fully, perhaps because such a complete definition is not possible at the moment of indication.

The term 'cruel punishment' can serve as an example of both a subject of permanent semeiosis and an indexical signification. At some time it may prove useful to create the sign 'cruel punishment' that indicates, let us say, 'that which causes suffering and is deliberately imposed by another human being. The content of the 'that' element (an index) is then discovered in a public effort of semeiosis, or, as Putnam put it, the social division of linguistic labor (Putnam 1975). The way the sign 'cruel punishment' was understood at the moment of its first use in the legal text is, in Peircean terms, a dynamical interpretant of this sign. Thus, the original public meaning the originalists prioritize is only a stage in the process of semeiosis that aims at reaching the final interpretant: the full understanding of the sign's meaning, i.e. the full understanding of what is 'cruel'. Under the spotlight of externalist semantics, the original public understanding of the term 'cruel' used by the lawmaker (a dynamical interpretant from the time of the text's enactment) loses its significance. However surprising it may sound, within the presented theoretical framework, the lawmaker's use of the term 'cruel' is one of many uses of this sign, and does not constitute a significant factor in defining its meaning.

Extrapolating from Peirce, legal interpretation should take into consideration the linguistic practice subsequent to the enactment within both the legal and general discourse, because alongside this practice our knowledge of real content of signs grow. Thus, the way we interpret the signs constituting the legal text today is more important that the way they were understood at the moment of the text's enactment. To be sure, our understanding is another dynamical interpretant, not the final one. But our linguistic practice is more developed and richer, because the number of usages of the interpreted word is bigger – it has grown from the moment of the text's enactment. The longer the chain of usages is, the better we understand the real value and the real function of a particular sign. With every instance of linguistic practice involving the sign we proceed further in the process of semeiosis, and we are closer to the final interpretant. Ultimately, when applying legal terms to the contemporary world, we endow them with the best meaning we have arrived at in the process of semeiosis – the meaning developed in the legal and linguistic practice of our community. As with the term 'electricity', our moral and legal terms (like 'cruelty') gain content by the permanent process of applying them to our reality and accumulating knowledge on the true nature of this reality. For instance, psychological research on the sources of suffering may provide new knowledge on what is cruel, and linguistic practice may as a consequence start applying the word 'cruel' in new areas.

4   Interpreting Legal Text Dynamically

Apart from exceptional situations in which a lawmaker coins a new word,[20] naming ceremonies for legal terms take place in general language or in specialized, legal language, often long before the lawmaker uses this word. In enacting a new law, the lawmaker includes into the legal language the words that have been used before, with their histories – their lineages.[21] The existing lineages and the proper functions of the words used make language autonomous from the lawmaker.

As the lawmaker uses existing words with their meanings (proper functions) already in place, he or she is dependent on the previous usages. The semantic situation of the lawmaker makes her equal to other users of language as far as the power to influence public meaning is concerned. In this regard, the lawmaker's situation does not differ much from that of the interpreter. Neither of them can impact the meaning of particular words by his or her individual understanding.[22] In order to make the lawmaker's use a crucial factor in defining the meaning, there must be something special in this use: it must be in some sense a milestone use which changes the way the public language is used. In the historical chain of usages, such milestone moments do not happen often, if at all. Like in the general theory of evolution, the creation and the evolution of language is a slow, incremental process that produces its outcomes little by little over long periods of time, not by spectacular one-off changes.

Between enactment and interpretation the words of a legal text are used many times and their lineages become much longer. The language is

---

20   On the face of it, some lawmakers' attempts to define legal terms may look like naming ceremonies. In fact, legal definitions very rarely create new terms. In the majority of cases lawgivers make the terms more precise or less vague by defining them. Moreover, in the definitions lawmakers use other terms taken from the public language, rooting them in other lineages. As such, the definitions can be treated as exercises in Peircean semeiosis, translating signs into other signs, rather than as original baptisms.

21   This claim is not so obvious even for the legal philosophers that apply externalist (realist) semantics to legal analyses, e.g. N. Stavropoulos suggests that lawmakers are original reference-fixers, i.e. that they perform a naming ceremony by using legal terms in the legal text (Stavropoulos 1996, p. 46). As indicated above, I find this position misguided.

22   This is not to say that in other aspects they are the same. The lawmaker's crucial advantage over the interpreter is that the former has the sole competence to select the words (signs) constituting legal texts. Those words, and not others, must then be interpreted by the latter.

constantly in operation: court verdicts, opinions presented in legal literature and commentaries are all instances of using the words from the legal text. Legal terms are in permanent circulation and are consistently grounded in preceding uses. Legal interpretation should therefore by necessity involve tracing how a particular term has been used in a particular linguistic community. Even originalists agree that this tracing should refer to the uses that had taken place before the utterance that is interpreted occurred (Solum 2015). If, however, legal text is to impact reality after it has been enacted, the question arises as to why neglect subsequent uses of the interpreted term? Within the theoretical framework supporting the static theories of interpretation this question seems irrational: the only factors that shape the meaning of the text – original intention or original convention – are historically located *before* the moment of enactment or *simultaneously* with it. Within externalist semantics the question is crucial: each subsequent use of the term enables the community to better understand the function of the term, and, by extension, its meaning. If the process of using the terms is the Peircean semeiosis, there is no reason to stop tracing the uses of legal terms at the moment of enactment – the process should be continued till the moment of interpretation, in order to maximize the interpreter's chance for gaining a full understanding of the terms.

But are those subsequent uses really relevant for legal interpretation? Despite all the theories, a particularly stubborn *advocatus diaboli* could still claim that for legal interpretation only one use of language counts: the lawmaker's one. After all, the enactment of a legal text is the lawmaker's utterance and this utterance takes place only once, at a particular point in time.

To rebut this challenge, one needs to dissect the concept of 'utterance'. Does the utterance in writing work in the same way as the utterance in speech? The latter is without doubt a one-off event; sounds of speech do not last sufficiently long to be applied in new contexts. Unlike speech, however, writing makes words long-lasting. A characteristic of written utterances, as opposed to spoken ones, is their capacity for multiple applications: while speech is a one-off exercise, limited to the time and place in which the speaker is located, written utterances are capable of being used in many different contexts (Goody 1986, p. 125). Using writing in law implicates that the practical consequences of legal acts extend beyond the moment of their enactment. Writing is a tool of transportation, making it possible for the tokens of words to appear in future situations and be applied to them.

The static theories of legal interpretation neglect the transportation function of writing and treat legal text as oral utterances: one-off events, located in a particular point in time. In fact, legal text can be treated as multi-utterances, according to the well-recognized adage: 'law is always speaking'.[23] Semantic externalism allows us to treat this adage not just as a metaphor but as a literal statement about the pragmatic function of legal texts: they 'speak' every time they are read. Therefore, their enactment is not the only moment the conventional meaning of their signs should be analyzed. The moment of the interpretation is equally, if not better suited for that purpose.

The always-speaking nature of law can be even better understood by using J.L. Austin's concept of illocutionary uptake (Austin 1975): the conventional effect a speech act causes. In speech, the illocutionary uptake occurs within a context when both speaker and hearer are present, and occurs only once; in writing it is otherwise.[24] The illocutionary acts performed in writing can result in multiple illocutionary uptakes. What is more, illocutionary uptake may occur in other places and in other locations than that in which the author of the act was located. The originalists assume that the illocutionary uptake occurring among the addressees that lived at the time of the enactment is privileged. This assumption is far from obvious once one adapts and applies Austin's theory to written communication. The potential of a written speech act for illocutionary multi-uptake is a strong argument for a non-originalist approach to the concept of 'utterance': one should not treat it as a one-off expression, but as a lasting sign that influences our reality in the long run.

Returning to the interpretation of legal text, its interpreter faces three facts which impact that text's meaning. First, he or she is exposed to a single utterance – one of the many of which this text is capable. Second, the way he or she understands the utterance is a function of the lineage of its terms. Third, that lineage is at a particular stage of its ongoing development on account of the process of semeiosis. All three facts combined provide the interpreter with a justification to endow legal text with a modified linguistic meaning: that prevailing at the moment of interpretation. In Peircean terms, the reader of a legal text forms an interpretant of it in their heads, because the text speaks to him or her in a particular context. The interpretant is constituted by the public meaning of this text resulting from the current (i.e. developed between the

---

23   Goldfarb (2013, p. 71) attributes the origins of the principle to an English barrister, George
      Coode, who in his treatise on legislative drafting dated 1845 recommended the use of the
      present tense in legislation, claiming that 'indicative language describing the case as *now*
      existing, or as having *now* occurred, is consistent with the supposition of *the law being
      always speaking*'.

24   True to its title, the speech act theory has been developed with speech as its main subject
      but is undertheorized as far as written communication is concerned. The speech-based
      version is the one applied by the majority of legal philosophers, including originalists, to
      legal language (Stubbs 1983).

moment of the first use of the interpreted term and the moment of interpretation) proper function of the signs of that text.

The whole enterprise of jurisprudence aims at improving the understanding of law as a set of words that influence the reality we live in. The process of
understanding is structured as Peircean semeiosis. In some aspects it is theoretical: the terms are defined and refined, translated into each other, contra-
dictions are removed and the relations between the concepts crystallize. But
there is a practical aspect to semeiosis, too. The courts apply the words of legal
text to the world: they qualify states of affairs as legal or illegal, find people
guilty or innocent, and authoritatively decide on the scope of statutory terms.
They extend these terms to new phenomena or restrict previous application,
to secure the proper function of those terms. External semantics argues that
both the theoretical and practical aspect of the semeiosis must be taken into
consideration. The fact that the semeiosis continues after the enactment constitutes an argument for dynamic interpretation, not against it. As long as a
legal text has practical significance, its terms should be interpreted according
to the current status of the semeiosis. And the practical significance of the
legal text lasts as long as the text is in force. Indeed, the very idea of 'being in
force' entails the potentiality of causing practical consequences. Following the
pragmatic maxim, those consequences cannot be neglected in the discussion
on the optimal approach to legal interpretation.[25]

The analysis presented above allows us to devise a theory that can potentially compete with the static theories of legal interpretation in general, and with
originalism in particular. Every static approach to legal interpretation anchors
the meaning in the moment of the text's utterance – in the legislative context,
upon its promulgation or ratification. The two versions of static theories within originalism agree that the moment of utterance is of utmost importance
for setting the meaning of the text. In both cases a historical fact is at play – a
fact of intending a particular meaning at a particular moment in time or a
fact of particular meaning being given to the words by a convention existing
at the time of enactment. As we have seen, the externalist semantics, based
on philosophical pragmatism, undermines the claim that either of the above-
presented historical facts are crucial or decisive to the meaning of legal texts.

In light of the above, we can revisit Solum's alluring example of a 13th century letter and reconsider the best way to interpret it. Solum presents this

---

25   The pragmatic maxim has been formulated by Peirce: 'Consider what effects, that might
      conceivably have practical bearings, we conceive the object of our conception to have.
      Then, our conception of these effects is the whole of our conception of the object'. (Peirce
      1878, p. 293)

example to prove that it goes without saying that we should adopt 13th century linguistic conventions to understand a letter from that period, and any other approach will prove useless, in particular interpreting the letter using 21st century linguistic conventions. Solum is fully right, but his example does not demonstrate anything about how we should interpret the law. How so? We interpret the 13th century letter according to 13th century linguistic conventions because the letter refers to the 13th century world. In other words, we interpret the letter in an originalist way, because to all intents and purposes it was read and used in that way. Its function does not exceed the timeframe of the 13th century, no pragmatic consequences of the letter arise after the 13th century. In particular, no human action is guided by the letter after the 13th century.

The legal text functions in a different way. A more appropriate historical metaphor would be to compare its words to marks on a 13th or rather 18th century map that is used today in treasure-hunting. The crucial mark on the map, the 'X' which marks the spot where treasure lies buried has a pragmatic function. That function is its potential to be used for practical purposes, a potential that exceeds the period in which the map was produced; the practical purpose of the map, after all, is to help find the treasure. The way X is understood influences the behavior of contemporary readers, guiding their actions today. In Peircean terms, the final interpretant of the 'X' is still to be found. Unlike the 13th century letter, whose pragmatic consequences (e.g. the actions called for by the letter or the information conveyed within it) are limited to its 13th century addressees, the ultimate pragmatic consequences of the map remain suspended until the treasure is found. To be successful in their treasure-hunting efforts, contemporary map-users have to locate the 'X' in the contemporary environment. This is no easy task as two changes must be considered: in the world and in the knowledge of the world. The mapping relation of 'X' has to be recognized within the current state of affairs. It seems obvious then that one should put the 'X' onto the contemporary map: using the map according to the original knowledge of the world and ignoring or dismissing its relation to the contemporary one will get the contemporary treasure hunter nowhere.

Interpreting legal text is more theoretically akin to reading an old map than an old letter. When reading the old map, the X mark should be extrapolated onto a contemporary map to guide the readers' actions; similarly, the words of the legal text must be put into a contemporary context that includes our existing knowledge of the world.[26]

---

26   In legal studies, the constant flux between the present and the past that constitutes interpretation is tackled by Aharon Barak: 'Although the text was created in the past, the questions to which it responds are in the present. It is a dialogue that has both static and

The difference between the letter and the map can be also explained in terms of J.L. Austin's theory of speech acts, and especially his concept of the perlocutionary act (Austin 1975). Austin's speech acts have three aspects: saying words (locutionary act), causing a conventional effect (illocutionary act) and impacting reality (perlocutionary act). In the case of the 13th century letter, no perlocutionary acts take place beyond the 13th century; in particular, no human action is guided by the letter nowadays. By contrast, the X sign on the map causes perlocutionary effects in the contemporary world: it impacts the behaviour of the people who read the map today and who arrange their actions according to the guidance the map provides.

To conclude, it would seem that the dynamic approach to legal interpretation enjoys at least as strong a theoretical justification in the philosophy of language as the static one. It may not satisfy the demands of the originalists, who insist we treat historical intentions or conventions prevailing in the period in which it is produced as the only linguistically justified sources for interpreting legal text; however, close examination reveals these demands to be somewhat arbitrary.

5   Possible Counter-Arguments to Semantic Externalism

Semantic externalism, which supports the theory outlined above, has been challenged by legal philosophers. Critics claim that it suffers from two fundamental weaknesses which preclude its application to legal language and the law in general. Such claims, though potentially destructive for the theoretical underpinnings of this paper, can be convincingly rebutted.

The first alleged weakness is an inability of semantic externalism to explain how the meaning of non-natural kind words is constituted. According to some authors (Patterson 1989), the externalist (realist) semantics that was originally applied to natural kind terms (gold, water) and proper names is of limited application to other kinds of terms, including legal and moral terms. The reason is that the latter terms refer to a reality that is mind-dependent, and thus subjectively projected by a language user. As such, this reality lacks a tangibility which the natural kinds possess.

---

dynamic aspects. Sometimes, a text carries meanings that its author did not anticipate and of which he or she was not aware. The dialogue between the text and the interpreter is never-ending [...] The text does not speak for itself. It responds to the questions that the interpreter asks of it. Such questions are external to the text. They are products of the present, and they are linked to our ability to understand the text in the present, against the backdrop of the past'. (Barak 2005, pp. 57–58)

A convincing rebuttal of the above-outlined criticism has already been presented. Firstly, even the original versions of the externalist semantics analysed examples of non-natural kinds (e.g. artefacts like pencils – Putnam 1975), and the application of the externalist semantics to legal and moral terms has been successfully demonstrated ever since (Burge 1979, Stavropoulos 1996). Secondly, a convincing refutation of the 'mind-dependence assault' has been offered by some authors, especially D. Brink (1989). Brink's counter-arguments have not been effectively rebutted by his critics, and run along the following lines. Legal and social kinds can be explained in terms of laws and generalisations, exactly as can chemical or biological kinds. As such, legal and social kinds are institutions that are:

> independent of particular people's conception of those institutions, practices and relations in the following senses: (i) those social phenomena are the objects of people's conceptions and so antedate those conceptions; (ii) people's conceptions about those phenomena can be mistaken about the real nature of the phenomena; (iii) when people's conceptions of those phenomena are correct it is in virtue of correctly describing the nature of those institutions, practices, and relations. (Brink 1989, p. 184)

On this basis, we can see that there is no real obstacle to being a semantic externalist with regard to legal or social kinds.

Another counter-argument to the 'mind-dependence' issue is that the newer versions of externalist semantics (Barwise/Perry, Millikan) are more focused on the function the referenced elements of reality have, not on their nature. Even if the internal structure of natural kinds and legal kinds differ, their function is structurally similar insofar as they cause tangible effects in reality, such as physical changes in the world or changes in human behaviour. Legal terms are capable of forming historical lineages of usage and those lineages are not functionally different from the lineages formed by the natural kind terms. We use the terms to qualify complex bits of reality, we have theories about their functions and we are able to tell whether the use of the non-natural kind terms is correct or not (as in the above-mentioned example of 'cruelty' by Bernstein). Why should we then treat the non-natural kind terms in a different way? Millikan's idea of proper function can be attributed to every linguistic instrument, including abstract and theoretical terms; as such it has a much wider application than the classical Kripke-Putnam semantics that focused on proper names and natural kinds, and to which the standard criticism of semantic externalism referred.

The second alleged weakness of semantic externalism is its perceived inability to take account of the phenomenon of the authority of the lawmaker (Bix

2003). The conviction concerning this alleged weakness results from a simple deduction. Since semantic externalism questions the influence of the author (speaker) on what his utterance means, proposing instead that one should focus on the autonomous meaning of the utterance, the personal authority of the legislator is undermined. As a consequence, the argument goes, semantic externalism undermines the key role of the lawmaker-sovereign as the creator of the law and as the person whose will is the source of normativity. That assertion requires comment.

First, let us make a distinction. The conviction that the essence of the law is normativity is not identical with the assertion that there exists but one possible source of that normativity. Internalist semantics, focused on the author, ascribes the source of meaning to the will of the author, and thereby upholds the traditional concept of normativity arising from the author of a legal text (Bix 2003). Shifting to the position of semantic externalism does not mean, however, that we need resign from normativity as such. Normativity is simply no longer located in the relationship between the lawmaker and the people bound by his or her laws, but rather in the relationship between the people and the text whose authority they recognise. The legal text has a meaning which is autonomous of its users: that meaning results from the history of the linguistic signs of which the text is composed and their proper function, which has been formed in the historical process of the use of those signs. Independently of this, acknowledgement that a given text is a legal text is made by a decision of the lawmaker. The lawmaker chooses a given text as a binding text, and therefore accepts the fact that a certain set of linguistic signs, together with their historical baggage and their function, are to be interpreted by addressees of the law.

The lawmaker does not create the meaning of a legal text but does make a selection of a certain combination of linguistic signs and establishes that combination as an artefact whose meaning is then determined by the interpreters. The solution to the normative problem, then, is to replace normativity stemming from the semantic intentions of the lawmaker with normativity resulting from the fact that a particular legal text, with its meaning formed in a historical process of language use, has been formally chosen by the lawmaker and made law. Such an approach to normativity makes semantic externalism fully applicable to legal language.

6   Conclusion

My central thesis in this paper is that the linguistic meaning of legal texts is continuously shaped in the social dimension, not created by one-off decisions of individual lawmakers. The meaning of the legal text is influenced by legal practice – the doctrinal and the judicial one – and this practice does not end at the moment of the enactment. In other words, 'law in action' influences the meaning of 'law on the books', and the interpreter should take this into consideration when interpreting legal texts. In many cases, such an approach necessitates updating the meaning of the legal text.

Contrary to a common presumption, giving legal texts contemporary meanings does not privilege the interpreter over the lawmaker. The power of these two figures over meanings is similar, in that it is almost non-existent. Rather, the power to establish the meanings of terms in a particular linguistic community lies with historically determined lineages and proper functions of the terms used. A change in meaning cannot be brought about by any one individual; therefore, it does not depend on any one individual's discretionary powers. Such a change is a slow, evolutionary process, based on rational acceptance by a linguistic community. As such, it can provide a basis for a legal interpretation that is relatively stable and controllable. Thus, the classic charges of subjectivity and destabilization raised against the dynamic theory of legal interpretation do not apply to the theory presented here. In fact, such charges were a reflection of the under-theorized nature of previous versions of the dynamic approach, which were supported by utilitarian or moral justifications rather than linguistic ones.

The title of this paper includes a question mark, and with good reason. We have seen that there exists a theoretical position in the philosophy of language that can compete with the theoretical framework for static theories of interpretation, especially originalism. The theory, which is not fully elaborated here due to the constraints of space, enjoys a robust support from semantic externalism and Peircean semiotics. A full elaboration of the theory would dispense with the need for the question mark.

Bibliography

Austin, J.L. (1975). *How to do Things with Words*. Oxford: Oxford University Press.

Barak, Aharon (2005) Purposive Interpretation in Law. Princeton and Oxford: Princeton University Press.

Barwise, J. and J. Perry (1983). *Situations and Attitudes*. Cambridge, Mass.: MIT Press.

Bernstein, R. J. (2010). *The Pragmatic Turn*. Cambridge-Malden: Polity.

Bix, B. (2003). Can Theories of Meaning and Reference Solve the Problem of Legal Determinacy? *Ratio Juris* 16 (3), 281–295.

Brink, D. O. (1989). Semantics and Legal Interpretation. Further Thoughts. *Canadian Journal of Law and Jurisprudence* 2 (2), 181–191.

Burge, T. (1979).Individualism and the Mental. *Midwest Studies in Philosophy* 4, 73–122.

Calabresi, S.G. (2007). *Originalism: A Quarter-Century of Debate*. Washington, DC: Regnery Pub.

Carroll, L. (1872). *Through the Looking-Glass*. New York: Dover Publications Inc.

Ekins, R. (2013). *The Nature of Legislative Intent*. Oxford: Oxford University Press.

Eskridge, W. Jr. (1987). Dynamic Statutory Interpretation. *Faculty Scholarship Series* 1505.

Fish, S. (2008). Intention is All There Is: A Critical Analysis of Aharon Barak's Purposive Interpretation in Law. *Cardozo Law Review* 29 (3), 1109–1146.

Goldfarb, N. (2013). 'Always speaking?' Interpreting the present tense in statutes. *Canadian Journal of Linguistics* 58 (1), 63–83.

Goody, J. (1986). *The Logic of Writing and the Organization of Society*. Cambridge: Cambridge University Press.

Kripke, S. (1980). *Naming and Necessity*. Cambridge, Mass.: Harvard University Press.

Millikan, R. (1984). *Language, Thought and Other Biological Categories*. Cambridge, Mass.: MIT Press.

Millikan, R. (2005). *Language: A Biological Model*. Oxford: Oxford University Press.

Nöth, W. (2014). The growth of signs. *Sign Systems Studies* 42 (2/3), 172–192.

Peirce, C. S. (1878). How to Make Our Ideas Clear. *Popular Science Monthly* 12, 286–302.

Peirce, C.S. (1931–36). *The Collected Papers*. Volumes 1–6. Eds. Charles Hartshorne and Paul Weiss. Cambridge Mass.: Harvard University Press.

Peirce, C. S. (1998). *The Essential Peirce*. Volume 2. Bloomington I.N.: Indiana University Press.

Putnam, H. (1975). The Meaning of 'Meaning'. *Minnesota Studies in the Philosophy of Science* 7, 131–193.

Patterson, D. (1989). Realist Semantics and Legal Theory. *Canadian Journal of Law and Jurisprudence* 2 (2), 175–179.

Rauti, A. (2012). Multiple Groundings And Deference. *The Philosophical Quarterly* 62 (246), 317–336.

Sbisà, M. (this volume). Varieties of speech act norms. In. M. Witek and I. Witczak-Plisiecka (eds.), *Normativity and Variety of Speech Actions*, pp. 23–50. Leiden: Brill (*Poznań Studies in the Philosophy of the Sciences and the Humanities* 112).

Scalia, A. (1989). Originalism: The Lesser Evil. *U. Cinn. L. Rev.* 57, 849–865.

Short, T.L. (2007). *Peirce's Theory of Signs*. Cambridge: Cambridge University Press.

Solum, L.B. (2008). Semantic Originalism, *Illinois Public Law Research Paper No. 07-24*.

Solum, L.B. (2011). What is Originalism? The Evolution of Contemporary Originalist Theory, https://papers.ssrn.com/sol3/papers.cfm?abstract_id=1825543 (last accessed: 14 May 2017).

Solum, L.B. (2015). The Fixation Thesis. The Role of Historical Fact in Original Meaning, http://papers.ssrn.com/sol3/papers.cfm?abstract_id=2559701 (last accessed: 12 September 2018).

Stavropoulos, N. (1996). *Objectivity in Law*. Oxford: Clarendon Press.

Strauss, D.A. (2010). *The Living Constitution*. Oxford: Oxford University Press.

Stubbs, M. (1983). Can I Have That in Writing? Some Neglected Topics in Speech Act Theory. *Journal of Pragmatics* 7, 479–494.

Witek, M. (this volume). Coordination and Norms in Illocutionary Interaction. In. M. Witek and I. Witczak-Plisiecka (eds.), *Normativity and Variety of Speech Actions*, pp. 66–97. Leiden: Brill (*Poznań Studies in the Philosophy of the Sciences and the Humanities* 112).

CHAPTER 9

Are Implicative Verbs Presupposition Triggers?

Evidence from Polish

Mateusz Włodarczyk

Abstract

In this paper we present results of the experiment on reinforceability of conversational implicatures and presuppositions. Within–subject analysis of variance (ANOVA) was used for statistical analysis. Four different presupposition triggers were used in the experiment: factive verbs, implicative verbs, change of state verbs and temporal clauses. Mean score of 3,31 on the redundancy scale for sentences with reinforced indirect messages linked with implicative verbs suggest that in contrast to presuppositions carried by other triggers, those indirect messages (or assumptions) can be reinforced without producing a sense of anomalous redundancy. We argue that the results can be explained using the notion of accommodation and that assumptions linked to implicative verbs could be treated as default meanings rather than presuppositions.

1   Introduction: Conversational Implicatures, Presuppositions and Reinforceability

The purpose of the present paper is to reconsider the status of indirect messages communicated with the use of implicative verbs.[1] Traditionally implicative verbs were treated as presupposition triggers (Karttunen 1971; Levinson 1983; van der Sandt 1988) but the experimental results presented in this paper suggest that unlike presuppositions carried by other triggers, assumptions linked to implicative verbs can be reinforced without producing anomalous redundancy (cf. Włodarczyk 2017). We examine the results of the experiment using the notion of accommodation. The structure of this paper is as follows: The first section discusses the phenomena of conversational implicatures

---

1   I am grateful to the journal editors, Iwona Witczak-Plisiecka and Maciej Witek, as well as to the anonymous reviewers for comments that greatly improved the earlier versions of the manuscript.

and presuppositions, and explains the notion of reinforceability used in the experiment. The second section proposes a definition of linguistic redundancy, describes the experimental procedure adopted in the survey and presents the obtained results. The last section discusses the concept of accommodation introduced by Lewis (1979) and considers how it can be used to describe and account for the experimental results. It also sketches the procedure for the follow up study regarding the accommodation of indirect messages communicated by implicative verbs. We then argue that implicative verbs, rather than being treated as presupposition triggers, can be better accounted for in terms of default meaning. It is worth noting that presuppositions and reinforcement can be understood as speech actions—things we do with words—and that the question posed in this paper can be reformulated as: what do we do with implicative verbs?

Let us start by briefly discussing conversational implicatures. They are perhaps the best known pervasive pragmatic phenomena. Conversational implicatures were first described by Paul Grice in *Logic and Conversation* (1975). They occur in situations in which what the speaker means goes beyond what she says. According to Grice, what the speaker says is closely connected to the conventional meaning of the words she uses, whereas what she implicates in saying what she says depends on the context of her utterance. Consider the following conversation between (a) and (b):

(1)

    a. I feel like having a pizza.

    b. There is a restaurant around the corner.

In a common conversation B would not be understood as merely stating the fact that there is a restaurant nearby but also *implicating* that the restaurant is serving a pizza. Grice (1989, p. 31) maintained that what is implicated is calculated from the fact that the speaker is saying what she says and that this inference process is governed by what he called the Cooperative Principle:

> Make your conversational contribution such as is required, at the stage at which it occurs, by the accepted purpose or direction of the talk exchange in which you are engaged (Grice 1989, p. 26).

The Cooperative Principle is mutually known among conversing agents, i.e. in (1) both (a) and (b) are assuming that their interlocutor is following it. This assumption is what enables the hearer to work out conversational implicature. Grice (1989, pp. 26–27) also distinguished four groups of maxims that further specify the rules which are assumed by interlocutors to be followed in conversation, and are crucial for working out implicatures:

(i)   Maxim of Quantity: Make your contribution as informative as is required;
       do not make your contribution more informative than is required;
(ii)   Maxim of Quality: Do not say what you believe to be false; do not say that
       for which you lack adequate evidence;
(iii) Maxim of Relation: Be relevant;
(iv)   Maxim of Manner: Be perspicuous: avoid obscurity of expression; avoid
       ambiguity; be brief; be orderly.

Implicature in (1) can be worked out if we assume that the speaker (b) is conforming to the maxim of relation: that she believes in what has to be assumed
(in this case that the restaurant is serving pizza) in order for her contribution
to be appropriate at this stage of the conversation. The best known characteristics of conversational implicatures are (Levinson 1983):

(i)   Cancelability (or defeasibility): implicatures can be denied in specific
       contexts;
(ii)   Non-detachability: implicatures are connected to the semantic content
       of what is said and not to the lexical items;
(iii) Calculability: the line of reasoning which leads from what is said to what
       is implicated can be shown for every instance of implicature;
(iv)   Non-conventionality: implicatures are not a part of conventional mean-
       ing of linguistic expressions.

Grice's original theory of conversational implicatures was later reinterpreted
and modified by Levinson (2000), Horn (1984; 1989), Gazdar (1979) and other
scholars working within the so-called neo–Gricean tradition. Following Grice,
they claim that the assumption of the speaker's rationality is essential for understanding her implicatures (Lepore and Stone 2015). Unlike Grice, however,
they attempt to account for many pragmatic effects in terms of language rules
and conventions. The most prominent alternative to the neo-Gricean theories
is Sperber and Wilson's (1986) Relevance Theory, which replaces Grice's maxims with the Principle of Maximal Relevance. Sperber and Wilson's theory represents the contextualist orientation in linguistics which allows for pragmatic
modifications of the truth-evaluable level of meaning (Jaszczolt 2010). In this
paper we will use Default Semantics, which is the neo-Gricean, contextualist
and dynamic theory developed by Kasia Jaszczolt (2005; 2010) to explain the
results of the experiment.

1.1   *Presuppositions*
Now let us focus on another kind of linguistic phenomenon: presuppositions.
It is worth noting that in this paper we will use the term 'presupposition' in its
technical sense discussed by Levinson in *Pragmatics* (1983). In other words,
we take presuppositions to be pragmatic assumptions that are connected to

specific linguistic constructions called presupposition triggers and can be de-
tected using specific tests (Levinson 1983). The phenomenon of presupposition
was first recognized by Gottlob Frege, who considered the following sentence:

(1)   Kepler died in misery
and observed that by uttering it we assume or take for granted that the name
'Kepler' designates something, but this assumption cannot be understood as
part of the sense of the sentence because it is preserved under negation (Frege
1948). So both sentence (2) and its negation share the same presupposition
that has to be satisfied for them to have logical value. Being constant under
negation is considered the main characteristic of presuppositions in a technical sense.

Presuppositions came back into view when Peter Strawson (1950) argued
against Bertrand Russell's theory of definite descriptions. According to Strawson, presupposing is a special kind of pragmatic inference that should be distinguished from entailment. He defined it as follows: statement S presupposes
statement S' if and only if the truth of S' is a necessary condition for the truth or
falsity of S. This definition gave rise to the semantic account of presupposition
(for a discussion of this topic, see Levinson 1983, pp. 169–177, and van der Sandt
1988, pp. 5–8). However, the semantic account fails to explain such properties
of presupposition as cancellability and projection (for the critique of semantic
theories of presupposition see Wilson 1975). In light of these problems pragmatic theories of presupposition were developed (Gazdar 1979; Karttunen and
Peters 1975; Stalnaker 1973) and on their grounds the notion of accommodation
was introduced. Some of the contemporary theories of presuppositions reject
the pragmatics/semantics distinction, and attempt to integrate both accounts
(Jaszczolt 2005). As has been mentioned above, one of the best known characteristics of presupposition is that the presupposition of (an utterance of) a
sentence is the same as the presupposition of (an utterance of) the negation of
that sentence. In addition, presuppositions are non-monotonic and thus cancellable (Jaszczolt 2005). They are also detachable, in contrast to implicatures,
which means that they are not linked to the meaning of lexical items, but to
the form. In short, both presuppositions and implicatures construed as prag-
matically determined meanings are cancellable. Unlike implicatures, however,
presuppositions are preserved under negation.

1.2   *Reinforceability*
Besides preservation under negation, there are other characteristics of presuppositions that make them different from implicatures. For example, Jerry Sadock (1987) hypothesized that implicatures are the only pragmatic or semantic

inferences that can be reinforced without producing a sense of anomalous re-dundancy. In other words, after communicating an assumption at the level of conversational implicature we can express it explicitly, for example in (1) speak-er (b) can overtly include in his utterance what he previously implicated with-out producing any kind of pragmatic anomaly. Since Sadock's hypothesis states that implicatures are the only inferences that can be reinforced, then it follows that presuppositions cannot be reinforced without causing anomalous redun-dancy unless we accept that presuppositions are a type of implicatures.

There are many different lexical elements, syntactic constructions and even intonation patterns (van der Sandt 1988) that can function as presupposition triggers. For instance, Levinson (1983) lists as many as twelve different pre-supposition triggers, and van der Sandt (1988) lists thirteen. And indeed, for many presupposition triggers Sadock's hypothesis seems to hold. In the fol-lowing examples *i*-sentences are sentences with various presupposition trig-gers, *ii*-sentences are presuppositions of the *i*-sentences, and *iii*-sentences are *i*-sentences with presuppositions overtly included[2]:

Temporal clauses:
3)
>   i.   Many years has passed since I saw Mary.
>   ii. I saw Mary.
>   iii. Many years has passed since I saw Mary and I saw Mary

Factive verbs:
4)
>   i.   Jim Lovell regrets not landing on the Moon.
>   ii. Jim Lovell didn't land on the Moon.
>   iii. Jim Lovell regrets not landing on the Moon and Jim Lovell didn't land on the Moon.

Change of state verbs:
5)
>   i.   John has stopped playing guitar.
>   ii. John had been playing guitar.
>   iii. John has stopped playing guitar and John had been playing guitar.

---

2   Saying that *ii*-sentences are presuppositions of *i*-sentences we are not committing ourselves to the view that presuppositions are properties of sentences. Following Stalnaker (1973), we assume that speakers have presuppositions in primary sense and sentences have presuppositions in derivative sense.

In all of the above examples presupposition-reinforcing *iii*-sentences, which have the form of conjunctions, appear to be anomalous. More precisely, in uttering the second argument of a conjunction we explicitly communicate what we have just presupposed in uttering its first argument, thereby producing an effect of giving redundant information that does not serve any communicative function and thus makes the whole sentence infelicitous. The situation is different in the case of implicatures. This time let us assume that *i*-sentence is a conversation between (a) and (b); *ii*-sentence is what (b) implicates by her utterance; and *iii*-sentence is a conversation between (a) and (b) in which (b) is reinforcing her implicature:

(6)
      i. a. Do you want to go to the cinema tonight?
           b. I have a headache.
     ii. I don't want to go to the cinema tonight.
   iii. a. Do you want to go to the cinema tonight?
           b. I have a headache, I don't want to go to the cinema tonight.

There seems to be no anomalous redundancy here. That is, overtly including implicatures in our utterance does not lead to a repetition of information—at least not on the level of what is said by the speaker. This suggests that information that is on the level of implicature can be freely reinforced without producing anomalous redundancy. In fact, one can even say that reinforcing implicatures may in some cases prevent miscommunication since implicatures have to be worked out and this process is prone to failure (for example, the hearer may not have the access to the necessary information).

So far, the above-cited examples seem to support Sadock's hypothesis. There is indeed a sense of anomalous redundancy when we reinforce presuppositions (in a null context at least). But as we have already mentioned, there are many different presupposition triggers and there is a possibility that presuppositions triggered by other types of lexical forms and syntactic structures can be reinforced without producing a sense of anomalous redundancy, or maybe some contexts allow for presuppositions to be reinforced.

1.3   *Implicative Verbs*

Let us consider a specific class of presupposition triggers called implicative verbs, which seem to be somewhat different from other triggers. Implicative verbs were first described by Lauri Karttunen (1971). Asserting the main sentence with an implicative verb as predicate commits the speaker to an implied

proposition, while questioning the main sentence leads to questioning the implied proposition as well (Karttunen 1971). But implicative verbs function also
as presupposition triggers. They carry a presupposition of some necessary and
sufficient condition that determines whether the event described in the complement took place (Karttunen 1971). Some of the implicative verbs are: *manage, forget, remember, bother, happen, see fit, get, dare, venture*. Below are examples of sentences with implicative verbs with presuppositions that they carry:

(7) John managed to stop before intersection (John tried to stop).
(8) Mary forgot to close the door (Mary ought to or intended to close
the door).
(9) Mark happened to be in the right place (Mark had no plans to be in
the right place).

We follow Levinson (1983, p. 181) in regard of what are the presuppositions of
specific implicative verbs. It is worth noting that presuppositions triggered by
some implicative verbs are more complex. For example, the verb 'to bother'
triggers to the effect that some conscious effort is needed on the part of the
subject and also that the subject's willingness is a crucial factor that determines
the outcome (Karttunen 1971). As we can see, implicative verbs work differently
from another class of verbs that function as presupposition triggers, viz., factive
verbs. Factive verbs simply presuppose the truth of their complement sentences
(Karttunen 1971) as we saw in (4). So in their case what is presupposed is composed out of concepts that are activated or encoded by lexical units occurring
in the sentence, while in the case of implicative verbs what is presupposed goes
beyond concepts encoded by lexical units. We will elaborate on this in section
3. But the main question here is: can we reinforce implicative verbs without
producing a feeling of anomalous redundancy? Let's consider the following sentences in which presuppositions triggered by implicative verbs were reinforced:

(10) John managed to stop before intersection and he tried to stop.
(11) Mary forgot to close the door and she intended to close the door.
(12) Mark happened to be in the right place and he had no plans to
be there.

Intuitively, these sentences are less anomalous than the sentences with different presupposition triggers. In fact, we could imagine contexts in which
reinforcing presuppositions triggered by implicative verbs can prevent miscommunication. For example, if our interlocutor has doubts about John willingness to stop before intersection we can include information that he indeed

tried to stop. In other words, there are reasons to believe that implicative verbs at least in some contexts can be reinforced. This observation was the starting point for constructing the experiment described in the following section.

2   Experiment

We will now describe the experimental procedure and methods of analysis applied in the survey and present the obtained results. Before we get into details, however, it is worthwhile to consider the nature of anomalous redundancy (and linguistic redundancy in general) and methods of measuring it.

2.1   *What Is Linguistic Redundancy?*

For the purpose of the experiment it is necessary to define *anomalous redundancy* and distinguish it from what we call *proper* or *justified redundancy*. There are many different definitions of redundancy, and the matter is further complicated by the fact that there seems to be a discrepancy between how this term is used in information theory and how it is used in linguistic theories. The definition of linguistic redundancy adopted in the experiment was primarily based on the work by Ernst-Jan C. Wit and Marie Gillette (1999), who proposed their own account of linguistic redundancy. Despite the fact that linguistic redundancy is commonly treated as a negative quality, a study of natural languages shows us that they are in fact highly redundant (Wit and Gillette 1999). The authors distinguish two types of linguistic redundancy: grammatical redundancy and context redundancy. Grammatical redundancy is obligatory and internal to language. It is also truly redundant: it serves only to repeat information already given by another feature. On the other hand, contextual redundancy is the repetition of information that is, in a grammatical sense, non-obligatory (Wit and Gillette 1999). With regard to this distinction we can say that reinforcing any semantic or pragmatic aspect of meaning should be classified as contextual redundancy: it is non-obligatory and it is not systematically generated by grammatical rules. According to Wit and Gillette (1999, pp. 9–12), contextual redundancy can be divided into four categories:

(*i*)   Identical or synonymous repetition: occurs when the expression contains two (or more) identical or synonymous words or subexpressions. Example: 'Beneath me was a deep, deep ocean';

(*ii*)   Isolating, salient repetition: occurs when the expression contains at least two subexpressions, one of which implicitly contains one or more features of the other. Example: 'I love the salty sea';

(*iii*) Contrasting repetition: occurs when two (or more) words or expressions that semantically constitute a contrast are repeated, or in some way redundantly coded.
Example: 'This is a rose, but it is blue, not red';

(*iv*) Distinguishing, differentiating repetition: occurs when the speaker disambiguates a word or an expression in an unambiguous context with another word or expression that is considered non-repetitive in the ambiguous context of that first word.

Example: 'Did you hear about the new discovery about Europa, Jupiter's moon?' If this should be a conversation between two astronomers, the information that the word 'Europa' refers to one of Jupiter's moons is probably not necessary. But if the conversation takes place between, for example, an astronomer and a non-astronomer, this piece of information may be necessary for the hearer to understand the utterance.

Now we can address the second question: what is the purpose of linguistic redundancy? Wit and Gillette (1999, pp. 9–11) propose the following classification of different functions of contextual redundancy:

(*i*)   Increasing comprehensibility;
(*ii*)   Resolving ambiguity;
(*iii*) Isolating a feature;
(*iv*)   Contrasting elements;
(*v*)   Emphasizing or intensifying;
(*vi*)   Creating poetic effect;

As we see, there are many functions of redundancy, but the first two are most important from reinforceability standpoint, and are in fact closely related to each other. To explain this, let us consider situations in which the utterer would like to reinforce her implicatures. It seems likely that resolving ambiguity is the prime candidate for triggering this process. It is plausible that one can be willing to dynamically increase the amount of information he provides if it leads to successful communication. So resolving ambiguity may be considered as one kind of motivation for reinforcement, but its main purpose is to increase comprehensibility in communication. In other words, the utterer evaluates the context of communication and recognizes that he can be misunderstood, so he states explicitly what was conveyed by his utterance. Obviously, this is only a preliminary conclusion and further study is necessary to determine the exact psychological process of reinforcing statements.

Taking the above-quoted distinctions into account, for the purpose of the experiment, normal or proper linguistic redundancy was defined as repetition of information that increases the comprehensibility of an utterance. By contrast, anomalous redundancy was defined as repetition of information that reduces the comprehensibility of an utterance (for a discussion see Włodarczyk 2017).

Reinforcing conversational implicatures gives rise to interesting cases of redundancy. The point is that what is conveyed by implicature is an inferred (or worked-out) meaning that goes beyond what is said. In other words, the process whereby the hearer determines the implicature communicated by the speaker is a complex non-demonstrative and non-monotonic inference that makes use of certain contextual assumptions. While in many cases this inference is very easy for the receiver to make, what is implicated by the utterer is still different from literal meaning (*what is said*), and as we already stated above, this difference is probably what allows us to reinforce implicatures in our utterances. Of course that does not mean that reinforcing implicatures cannot lead to redundancy—the definition of redundancy applies to repetition of information, and if we overtly include in our utterance what is conveyed by an implicature we basically repeat information. However, in case of implicature, reinforcement, whether redundancy is anomalous or not is probably mostly context-dependent i.e. it is directly related to the success of the receiver in making adequate inference. Perhaps in some cases (when, for example, working out implicature is sufficiently easy for the hearer) reinforcing implicature could lead to anomalous redundancy; however, results of the experiment do not support this hypothesis and it would be necessary to conduct another study to find out if there are conditions where situation like that could occur. The situation is different with presuppositions. As we have already seen, it seems that for many presupposition triggers reinforcing leads to repetition of information that was already encoded by lexical units of a sentence. Implicative verbs are of course an exception. Now, considering the above distinctions of categories of contextual redundancy we could say that reinforcing implicatures is an example of distinguishing repetition and reinforcing presuppositions is an example of a synonymous repetition. It is not clear, however, how to classify reinforcing indirect messages communicated with the help of implicative verbs according to that division.

The definition of proper/anomalous redundancy was used to create a scale on which subjects were rating the experimental material. Positions on a scale (1–5) were described as follows (see also Włodarczyk 2017):

(1) Additional content is not a repetition of information already communicated and it increases the comprehensibility of the whole utterance.

(2) Additional content is not a repetition of the information already communicated but it does not increase the comprehensibility of the whole utterance.

(3) Additional content is neutral in terms of repetition of information and the comprehensibility of the utterance.

(4)   Additional content repeats the information already communicated but it
      does not reduce the comprehensibility of the whole utterance.
(5)   Additional content repeats the information already communicated and
      it reduces the comprehensibility of the whole utterance.

The scale was constructed so as to fit the predicted characteristics of both conversational implicatures and presuppositions: implicatures should score on a lower end of the scale: reinforcing them should cause minimal (if any) redundancy, and in many cases this should increase comprehensibility, especially in a situation where context is limited; presuppositions, by contrast, should score at the higher end of the scale: reinforcing them usually leads to redundant repetition of information that can cause confusion in communication.

2.2   *Experimental Procedure*

The experimental procedure was constructed following a study done by Joanna Rączaszek-Leonardi and Nicoletta Caramelli (Rączaszek-Leonardi 2011). Test subjects were presented with 50 different dialogues containing five different types of messages (one in each dialogue): conversational implicatures and presuppositions triggered by factive verbs, temporal clauses, implicative verbs, and change of state verbs. As conversational implicatures naturally occur in dialogues, it was also necessary to construct dialogues containing sentences with presuppositions, for experimental material to be uniform. The experimental material was presented as a slideshow using multimedia projector. Each dialogue was presented in two versions: unreinforced and reinforced. Both versions were shown for seven seconds, and in the reinforced version additional information was highlighted to prevent confusion. After that information to rate each dialogue on a five-point scale was presented for 10 seconds and then a blank slide was showed for 3 seconds. The experiment lasted for 22 minutes and 30 seconds. Test subjects (N = 48) were students from the University of Szczecin and the West Pomeranian University of Technology. Before the experiment a pilot study was conducted (N = 5) with a goal of gathering feedback on clarity of the experimental procedure. The examples of dialogues used in the experiment can be found in Appendix 1.

2.3   *Statistical Analysis and Results*

One factor, within-subject analysis of variance (ANOVA), was used to analyze the results. This form of analysis is used when subjects are tested on all levels of an independent variable. The greatest advantage of using this form of analysis is that it minimizes the effect of individual differences and increases the probability that manipulation of independent variable is the source of variation in results. Shapiro-Wilk test and Mauchly's test were conducted before the analysis to check for normal distribution and sphericity of the data,

TABLE. 9.1   Mean results for linguistic constructions

Message type	Mean	Standard deviation	N
1. Implicatures	1.6417	.51523	48
2. Factive verbs	4.4042	.44719	48
3. Temporal clauses	4.5250	.46927	48
4. Change of state verbs	4.2417	.64009	48
5. Implicative verbs	3.3125	.90027	48

respectively. Results showed that both assumptions are violated. However, normal distribution assumption can be violated if N> 30 and within-subjects ANOVA does not require sphericity of the data. Firstly, we present means and standard deviations for all message types used in the experiment:

As we see in Table 9.1, standard deviation for implicative verbs was higher than for the other message types. One possible explanation is that sentences containing implicative verbs were harder to rate for test subjects, as they presented a unique case in comparison to clearly anomalous redundancy of other types of reinforced presuppositions on the one hand, and lack of anomalous redundancy in case of reinforced implicatures on the other.

Results of the f-statistic are as follows:

TABLE. 9.2   Test of within-subjects effects

Source		Type III sum of squares	Df	Mean square	F	Sig.	Partial eta squared
Construction	Sphericity assumed	279.775	4	69.944	239.774	.000	.836
	Greenhouse-Geisser	279.775	2,845	98.024	239.774	.000	.836

As we can see, the results of within-subject ANOVA with a Greenhouse-Geisser correction shows a significant effect of Message type $(F(4, 43) = 239,774; p < 0.01; \eta^2 = 0,84)$. Bonferroni post hoc test was conducted to discover how specific means differed:

TABLE. 9.3   Pairwise comparison

Message type (I)	Message type (J)	Mean difference (I-J)	Std. error	Sig.	95% Confidence interval for difference	
					Lower bound	Upper bound
Implicatures (1)	2	−2.763*	.102	.000	−3.064	−2.461
	3	−2.883*	.111	.000	−3.212	−2.555
	4	−2.600*	.112	.000	−2.929	−2.271
	5	−1.671*	.149	.000	−2.111	−1.231
Factive verbs (2)	1	2.763*	.102	.000	2.461	3.064
	3	−.121	.059	.465	−.295	.053
	4	.163	.093	.855	−.110	.435
	5	1.092*	.132	.000	.702	1.482
Temporal clauses (3)	1	2.883*	.111	.000	2.555	3.212
	2	.121	.059	.465	−.053	.295
	4	.283*	.086	.018	.031	.536
	5	1.213*	.120	.000	.858	1.567
Change of state verbs (4)	1	2.600*	.112	.000	2.271	2.929
	2	−.163	.093	.855	−.435	.110
	3	−.283*	.086	.018	−.536	−.031
	5	.929*	.112	.000	.601	1.258
Implicative verbs (5)	1	1.671*	.149	.000	1.231	2.111
	2	−1.092*	.132	.000	−1.482	−.702
	3	−1.213*	.120	.000	−1.567	−.858
	4	−.929*	.112	.000	−1.258	−.601

Differences between conversational implicatures and presuppositions were statistically significant (Table 9.3). As expected, implicatures had the lowest mean score (1,64) among all types of messages used in the experiment. When we take the description of the scale into consideration, the results show that additional information that was included in reinforced versions of sentences was not treated by the test subjects as a repetition of the information already communicated and that it increased the comprehensibility of the whole utterance. On the other hand, utterances involving three presupposition triggers (factive verbs, temporal clauses and change of state verbs) were systematically rated on the high end spectrum of the scale, which means that additional information in the case of these linguistic constructions was considered as an unnecessary repetition of information and that it reduced comprehensibility.

An interesting result of the study is that utterances involving implicative verbs were rated as neutral (mean score of 3,31), and the difference between them and utterances containing other presupposition triggers as well as those communicating conversational implicatures was statistically significant. In case of implicative verbs the additional information was not treated as repetition of information and it had no effect on the comprehensibility of sentences. The test results confirm the Sadock hypothesis, according to which conversational implicatures can be reinforced without producing a sense of anomalous redundancy. It also confirms that presuppositions triggered by factive verbs, change of state verbs and temporal clauses cannot be reinforced without producing a sense of anomalous redundancy. However, the Sadock hypothesis is false with regard to implicative verbs, in which presuppositions *can* be reinforced without producing a sense of anomalous redundancy. The fact that implicative verbs also differ from conversational implicatures suggest that they cannot be simply classified as the same type of pragmatic phenomena. We will now try to explain the experimental results using the concept of accommodation.

3 Accommodation

In this section we discuss the concept of accommodation and clarify how it can be used to explain the results. The notion of accommodation is commonly applied in many contemporary models of presuppositions (Beaver 2001; von Fintel 2006; Jaszczolt 2005; Karttunen 1974; van der Sandt 1992; for a discussion of the phenomenon of accommodation, see also section 7 of Sbisà this volume) and it is instrumental in explaining the phenomenon of informative presuppositions. To understand what informative presuppositions are, we must first define—following Stalnaker (1973; 2002)—the concept of pragmatic presupposition and consider its relation to the idea of common ground. The pragmatic account of presuppositions comes from Stalnaker (1973), who proposed it as an alternative to semantic theories. Firstly, we need to establish what common ground is. By common ground of a conversation we understand a set of propositions that the participants in a conversation at that time mutually take for granted and which are not subject to further discussion (von Fintel 2006). Common ground can be updated by what is asserted in an utterance: if

. what the speaker asserts is accepted by her interlocutors, the asserted proposition becomes part of the common ground. Therefore, sentences can have
pragmatic presuppositions in the sense of imposing certain requirements on
the common ground (von Fintel 2006). That is, if a sentence containing presupposition is uttered, then it is necessary for common ground to include presupposed proposition or otherwise the utterance will be infelicitous. The next
question is: what is the source of pragmatic presuppositions? Stalnaker did
not specify the source of pragmatic presuppositions and the relation between
them and meanings of natural language sentences. Kai von Fintel (2006, p. 3)
proposes that presuppositional component meaning is hardwired in semantics of expression which can be done by using either three-valued semantics or
by context-change potential based semantics. But what exactly happens when
we utter a sentence whose presupposition is not part of the common ground?
Let us consider an utterance of the following sentence:

(13) I have to pick up my sister from the airport.

In a null context this utterance fails to constitute an appropriate or felicitous
one because it presupposes that the utterer has a sister while this proposition is
not part of the common ground in question. But we encounter many sentences
of that type in everyday communication and they usually do not produce any
kind of infelicity or inappropriateness. Normally, after hearing sentence (13)
we simply accept the information that our interlocutor has a sister. That is, we
update the common ground of the conversation by adding this proposition to
it. In short, the common ground among the conversing agents can be updated
not only by what the speaker asserts, but also by what she or her assertion
presupposes. This of course poses a serious problem for any common ground
theory, according to which utterances carrying presuppositions that are not
part of common ground are infelicitous (Levinson 1983; see Witek 2016 for discussion about appropriateness rules and Maxim of Appropriateness). David
Lewis proposed that in such situations the process of accommodation takes
place, and he formulated the rule of accommodation for presuppositions:

> If at time *t* something is said that requires presupposition P to be accept-
> able, and if P is not presupposed just before *t*, then—*ceteris paribus* and
> within certain limits—presupposition P comes into existence at *t* (Lewis
> 1979, p. 340).

If we accept this rule we can still use the common ground theory of presuppositions and acknowledge the fact that in some cases presupposition can be

informative, i.e. can be accommodated. The idea of accommodation is the key element of most of the contemporary models of presuppositions; for example, it is used in Dynamic Semantics Discourse Representation Theory, and in Default Semantics. According to these models presuppositions function similarly to an anaphoric expression, but in the cases when they cannot be bound to the discourse referent the presupposed proposition is accommodated (Beaver and Geurts 2014). This trend was set by Rob van der Sandt (1992), and one could say that it is a standard way of handling presuppositions in models deriving from Dynamic Semantics.

3.1   *Accommodation and Implicative Verbs*
Our hypothesis is that the process of accommodation is responsible for producing a sense of anomalous redundancy while presupposition is being reinforced, and that it can explain the present experimental results. Let us look once again at the definition of accommodation: if what is presupposed by an utterance is not part of the common ground, then the presupposition normally—'ceteris paribus and within certain limits'—becomes a part of the common ground. So when the presupposition is reinforced, i.e. the proposition that was presupposed is explicitly expressed, a sense of anomalous redundancy occurs. It occurs because this proposition has been already accommodated. Now, the lack of anomalous redundancy in cases involving the use of an implicative verb could be explained if they were not accommodated. This is our main point here: if there is no accommodation, there is no anomalous redundancy. Currently there is no sufficient data to properly support this hypothesis, but there is one observation that makes it plausible: it is the way in which implicative verbs represent propositions that are allegedly presupposed. As we already mentioned, if we look at other presupposition triggers (for example: quantifiers, temporal clauses, factive verbs or change of state verbs), we can see that what is presupposed is composed of concepts encoded by lexical units used in the utterance carrying the presupposition in question. For example, if we utter a sentence such as (14):

(14) John regrets that he drank orange juice.

then what is presupposed is that John drank orange juice, and there is literal, direct reference to this fact: words like 'John', 'drank', and 'orange juice' that encode concepts contributing to the presupposed proposition are already present in sentence (14). This is also true for temporal clauses and change of state verbs, and in fact for many different presupposition triggers that were not included in the experiment. But it is not true for implicative verbs. Let's look at the following sentence:

(15) I remembered to lock the door.

We recall that utterances with the verb 'remember' presuppose that the speaker was obligated or expected to carry out a certain task. But in this case there is no direct, literal reference to this obligation or expectation: there are no words like 'obligation' or 'expectation' which encode the key aspects of presupposed content in the sentence. The observed differences have consequences for the difficulty (for the hearer) to determine the proposition that has to be accommodated. In case of most presupposition triggers it is quite easy for the receiver to determine what has to be accommodated, because this information is already encoded in the sentence. In case of implicative verbs, it may be more challenging for the receiver to determine what has to be accommodated because the presupposed proposition goes beyond what is encoded in the sentence, and this information is specific for given implicative verb (i.e. obligation to do X in case of 'remembered to X' or at least attempting to Y in case of 'did not manage to Y'). So it seems that as far as implicative verbs are concerned, there is a wider gap between what is presupposed and what is literally said. That the subject was in some way obligated to close the door can be probably inferred from this utterance, but this already complicates the process of accommodation.

To summarize: the results of the experiment show that utterances involving implicative verbs were rated as neutral both in terms of repetition of information and increasing comprehensibility (mean score: 3,31, as shown in the table 9.1). Utterances containing other presupposition triggers where rated significantly higher on the scale. This difference in the results has to be elucidated. We propose a following explanation: anomalous redundancy that appears when presuppositions are reinforced is an effect of the process of accommodation. Lack of anomalous redundancy in case of reinforcing indirect messages communicated by implicative verbs is caused by lack of accommodation of said indirect messages. This hypothesis is supported by an observation that there is a difference in the way those indirect messages are encoded by lexical units. However, there is a need for explaining why assumptions associated with or triggered by implicative verbs are not accommodated. It is also necessary that we conduct another experiment specifically designed to test accommodation of assumptions associated with implicative verbs. We will now describe how that experiment could be constructed.

We recall that the phenomenon of informative presuppositions can be accounted for in terms of accommodating mechanisms responsible for updating the common ground with presupposed propositions. This provides us with a way to operationalize this process because if a proposition is part of the common ground then it can be accessed by the hearer. So in order to verify the fact that the use of a given presupposition trigger leads to updating the common ground, we must check whether hearers can access this new information. Of course there is a possibility that propositions that are presupposed by utterances containing implicative verbs can be accessed by a hearer even when they are not accommodated (for example by inference). Additional measurements are then in order. The proposed experiment should proceed as follows: a subject will be presented with a sentence containing presupposition trigger or conversational implicature, then a set of questions related to presented sentence will be displayed. Some of the questions will be designed to test if accommodation of presupposition occurred. For example, for utterances containing change of state verbs like in (16):

(16) John stopped playing guitar.

the question may take the following form: has John been playing guitar? Negative answer for this kind of questions regarding sentences with implicative verbs will be clear evidence that presuppositions that are triggered by these verbs are not accommodated. Additionally, the reaction time will be measured: a significant difference between the time needed to give an answer for questions related to sentences with implicative verbs and for questions related to other presupposition triggers can be treated as evidence for there being a difference in the process of accessing information provided by different sentences. One possible explanation of such a difference will be that this information is accessed through a process other than accommodation.

It is worth noting that some researchers classify implicative verbs as conventional implicatures (Abbott 2006, Potts 2007). The proposed experiment could also include sentences with paradigmatic cases of conventional implicatures. If there appear to be differences between conventional implicatures and implicative verbs in the final results of the experiment, this will suggest that these two phenomena do not fall into the same pragmatic category.

3.2. Implicative Verbs Presuppositions as Default Meaning?
There are two ways in which the lack of accommodation of assumptions triggered by implicative verbs can be handled in the case when experimental results support this hypothesis. First, one may maintain the claim that they are presupposition triggers. To do that one has to explain why presuppositions triggered by implicative verbs are not accommodated in the same way as other

presupposition triggers. It is worth noting, however, that this will be hard to do in the framework of pragmatic presuppositions because the process of accommodation functions as a context–repair process. If requirements imposed on common ground by utterances containing presupposition triggers in the form of implicative verbs are not met, those utterances cannot update the common ground between conversing agents. The other option is to assume that implicative verbs are not presupposition triggers. Then of course one will have to provide an alternative explanation of the relation between utterances containing implicative verbs and propositions that were assumed to be their presuppositions. In the remaining part of this section we will briefly discuss Defaults Semantics (Jaszczolt 2005; 2010) and show how the concept of defaults can be used to provide an alternative explanation for implicative verbs.

Default Semantics (henceforth DS) departs from postulating different levels of an utterance interpretation, which is the hallmark of many theoretical accounts of utterance meaning, and instead assumes that there is just one representation of utterance meaning to which various types of information contribute (Jaszczolt 2005, p. 3). The meaning of an utterance is thus described as a *merger representation*. It is important to note that the terms 'primary meaning' and 'secondary meaning' used in DS differ from Grice distinction of 'what is said' and 'what is implicated': what is conversationally implicated *may be* the primary meaning, and the representation of primary meaning need not be isomorphic with the representation of the uttered sentence (Jaszczolt 2010). One of the types of information that contribute to the meaning of an utterance are defaults, defined as '(...) salient interpretations arrived at without the help of the context of the particular situation in which the utterance was uttered' (Jaszczolt 2005, p. 5). The concept of defaults was used previously by Kent Bach (1994; 2001) and Stephen Levinson (1995; 2000) and in theories like Discourse Representation Theory (Kamp and Reyle 1993) and Segmented Discourse Representation Theory (Asher and Lascarides 1998; 2003); but Default Semantics differs from these theories in some points. One of the main differences is that DS does not recognize the privileged role of syntax in constructing merger representations and that the compositionality does not need to be imposed at the level of the output of syntax (Jaszczolt 2010). More importantly, DS offers a wide classification of different defaults that can be used to describe implicative verbs.

In DS, the sources of information that contribute to the merger representation are as follows (Jaszczolt 2010):
(*i*)   World knowledge;
(*ii*)   Word meaning and sentence structure;
(*iii*) Situation of discourse;

(*iv*)   Stereotypes and presumptions about society and culture;

(*v*)   Properties of human inferential system.

The merger representation of both the primary and secondary meaning of an utterance is produced by a set of processes onto which different sources of information are mapped. The types of processes that construct primary meanings are as follows (Jaszczolt 2010, p. 10):

(*i*)   Combination of word meaning and sentence structure.

(*ii*)   Social, cultural and world-knowledge defaults.

(*iii*)   Cognitive defaults.

(*iv*)   Conscious pragmatic inference.

We propose that the propositions that are associated with implicative verbs can be best understood as social, cultural and world-knowledge defaults used in interpretation of utterances containing them. Social and cultural defaults are interpretations caused by social and cultural stereotypes and they are non-inferential, instantaneous and automatic. For example, in sentence (17):

(17)   We advertised for a new nanny;

the default interpretation is that the speaker means a *female* nanny. Perhaps the same process can be used to explain why interpretation of sentences with implicative verbs like 'remember', cf (18):

(18)   I remembered to close the door;

includes that 'I' was obligated to close the door. That someone saying 'I remembered X' was obligated to X is standard, non-controversial interpretation of this particular implicative verb and it stems from knowledge about regular human behavior. But it is not necessary that we interpret sentence (18) in that way. In fact, this interpretation can be invalidated as shown in sentence (19) (note: we cannot do this with sentences like 'I have to pick up my sister from the airport'):

(19)   I remembered to close the door; but I was not obligated to close them.

But how treating proposition associated with implicative verbs as default interpretations can explain that those verbs can be reinforced? We recall that accommodation is a context-repair process; that is, it prevents communication failure in situations where common ground does not meet requirements imposed on it by sentences with presupposition triggers. So when accommodation occurs it is *necessary* for the communication to be successful. Accommodation results in adding the presupposed proposition to the common ground

between conversing agents. As the corollary of this, reinforcing presuppositions will lead to redundancy, since the presupposed content has already been
accepted as part of the common ground. The main point here is that in the
case of many presupposition triggers the hearer is forced to accommodate presupposed proposition to make sense of a conversation. The situation is different in the case of social and cultural defaults. Defaults do not initiate a context-
repair process; they are just preferred interpretations of utterances. The hearer
can choose another interpretation and this will not produce a communication
failure. So if the speaker reinforces the default meaning of an implicative verb
like 'remember' this can be treated by the hearer as an additional clue in interpretation and it will not lead to a sense of anomalous redundancy. Thus,
by not treating implicative verbs as presupposition triggers and interpreting
them in terms of defaults we can maintain that they can have specific propositions associated with them and that they can be reinforced without producing
a sense of anomalous redundancy. To answer the question posed in the beginning: what do we do with implicative verbs? According to Stalnaker (2002,
p. 707), speaker presupposition can be defined as a propositional attitiude of
an individual speaker; it can be identified with what the speaker believes to
be a common belief. On this account speaker presupposition can be used to
update the context (or to make a context change) of a conversation almost
as efficiently as by assertions. But for this update to be successful the process
of accommodation must take place. If the indirect messages associated with
implicative verbs are not accommodated, the utterer cannot expect to make
context change by using them in a conversation as easily as by using different
presupposition triggers.

Appendix 1: Examples of Dialogues Used in Experiment (with Polish Translation)

Change of state verbs:

(1)   a: I heard that Stanisław found a new hobby. (Słyszałem, że Stanisław znalazł
       sobie nowe hobby)

      b: Yes, he started building plastic models [and he builds plastic models]. (Tak,
       zaczął składać modele [i składa modele])

(2)   a: Karol stopped smoking cigarettes [and he smoked cigarettes]. (Karol przestał
       palić papierosy [i palił papierosy])

      b: Yes, and he plans to eat healthier too. (Ponoć ma również zamiar zdrowiej się
       odżywiać)

(3)   a: Albert finished writing his master's thesis [and he was writing his master's the-
       sis]. (Albert skończył pisać pracę magisterską [i pisał pracę magisterską])

      b: I envy him. (Zazdroszczę mu)

Factive verbs:

(4) a: Joanna is sad because Jan left [and Jan left] (Joanna smuci się ponieważ Marek wyjechał [i Marek wyjechał.])

 b: What can we do too cheer her up? (Co możemy zrobić, żeby poprawić jej humor?)

(5) a: I'm glad that we were able to finally meet [and we finally meet].

 b: I hope that soon we will do it again. (Mam nadzieję, że niedługo to powtórzymy.)

(6) a: How was your holiday? (Jak urlop?)

 b: We were all happy that we went to the mountains because each of us loves climbing [and we went to the mountains].(Wszyscy cieszyli się, że wyjechaliśmy w góry, ponieważ każdy z nas uwielbia wspinaczki [i wyjechaliśmy w góry.]).

Implicative verbs:

(7) a: Why is Marta so happy? (Czemu Marta jest taka wesoła?)

 b: She avoided coming to work tomorrow [and she ought to come to work tomorrow]. (Uniknęła przychodzenia jutro do pracy [i powinna była jutro przyjść do pracy])

(8) a: Why did the lions escaped their cages? (Czemu lwy uciekły ze swoich klatek?)

 b: Krzysztof forgot to close the door [and he ought to close the door] (Krzysztof zapomniał zamknąć za sobą drzwi [i powinien był zamknąć za sobą drzwi])

(9) a: Mariusz managed to finish the race in the first place [and he tried to finish the race in the first place] (Mariusz zdołał zakończyć wyścig na pierwszym miejscu [i próbował zakończyć wyścig na pierwszym miejscu])

 b: We should congratulate him. (Powinniśmy mu pogratulować)

Temporal clauses:

(10) a: Before I became a pirate I was an officer on a warship [and I became a pirate]. (Zanim zostałem piratem byłem oficerem na statku wojennym [i zostałem piratem])

 b: So that's where your experience comes from. (To stąd wzięło się twoje doświadczenie)

(11) a: Many years has passed since I last saw Tomek [and I saw Tomek]. (Wiele lat minęło od kiedy ostatni raz widziałem Tomka [i widziałem Tomka])

 b: He has changed. (Zmienił się)

(12) a: The kids were bored while it was raining [and it was raining]. (W czasie gdy padał deszcz, dzieciaki strasznie się nudziły [i padał deszcz.])

 b: When I was in their age I was never bored. (Gdy ja byłem w ich wieku nigdy się nie nudziłem)

Conversational Implicatures:

(13)   a: What happened to our dinner? (co się stało z naszą kolacją)

      b: The dog looks very happy [he probably ate it]. (Pies wygląda na bardzo szczęś-
liwego [pewnie ją zjadł])

(14)   a: Do I look good in this dress? (Czy dobrze wyglądam w tej sukience?)

      b: I always thought that red suits you [you look very good in that red dress]. (Za-
wsze uważałem, że w czerwonym Ci do twarzy [wyglądasz bardzo dobrze w
tej czerwonej sukience])

(15)   a: Maybe we can order a steak? (Może zamówimy stek?)

      b: Ewelina is a vegan [we cannot order a steak]. (Ewelina jest weganką [nie
zamówimy steku])

Bibliography

Abbott, B. (2006). Where have some of the presuppositions gone. B.J. Birner and G.L.
Ward (eds.), *Drawing the boundaries of meaning: Neo-Gricean studies in pragmatics
and semantics in honor of Laurence R. Horn*, 1–20. Amsterdam: John Benjamins Publishing Company.

Asher, N. and A. Lascarides (1998). Bridging. *Journal of Semantics* 15, 83–113.

Asher, N. and A. Lascarides (2003). *Logics of Conversation*. Cambridge University Press.

Bach, K. (1994). Semantic Slack: What Is Said and More. In: S.L. Tsohatzidis (ed.), *Foundations of Speech Act Theory: Philosopical and Linguistic Perspectives*, pp. 267–291.
London: Routledge.

Bach, K. (2001). You don't say?. *Synthese* 128, 15–44.

Beaver, D. (2001). *Presupposition and Assertion in Dynamic Semantics*. Stanford: CSLI
Publications.

Beaver, D. and B. Geurts (2014). Presupposition. In: E. N. Zalta (ed.), *The Stanford Encyclopedia of Philosophy* (Winter 2014 Edition).

von Fintel, K. (2006). What is presupposition accommodation, again?. *Philosophical
perspectives* 22 (1), 137–170.

Frege, G. (1948). Sense and reference. *The Philosopical review* 57 (3), 209–230.

Gazdar, G. (1979). *Pragmatics: Implicature, Presupposition and Logical Form*.
New York: Academic Press.

Grice, P. H. (1975). Logic and Conversation. In: P. Cole and J. Morgan (eds.), *Syntax and
Semantics III: Speech acts,* pp. 41–58. New York: Academic Press.

Grice, P. H. (1989). *Studies in the Way of Words*. Cambridge, MA: Harvard University Press.

Horn, L. R. (1984). Toward a New Taxonomy for Pragmatic Inference: Q-based and R-
Based Implicature. In: D. Schffrin (ed.), *Georgetown University Round Table on Languages and Linguistics*, pp. 11–42. Washington D.C.: Georgetown University Press.

Horn, L. R. (1989). *A Natural History of Negation.* Chicago: University of Chicago Press.

Jaszczolt, K. M. (2005). *Default Semantics: Foundations of a Compositional Theory of Acts of Communication.* Oxford: Oxford University Press.

Jaszczolt, K. M. (2010). Default Semantics. In: B. Heine and H. Narrog (eds.), *The Oxford Handbook of Linguistic Analysis,* pp. 193–221. Oxford: Oxford University Press.

Kamp, H. and, U. Reyle (1993). *From Discourse to Logic: Introduction to Model-theoretic Semantics of Natural Language, Formal Logic and Discourse Representation Theory.* Dordrecht: Kluwer.

Karttunen, L. (1971). Implicative Verbs. *Language* 47, 340–358.

Karttunen, Lauri. 1974. Presupposition and linguistic context. Theoretical Linguistics 1(1), 181–194.

Karttunen, L. and S. Peters (1975). Conventional Implicature in Montague grammar. In: *BLS 1: Proceedings of the First Annual Meeting of the Berkeley Linguistics Society,* pp. 266–278.

Lepore, E. and M. Stone (2015). *Imagination and Convention: Distinguishing Grammar and Inference in Language.* Oxford: Oxford University Press.

Levinson, S. C. (1983). *Pragmatics.* Cambridge: Cambridge University.

Levinson, S. C. (1995). Three levels of meaning. In: F.R. Palmer (ed.), *Grammar and Meaning. Essays in Honour of Sir John Lyons,* pp. 90–115. Cambridge: Cambridge University Press.

Levinson, S. C. (2000). *Presumptive Meanings: The Theory of Generalized Conversational Implicature.* Cambridge, MA: MIT Press.

Lewis, D. (1979). Scorekeeping in a Language Game. *Journal of Philosophical Logic* 8, 339–359.

Potts, C. (2007). Into the Conventional-Implicature Dimension. *Philosophy compass* 2(4), 665–679.

Rączaszek-Leonardi, J. (2011). *Zjednoczeni w mowie. Wzlędność językowa w ujęciu dynamicznym.* Warszawa: Wydawnictwo Naukowe Scholar.

Sadock, J. (1987) On Testing for Conversational Implicature. In: P. Cole (ed.), *Syntax and Semantics Volume 9: Pragmatics,* pp. 281–298. New York: Academic Press.

van der Sandt, R. A. (1988). *Context and Presupposition.* London: Croom Helm.

van der Sandt, R. A. (1992). Presupposition projection as anaphora resolution. *Journal of Semantics* 9, 333–377.

Sbisà, M. (this volume). Varieties of speech act norms. In. M. Witek and I. Witczak-Plisiecka (eds.), *Normativity and Variety of Speech Actions,* pp. 23–50. Leiden: Brill (*Poznań Studies in the Philosophy of the Sciences and the Humanities* 112).

Sperber, D. and D. Wilson (1986). *Relevance: Communication and Cognition.* Oxford: Blackwell.

Stalnaker, R. (1973). Presuppositions. *Journal of Philosophical Logic* 2, 447–457.

Stalnaker, R. (2002). Common Ground. *Linguistics and Philosophy* 25 (5–6), 701–721.

Strawson, P. (1950). On referring. *Mind* 59 (235), 320–344.

Wilson, D. (1975). *Presuppositions and Non-Truth-Conditional Semantics*. London: Academic Press.

Wit, E. C. and M. Gillette (1999). *What is linguistic redundancy?* University of Chicago.

Witek, M. (2016). Accommodation and Convention. *Polish Journal of Philosophy* 10 (1), 101–116.

Włodarczyk, M. (2017). Presupozycje a wzmocnienie. *Rocznik Kognitywistyczny* 10, 39–55.

Index